Kerry writes at an interesting time with his books very much interwoven with his blog. This is a revolutionary approach to law and learning. You will see it here first. It is the future....
Gordon Exall, Barrister, Hardwicke Chambers

Of those who predict the future of the entire legal profession, time and again Kerry Underwood has called it right. He equally appreciates and strives to uphold the importance of the need to provide everyone with fair access to justice.
Kerry is our leading legal philosopher.
Professor Dominic Regan

An invaluable work for all those engaged in lower value personal injury claims.
Andrew Wilson, Barrister

There is so much crap being hurled at Claimant PI lawyers at the moment, with the government, seemingly intent on destroying the legal profession, it is difficult to know where to look. One could bury ones head in the sand..... but for those with an aversion to death, consult Kerry's new oracle, in conjunction with his blog. You know it makes sense!
Andrew Twambley, CEO, InjuryLawyers4U

G000245104

Comment re Second Edition of Fixed Costs

Both in style and content, this book deals with the subject with such clarity that is makes a complicated subject so understandable, one wonders what all the fuss is about. For anyone new to the concept of fixed costs it is the ideal starting point, for anyone who has grappled with them it clears a path through the confusion and controversy.
His Honour Michael Cook

What people said about Kerry's course on this subject

- *Most of the big decisions in my firm follow a Kerry Underwood course.*
- **Utterly brilliant!**
- *You give us the courage to keep going.*
- **Superb, inspirational course.**
- *What an original presentation. Loved your energy, passion and dynamism. Most unconventional but refreshing and original.*
- **Amazing course**
- *Extremely informative, the best and most useful course from a business point of view I have ever attended.*
- **Loved the course – so did my staff.**
- *Truly amazing content and presentation*
- **Absolutely brilliant. A must for all PI litigators.**
- *Great day with Kerry who spoke brilliantly. A wealth of knowledge and a great teacher. Many thanks!*
- **Brilliant – thanks Kerry. Really informative day and brilliantly delivered**
- *Thanks very much for all that you do.*
- **I find Kerry a most charismatic lecturer with an exceptional knowledge of the subject.**
- *Inspiration – Lee Mack meets Lord Denning!! Best on the circuit.*
- **Excellent course. Extremely useful and informative.**

- *Excellent presentation as always*
- **Very entertaining, well presented course.**
- *An essential part of any Civil Litigator's CPD requirements – attending an annual course with Kerry Underwood!*
- **Lots of those golden nuggets! Thank you.**
- *Very good course and going back to my firm with lots of thoughts, ideas and rethinking way we do some things.*
- **A very stimulating day, and with some brilliant points put forward.**
- *Very informative and engaging.*
- **Very good, well run and very detailed and well-presented course. Highly recommended.**
- *Very pragmatic advice with obvious real world experience.*
- **Excellent presentation and practical advice.**
- *Really helpful and will assist in informed discussion about the way in which we operate. Thank you.*
- **A different approach and attitude to low value cases.**
- *The business related guidance and business model suggested is so beneficial and so different from other CPD courses.*
- **Your talk was brilliant – great fun and informative.**
- *Most interesting and informative course I have been on.*
- **Really informative, fantastic materials.**

- *Some extremely helpful and useful points to note about how to run these cases effectively. Just what it said on the tin! Many thanks.*
- **Excellent speaker, highly recommended!**
- *Great course. Very useful and informative.*
- **Relevant, topical and highly informative. Excellent value as always.**
- *Enjoyable and delivered in simple speak.*
- **Very authoritative on issues that are of great significance at the moment.**
- *I love Kerry's courses – I may already know the subject, but he makes me look at it in a different – and hopefully more profitable – way.*
- **Fantastic and worthwhile course.**
- *Great value for money – as usual with KU!*
- **Kerry is always happy to answer any questions and discuss tricky points.**
- *Brilliant.*
- **Absolutely invaluable.**
- *Brilliant course. First one I have attended but it won't be the last.*
- **The right balance of knowledge, professionalism and humour. Excellent seminar.**

Reviews for the book Qualified One Way Costs Shifting, Section 57 and Set-Off

"This book is worth so much more than the price."

Professor Dominic Regan

"Comprehensive, authoritative, highly practical and always straight to the point..."

Rachel Rothwell, Editor, Litigation Funding

"This is a guide that will be invaluable"

PJ Kirby QC, Hardwicke Chambers

"Personal injury lawyers should keep this book by their side."

Mark Harvey, Head of Litigation, Hugh James Solicitors

"Thorough and readable, essential reading"

Gordon Exall, Barrister, Hardwicke Chambers

"This is the QOCS Bible." Sofia Ashraf, Barrister

"Very knowledgeable and entertaining to boot."

Anthony McCarthy, Macks Solicitors

"There is just no need to look elsewhere."

Andrew Twambley, CEO, InjuryLawyers4U

"Admirably thought through and I will be delving into it repeatedly."

Ian Foster, Law Costs Draftsman

Kerry Underwood on Personal Injury Reforms

10.00am to 4.30pm – 5.5 hours CPD

This course looks in detail at the personal injury reforms following the government's response to the consultation paper on 23 February 2017.

Topics covered include:

- Personal injury small claims limit
- Running personal injury small claims profitably
- Small claims track procedure
- Restriction of general damages in whiplash claims
- The tariff system
- Extension of fixed costs to all personal injury work
- Increase in value of claims covered by fixed costs
- Update on funding and costs including:
- Part 36
- Assignment of Conditional Fee Agreements
- Portals and Fixed Costs case law

Fee is £240 including VAT, subsequent delegates 10% discount.

BIRMINGHAM	WEDNESDAY	10 MAY	
LEEDS+	THURSDAY	11 MAY	
NEWCASTLE*	FRIDAY	12 MAY	
LIVERPOOL**	TUESDAY	16 MAY	SOLD OUT
MANCHESTER	WEDNESDAY	17 MAY	SOLD OUT
CARDIFF***	FRIDAY	19 MAY	SOLD OUT
PLYMOUTH****	TUESDAY	23 MAY	
EXETER****	THURSDAY	25 MAY	
LIVERPOOL**	TUESDAY	27 JUNE	
MANCHESTER	WEDNESDAY	28 JUNE	
CARDIFF***	THURSDAY	4 JULY	

*Sponsored by Trinity Chambers
** with Liverpool Law Society
***Sponsored by 9 Park Place Chambers
****Sponsored by Foot Anstey
+Sponsored by Zenith Chambers

To book contact Kerry Underwood on 01442 430900 or email kerry.underwood@lawabroad.co.uk

"Superb, inspirational course."

"You give us the courage to keep going."

"Utterly brilliant"

"What an original presentation. Loved your energy, passion and dynamism. Most unconventional but refreshing and original."

"Truly amazing content and presentation"

"Absolutely brilliant. A must for all PI litigators."

"Amazing course"

"I find Kerry a most charismatic lecturer with an exceptional knowledge of the subject."

"Inspiration – Lee Mack meets Lord Denning!! Best on the circuit."

"Kerry is the best presenter I have ever heard – fantastic"

"Most of the big decisions in my firm follow a Kerry Underwood course."

"Great day with Kerry who spoke brilliantly. A wealth of knowledge and a great teacher. Many thanks"

Personal Injury Small Claims, Portals and Fixed Costs

Volume 2 of 3

Kerry Underwood

Partner, Underwoods Solicitors

To

Doné

Law Abroad PLC

Copyright © 2017 Kerry Underwood. All rights reserved.

First softback edition printed 2017 in the United Kingdom.

This book contains Public Sector information licensed under the Open Government Licence V3.0.

A catalogue record for this book is available from the British Library.

ISBN 978-0-9935349-3-5

No part of this book shall be reproduced or transmitted in any form or by any means, electronic or mechanical, including photocopying, recording, or by any information retrieval system without written permission of the publisher.

Published by Law Abroad Publishing, part of Law Abroad PLC.

For more copies of this book, please email: claire.long@lawabroad.co.uk

Tel: 01442 430 900

Designed and set by Law Abroad Publishing, part of Law Abroad PLC, 79 Marlowes, Hemel Hempstead, Hertfordshire, HP1 1LF

http://www.underwoods-solicitors.co.uk/

Printed in Great Britain by Halstan & Co Ltd, 2 – 10 Plantation Road, Amersham, Buckinghamshire, HP6 6HJ.

Whilst every care has been taken to ensure the accuracy of this work, no responsibility for loss or damage occasioned to any person acting or refraining from acting as a result of any statement on it can be accepted by the author or publishers.

The moral right of the author has been asserted.

THANK YOU!

Special thanks to:

Doné Barnard
Jamiel Zaman

Thanks to:

9 Park Place Chambers, Cardiff
Brandon Abrahams
Nicholas Bacon QC
Cynthia Barnes
British International School of Stavanger, Norway
Caylee Burton
His Honour Michael Cook
Jo Downey
Gordon Exall
Foot Anstey
Simon Gibbs
Iain Goldrein QC
JP La Grange
Mark Harvey
Hemel Hempstead Town Football Club
PJ Kirby QC
Lawshare, Manchester
Michael Lieberman
Liverpool Law Society
Claire Long
Robert Males
Roger Mallalieu
Maninder Mann
Jan Miller
Tracy Ontong
Parklane Plowden Chambers, Leeds
Anna Patsalides
Mike Penning MP
David Pilling
Phoebe Ranger
Professor Dominic Regan
Sarah Robson
Rachel Rothwell
Michael Stubbs
Stuart Thompson
Trinity Chambers, Newcastle
Andrew Twambley
Leah Waller
Ben Williams QC
Andrew Wilson
Duncan Wood
My Blog Subscribers
My followers on Twitter

I am particularly grateful to David Pilling for proof reading this book, and to Nicholas Bacon QC for suggesting a number of amendments.

Any remaining mistakes are mine.

The Author

Kerry Underwood is a solicitor and is Senior Partner of Underwoods Solicitors. He is a lecturer, writer, broadcaster and former Employment Judge.

Kerry writes and edits the Costs and Funding section of Butterworths Personal Injury Litigation Service and is a regular contributor to Litigation Funding, New Law Journal, Solicitors Journal and the Law Society's Civil Justice Section Newsletter.

He pioneered Conditional Fee Agreements, TV advertising by lawyers and off-shoring work to South Africa.

Former Councillor and Parliamentary Candidate.

Kerry travels extensively and home is his beloved adopted town of Hemel Hempstead. Underwoods Solicitors sponsor Hemel Hempstead Town Football Club and Hemel Stags Rugby League Club. Underwoods Solicitors are Hemel Hempstead Business Ambassadors and Kerry is on the Board of that organisation.

Interests include football, cricket, gardening and reading.
Nelson Mandela, TS Eliot and Elvis are amongst his heroes.
Kerry supports Queen's Park Rangers.
Follow Kerry on Twitter @kerry_underwood
See Kerry's blog at: www.kerryunderwood.wordpress.com

Other titles by Kerry Underwood

Qualified One-Way Costs Shifting, Section 57 and Set-Off
Wasted Costs and Third Party Costs
Selected Writings Volume 1
Selected Writings Volume 2

Non-Law Books

My Dad and Other Writings

Shape without form, shade without colour,
Paralysed force, gesture without motion;

T.S. Eliot
The Hollow Men

Without lawyers, judges and courts, there is no access to justice and therefore no rule of law, and without the rule of law, society collapses

Lord Neuberger
Supreme Court President
10 April 2015

PARTS AND CHAPTERS

VOLUME 1

PART I – INTRODUCTION

PART II – DRIVERLESS CARS

PART III – SOFT TISSUE INJURY CLAIMS and MEDCO

PART IV – PERSONAL INJURY SMALL CLAIMS

PART V – FUNDING ISSUES IN PERSONAL INJURY CLAIMS GENERALLY

VOLUME 2

PART VI – THE PORTALS

PART VII – THE OLD "PREDICTIVE" COSTS REGIME

PART VIII – FROM PORTALS TO FIXED RECOVERABLE COSTS

VOLUME 3

PART IX – FIXED RECOVERABLE COSTS

PART X – EXTENDING FIXED RECOVERABLE COSTS

PART VI

THE PORTALS

Chapter 26

Portals: An Introduction

PORTALS: AN INTRODUCTION

Throughout this Part I use the shorthand terms "old predictive costs regime", "old RTA portal", "RTA portal" and "EL/PL portal".

Technically the portals are Pre-Action Protocols and there are two of them and their full names are the Pre-Action Protocol for Low Value Personal Injury Claims in Road Traffic Accidents and Pre-Action Protocol for Low Value Personal Injury (Employers' Liability and Public Liability) Claims.

They are universally known as the Road Traffic Accident Portal on the one hand and the Employers' Liability/Public Liability Portal on the other hand and these descriptions are generally shortened to RTA Portal and EL/PL Portal.

The claims process is commenced online by way of a Claim Notification Form (CNF).

Both portals cover work valued at between £1,000.01 and £25,000.00 and personal injury claims falling within these bands and these definitions are subject to an entirely different process as compared with other personal injury claims and other civil litigation generally.

Industrial disease claims, although coming within the EL/PL portal, are subject to a slightly different process.

The personal injury small claims limit is currently £1,000.00 and personal injury small claims are not included within the portal process.

The value is ascertained on a full liability basis, including pecuniary losses but excluding interest. In the RTA portal the value of vehicle related damages is also excluded for valuation purposes, although such damages can be claimed within the portal process.

Essentially the portals are pre-action protocols for what would be fast-track personal injury claims and around one million claims a year now go through the portal process. The detailed statistics are set out in chapter 28.

The portals are highly detailed, well-written and are formally made part of the system by the Civil Procedure Rules. I deal with the process in greater detail in chapter 29.

Their use is not compulsory, but failure to use them will generally lead to punishment in costs, as will unreasonably exiting the portal and I deal with that elsewhere.

The full text of the RTA Portal is set out in Chapter 33 and the full text of the EL/PL Portal is set out in Chapter 34. These portals came into effect on 31 July 2013, but prior to that there was the old RTA portal covering claims between £1,000.01 and £10,000.00 and that ran from 30 April 2010 to 30 July 2013.

The text of this old RTA portal is set out in the blog accompanying this book. To access the blog go to www.kerryunderwood.wordpress.com.

You can subscribe to the blog by visiting the above address and scrolling down to the bottom of the archive posts list on the right hand side of the page where it says email subscriptions.

Type your email address and click subscribe; once you receive the email click the link in the email and you have subscribed.

That gives you constant free access to all of the posts and each new post will be emailed to you.

The old RTA portal applies where the accident occurred on or after 30 April 2010 and the Claim Notification Form was submitted by 30 July 2013.

The new RTA portal applies where the accident occurred on or after 30 April 2010 but the Claim Notification Form was not submitted before 31 July 2013.

For claims over £10,000.00 the portal process started on 31 July 2013 and thus if the cause of action was before that date and the value is over £10,000.00, then the matter does not go onto a portal.

Thus for RTA claims occurring on or after 30 April 2010 and worth between £1,000.01 and £10,000.00, the portal that applies is determined by the date of the CNF, not the date of the accident.

On 30 April 2013 fixed costs in the old RTA portal were cut, although the portal remained essentially unchanged until 31 July 2013.

The relevant costs figures are determined by the date of the CNF, not the date of the cause of action.

EL/PL portal except industrial disease claims

The date of the cause of action determines whether the matter goes onto the portal. If it was before 31 July 2013 then it does not go on; if it was on or after 31 July 2013, then it does go on.

Industrial disease claims

The relevant date is that of the Letter of Claim, as by definition in an industrial disease claim there will not normally be a single event giving rise to a claim.

Thus if the Letter of Claim was sent on or before 30 July 2013, then the matter does not enter the portal.

If the Letter of Claim was sent on or after 31 July 2013, then the matter enters the EL/PL portal whenever the potential cause of action arose.

Thus the key date for an EL/PL claim is the date of the cause of action, **not** the date of notification.

In an industrial disease claim the key date is that of the Letter of Claim.

The portals are separate from the Pre-Action Protocol for Personal Injury Claims, which still operates as and when a claim exits one of the portals, and the full text of that protocol is set out in Chapter 36.

Recoverable costs in the portals are fixed and low, but the procedure is quick and simple. I deal elsewhere in detail with costs in the portal.

I also deal elsewhere with exclusions from the portals, but the key points to note are that bankrupts and those lacking capacity are excluded, but that children's claims go through the portals.

Limitation

If a matter is close to limitation then there is a procedure for issuing proceedings and those proceedings are then stayed so that the portal process can be engaged.

This is dealt with in Practice Direction 8B, which I consider in detail elsewhere but the text of the whole Practice Direction appears at Chapter 35.

Stages

The process consists of three stages, the first two of which are pre-action and involve no court fee. Stage 3 requires the issuing of proceedings under Part 8 of the Civil Procedure Rules and involves payment of a court fee.

The process is started by the electronic completion and filing of a Claim Notification Form which stands as the Letter of Claim should proceedings become necessary.

Any matter exiting the portals is in principle subject to Fixed Recoverable Costs, which came in on 31 July 2013, with the single exception of industrial disease cases, and there are penalties for unreasonably exiting the portal and also for not bringing in the portal a claim which should have been brought within the portal.

However in *Qader & Others v Esure Ltd & Khan v McGee [2016] EWCA Civ 1109, 16 November 2016*

the Court of Appeal held that the Fixed Recoverable Costs scheme does not apply to a claim started in the RTA portal and which exited the portal and was allocated to the multi-track after proceedings were issued under Part 7 of the Civil Procedure Rules.

Any doubts about the Qader decision have been ended by Rule 8.1 of The Civil Procedure (Amendment) Rules 2017, effective 6 April 2017, which provides that fixed recoverable costs only apply " for as long as the case is not allocated to the multi-track."

Rule 8 also amends the tables in CPR 45.29 to omit the words "but not more than £25,000.00" to make it clear that ex-portal claims which are not allocated to the multi-track are subject to Fixed Recoverable Costs, whatever their value.

As things stand an ex-portal matter settled pre-allocation is subject to Fixed Recoverable Costs, whatever its value.

The original Road Traffic Accident Portal came into effect on 30 April 2010 in relation to qualifying road traffic accidents, that is those which occurred on or after that date and covered claims up to £10,000.00.

On 31 July 2013 the road traffic portal jurisdiction was increased to £25,000.00 and that portal appears as Annex B of the 65th update – Practice Direction Amendments.

On the same day the Employers' Liability and Public Liability Portal came into being with the same jurisdiction or limit of £25,000.00 and that portal appears at Annex C of the 65th update – Practice Direction Amendments.

Exclusions from the portal process

There are extensive exclusions of cases from the portal process, even though they qualify on work type and value. I deal with exclusions from the portals in chapter 29.

Exiting the portal process

I deal with this subject in chapter 41.

Chapter 27

Key Dates and Costs

KEY DATES AND COSTS

Key Dates: Both Portals

The full title of what is commonly known as the Road Traffic Accident Portal is the Pre-Action Protocol for Low Value Personal Injury Claims in Road Traffic Accidents and the full text of that protocol appears in Chapter 34.

The full name of what is commonly EL/PL Portal is the Pre-Action Protocol for Low Value Personal Injury (Employers' Liability and Public Liability) Claims and the full text of that protocol appears at Chapter 35.

Road Traffic Portal

An accident which occurred prior to 30 April 2010 does not enter the portal, but may be subject to The Old Predictive Costs Regime – see Chapter 37.

30 April 2010 onwards

£1,000 – £10,000 damages

Claim Notification Form pre 30 April 2013	= old, higher costs	- old portal
Claim Notification Form 30 April 2013 onwards	= new, lower costs	- old portal
Claim Notification Form from 31 July 2013	= new, lower costs	- new portal

£10,000.01 – £25,000

Cause of action pre 31 July 2013	= does not enter any portal
Cause of action 31 July 2013 onwards	= enters new portal

Fixed Cost Medical Report	from 1 October 2014
MedCo	from 6 April 2015
Previous claim history (Searches of askCUEPI.com)	from 1 June 2015

Employers' Liability and Public Liability except industrial diseases

Cause of action pre 31 July 2013 = does not enter portal

Cause of action 31 July 2013 onwards = enters portal

Industrial diseases

Letter of claim pre 31 July 2013 = does not enter portal

Letter of claim 31 July 2013 onwards = enters portal

Thus the key date for Employers' Liability and Public Liability claims is the cause of action, **NOT** the date of notification.

In an industrial disease claim the key date is the date of the **letter of claim.**

Thus the Employers' Liability/Public Liability portal applies where the cause of action arose on or after 31 July 2013, or in the case of a disease claim, where the letter of claim is sent on or after 31 July 2013. (Paragraph 4.1(1) of the EL/PL Portal).

£25,000 is the valuation on a full liability basis including pecuniary losses, but excluding interest. (Paragraph 4.1(3)).

The protocols are generally well-written, clear and logical, but one small point to note concerns paragraph 4.1 of the RTA portal which states that the portal applies to accidents where the CNF is submitted on or after 31 July 2013.

On the face of it, this picks up pre 31 July 2013 accidents up to £25,000. In fact it does not, due to paragraph 1.2(1)(b) of the RTA portal which provides that the portal's upper limit is £10,000 for pre 31 July 2013 accidents.

Thus from 31 July 2013 the starting point is that all road traffic, public liability and employers' liability claims up to £25,000 go on to one of the two portals where the cause of action arose on or after 31 July 2013, but in relation to industrial disease cases the portal applies where the Letter of Claim was sent on or after 31 July 2013, irrespective of the date of the cause of action.

Conditional Fee Agreements

The key date is 1 April 2013.

If the CFA is pre-1 April 2013 then the success fee is recoverable from the other side; if not then it is not. The date of the CNF and whether the case is portalled or not, or goes into Fixed Recoverable Costs or not, is irrelevant to the issue of recoverability of the success fee.

After-the-Event Insurance

Exactly the same conditions apply as for conditional fee agreements in relation to recoverability of After-the-event (ATE) insurance premiums.

Exceptions

Mesothelioma

In the personal injury field success fees and After-the-Event insurance premiums remain recoverable in mesothelioma cases, whenever the Conditional Fee Agreement was entered into and whenever the ATE insurance was taken out.

Mesothelioma claims are currently excluded from the EL/PL Portal process. (Paragraph 4.3(10)).

Clinical Negligence

In clinical negligence cases the After-the-Event insurance premium remains recoverable in relation to the cost of a medical reports dealing with liability and causation.

On 30 January 2017 the Department of Health published its consultation paper covers England and Wales only: **Introducing Fixed Recoverable Costs in Lower Value Clinical Negligence Claims.**

Clinical negligence cases are currently excluded from the EL/PL Portal process. (Paragraph 4.3(9)).

However in October 2016 the Government announced that it proposed to extend the Fixed Recoverable Costs Scheme to clinical negligence cases, which presumably will then be the subject of a separate pre-action portal.

Lord Justice Jackson's review of Fixed Recoverable Costs is also looking at clinical negligence claims and his report is due out by 31 July 2017.

At present all exceptions to the abolition of recoverability of success fees and After-the-Event insurance premiums are themselves excluded from the portal process.

Small Claims

Small claims, that is currently all personal injury claims where general damages are £1,000 or less, are excluded from the portals. (Paragraph 4.1(4) of RTA portal and Paragraph 4.1(4) of the EL and PL portal).

It remains to be seen if this will be the case as and when the small claims limit is raised to £5,000 for road traffic cases and £2,000 for other matters.

Success Fees

Conditional Fee Agreement before 1 April 2013: Recoverable

Conditional Fee Agreement on or after 1 April 2013: Not Recoverable

Note that in mesothelioma claims the success fee remains recoverable whenever the conditional fee agreement was entered into. Mesothelioma claims are not subject to the portals or the existing fixed costs regime.

Whether or not a matter is capable of going on the portal, stays in or exits the portal, goes or does not go to fixed costs etc, is irrelevant in so far as recoverability of the success fee from the losing party is concerned.

Paragraph 7.44 of the RTA portal reads:

"7.44 Any offer to settle made at any stage by either party will automatically include, and cannot exclude—

....

(4) where applicable, any success fee in accordance with rule 45.31(1) (as it was in force immediately before 1 April 2013)."

Paragraph 7.41 of the EL/PL portal is in identical terms.

CPR 48 also contains transitional provisions in relation to this issue:

"48.1

(1) The provisions of CPR Parts 43 to 48 relating to funding arrangements, and the attendant provisions of the Costs Practice Direction, will apply in relation to a pre-commencement funding arrangement as they were in force immediately before 1 April 2013, with such modifications (if any) as may be made by a practice direction on or after that date.

(2) A reference in rule 48.2 to a rule is to that rule as it was in force immediately before 1 April 2013."

There can be very few claims still in the portal or fixed costs regime where the conditional fee agreement was entered in to prior to 1 April 2013, so here I have not set out the full and lengthy fixed recoverable success fee scheme.

If you have such a case and need advice then phone me on 01442 430900.

Note that a pre – 1 April 2013 conditional fee agreement with recoverable success fee automatically disqualifies a client from the protection of Qualified One Way Costs Shifting.

COSTS SUMMARY: ALL PORTALS

Portal costs are dealt with within CPR 45.18

ROAD TRAFFIC – Pre 30 April 2013

From £1,000.00 to £10,000.00	£
Stage 1 -	£400.00
Stage 2 -	£800.00
Total	**£1,200.00**

The post 29 April 2013 road traffic accident fees are:-

From £1,000.00 to £10,000.00	£
Stage 1 -	£200.00
Stage 2 -	£300.00
Total	**£500.00**

(The Civil Procedure (Amendment No. 3) Rules 2013, SI 2013 No 789 (L.7))

The post 30 July 2013 fees are:-

From £10,000.00 to £25,000.00	£
Stage 1 -	£200.00
Stage 2 -	£600.00
Total	**£800.00**

EL/PL

Fixed recoverable costs for claims within EL/PL protocols

From £1,000.00 to £10,000.00	£
Stage 1 -	£300.00
Stage 2 -	£600.00
Total	**£900.00**

From £10,000.00 to £25,000.00	£
Stage 1 -	£300.00
Stage 2 -	£1,300.00
Total	**£1,600.00**

These figures are taken from Table 6 and Table 6A which appears in CPR 45.18 and I set out those tables at the end of this chapter.

In both portals the Stage 1 fee is payable 10 days after receiving the Stage 2 Settlement pack and the Stage 2 fee is payable 10 days after settlement is agreed.

ALL PORTALS

Stage 3 Hearings

In all cases in all portals, whatever the value of the claims, the Stage 3 fee is £250 for a paper hearing and a further £250 for an oral hearing, giving a total of £500.

VAT

All fixed costs at all stages are exclusive of VAT (CPR 45.16(6)), and thus VAT must be added to all portal and fixed recoverable costs figures.

Type A, B and C fixed costs

Type A

Type A fixed costs are the legal representative's Stage 3 costs for a paper hearing and in the Road Traffic Accident portal are £250.00 plus VAT.

In the Employers Liability and Public Liability portal, which came into place on 31 July 2013, Type A fixed costs are £250.00 plus VAT.

Type B

Type B costs are *additional* advocate's costs for conducting an oral Stage 3 hearing and are also £250 for Road Traffic Accident portal cases and are the same for the Employers' Liability and Public Liability portals, giving a total fee of £500 for an oral Stage 3 hearing in all portals.

Type C

Type C fixed costs are the costs for the advice on the amount of damages where the claimant is a child and are £150 in the Road Traffic Accident portal and are the same in the new Employers' Liability and Public Liability portals.

Note that neither of the portals applies to protected parties within the meaning of CPR 21.1(2), for example a person lacking capacity within the meaning of the Mental Capacity Act 2005, (paragraph 4.3(2) of the EL and PL portal and paragraph 4.5(2) of the RTA portal).

Although children are dealt with in CPR 21 they are not protected parties. The heading of CPR 21, and the term used throughout, is Children *and* Protected Parties. (My italics).

Note also that while both the portal and the Fixed Recoverable Costs Scheme allow for an additional fee in relation to a matter involving a child, there appears to be no provision for such an additional fee if the matter is settled after exiting the portal, but before proceedings are issued.

In practice it may be that costs for issuing and seeking approval of the settlement will be treated as an interim application post *Sharp v Leeds City Council,* 1 February 2017, [2017] EWCA Civ 33 and the fee for any advice recovered as a disbursement reasonably incurred as a result of a particular feature of the dispute per CPR 45.29I(h).

There appears to be nothing to stop a claimant issuing proceedings while the matter is still in one of the portals, provided that the appropriate time has expired since lodging the Claim Notification Form, which stands as the Letter of Claim.

Claimants may wish to do this in children cases to avoid the lacuna whereby no additional fee is payable in a child case where the matter has exited the portal but not yet been issued.

London enhancement

The 12.5% uplift continues to apply where the claimant lives or works in an area set out in Practice Direction 45 and instructs a legal representative who practices in that area. (CPR 45.18(5)).

Paragraph 2.6 of Practice Direction 45 states that:-

"The area referred to in rules 45.11(2) and 45.18(5) consists of (within London) the county court districts of Barnet, Bow, Brentford, Central London, Clerkenwell and Shoreditch, Edmonton, Ilford, Lambeth, Mayors and City of London, Romford, Wandsworth, West London, Willesden and Woolwich and (outside London) the county court districts of Bromley, Croydon, Dartford, Gravesend and Uxbridge"

Legal representatives only get costs

The fixed recoverable costs, set out in CPR 45.18, apply only in relation to a claimant who has a legal representative. (Paragraph 4.6 of the RTA portal and Paragraph 4.4 of the EL and PL portal).

Thus no-one but a legal representative can get portal costs, although claimants in person may use the portals (see Paragraph 5.10 of each portal). Thus a Claims Management Company cannot recover portal costs.

In the Small Claims court anyone, including a Claims Management Company, can act for a fee.

Where the claimant reasonably believes that the claim is valued at between £1,000.01 and £25,000 but it subsequently becomes apparent that the value of the claim is less than £1,000, the claimant is entitled to the Stage 1 and (where relevant) the Stage 2 fixed costs (Paragraph 5.9 of each portal).

Children

The rules relating to costs in cases involving children depend on when and how the matter is resolved. They are of considerable complexity. This is an outline. I look at the whole issue of cases involving children in more detail in chapter 39.

An additional Type C payment of £150 plus VAT remains payable in cases involving children. Cases involving protected parties, either as claimant or defendant, do not go in to the portals.

In a portal case involving a child which proceeds to Stage 2 and is settled, an application must still be made to the court for approval and the court requires the following information, as set out in Practice Direction 8B:-

- the draft consent order;
- advice by counsel, solicitor or other legal representative on the amount of damages;
- a statement verified by a statement of truth signed by the litigation friend which confirms whether the child has recovered in accordance with the prognosis and whether there are any continuing symptoms. This statement will enable the court to decide whether to order the child to attend the settlement hearing;

If the court approves the settlement at a settlement hearing it will order the defendant to pay

(a) Stage 1 and 2 fixed costs;

(b) Stage 3 Type A, B and C fixed costs; and

(c) disbursements allowed in accordance with rule 45.19 (CPR 45.21(2)).

Where the court does not approve the settlement at a settlement hearing, it will order the defendant to pay Stage 1 and 2 fixed costs (CPR 45.21(3)).

Where the court approves the settlement at a second settlement hearing the court will order the defendant to pay:

(a) Stage 3 Type A and C fixed costs for the first settlement hearing;

(b) CPR 45.19 disbursements; and

(c) Stage 3 Type B fixed costs for one of the hearings.

(CPR 45.21(5)).

The court has a discretion also to order either party to pay an amount equivalent to either or both the Stage 3 Type A or Type B fixed costs where the court does not approve the settlement at the first settlement hearing, but does approve the settlement at a second settlement hearing (CPR 45.21(6)).

Infant settlement at Stage 3 of portal

CPR 45.22 applies where the claimant is a child and the matter is settled after proceedings are started under the Stage 3 procedure and the settlement is more than the defendant's Road Traffic Accident protocol offer and an application is made to the court to approve the settlement.

A Stage 3 hearing to approve infant settlement or to assess damages must always be an oral hearing and will not be dealt with on the papers.

Where the court approves the settlement at the hearing it will order the defendant to pay:

(a) Stage 1 and 2 fixed costs;

(b) Stage 3 Type A, B and C fixed costs; and

(c) CPR 45.19 disbursements.

(CPR 45.22(2)).

Where the court does not approve the settlement at the settlement hearing it will order the defendant to pay Stage 1 and 2 fixed costs. (CPR 45.22(3)).

Where the court does not approve the settlement at the first settlement hearing, but does approve it at the Stage 3 hearing, it will order the defendant to pay:

(a) Stage 3 Type A and C fixed costs for the settlement hearing; and

(b) CPR 45.19 disbursements; and

(c) Stage 3 Type B fixed costs for one of the hearings.

The court has a discretion to also order either the defendant or the claimant to pay an amount equivalent to either or both of Stage 3 Type A and Type B costs where the court does not approve the settlement at the first settlement hearing but does approve the settlement at the Stage 3 hearing (CPR 45.22(6)).

Where the settlement is not approved at the Stage 3 hearing, the court will order the defendant to pay the Stage 3 Type A fixed costs (CPR 45.22 (7)).

Where the claimant is a child, and at a settlement hearing, or Stage 3 hearing, the court orders that the claim is not suitable to be determined under the Stage 3 procedure, it will order the defendant to pay:

(i) Stage 1 and 2 fixed costs; and

(ii) Stage 3 Type A, B and C fixed costs.

Where the court is to assess damages then an application to the court to determine the amount of damages must be started by a claim form. On issuing the claim form the claimant must state the date when the Court Proceedings Pack (Part A and Part B) Form was sent to the defendant, and supply copies of medical reports, evidence of special damages, evidence of disbursements and the value of the claim.

Note also that while both the portal and the Fixed Recoverable Costs Scheme allow for an additional fee in relation to a matter involving a child, there appears to be no provision for such an additional fee if the matter is settled after exiting the portal but before proceedings are issued.

There appears to be nothing to stop a claimant issuing proceedings while the matter is still in one of the portals, provided that the appropriate time has expired since lodging the Claim Notification Form, which stands as the Letter of Claim.

Claimants may wish to do this in children cases to avoid the lacuna whereby no additional fee is payable in a child case where the matter has exited the portal but not yet been issued.

Solicitor and own client costs

All matters set out above are fixed RECOVERABLE costs. Solicitors are allowed to charge client costs over and above these rates.

Section 74 of the Solicitors Act 1974

Section 74(3) of the Solicitors Act 1974 provides:-

"(3) The amount which may be allowed on the assessment of any costs or bill of costs in respect of any item relating to proceedings in a county court shall not, except in so far as rules of court may otherwise provide, exceed the amount which could have been allowed in respect of that item as between party and party in those proceedings, having regard to the nature of the proceedings and the amount of the claim and of any counterclaim."

This is an important and little known provision, which on its face prevents a solicitor charging any client any element of solicitor and own client costs in any County Court matter, including small claims and fixed costs matters as well as non-fixed costs matters in both the fast-track and multi-track in the County Court.

It allows a charge on defeat, but only to the extent that between the parties recovery would have been made in the event of a win.

However Section 74(3) has the escape clause "except in so far as rules of court may provide otherwise..."

They do.

CPR 46.9 reads:-

"**Basis of detailed assessment of solicitor and client costs**

46.9

(1) This rule applies to every assessment of a solicitor's bill to a client except a bill which is to be paid out of the Community Legal Service Fund under the Legal Aid Act 1988 or the Access to Justice Act 1999 or by the Lord Chancellor under Part 1 of the Legal Aid, Sentencing and Punishment of Offenders Act 2012.

(2) Section 74(3) of the Solicitors Act 1974 applies unless the solicitor and client have entered into a written agreement which expressly permits payment to the solicitor of an amount of costs greater than that which the client could have recovered from another party to the proceedings.

(3) Subject to paragraph (2), costs are to be assessed on the indemnity basis but are to be presumed –

(a) to have been reasonably incurred if they were incurred with the express or implied approval of the client;

(b) to be reasonable in amount if their amount was expressly or impliedly approved by the client;

(c) to have been unreasonably incurred if –

(i) they are of an unusual nature or amount; and

(ii) the solicitor did not tell the client that as a result the costs might not be recovered from the other party.

(4) Where the court is considering a percentage increase on the application of the client, the court will have regard to all the relevant factors as they reasonably appeared to the solicitor or counsel when the conditional fee agreement was entered into or varied."

Thus the Act, read in conjunction with this rule, does allow the solicitor to charge the client more than would have been recovered, but only if there is a written agreement expressly permitting payment of a greater sum.

CPR 46.9(4) refers to Conditional Fee Agreement success fees.

The appropriate wording should go in every retainer/Client Care Letter/agreement dealing with County Court or potential County Court litigation.

I suggest the following:-

"**Section 74 Solicitors Act 1974 agreement**

This agreement expressly permits the solicitors to charge an amount of costs greater than that which you will recover or could have recovered from the other party to the proceedings and expressly permits payment of such sum.

This part of this agreement is made under section 74(3) of the Solicitors Act 1974 and the Civil Procedure Rules 46.9 (2) and (3).

In so far as any costs or disbursements are of an unusual nature or amount these costs might not be recovered from the other party."

This law only applies to County Court matters and therefore this wording does not have to be put in matters which do not come before the County Court, for example CICA claims.

I have included it where appropriate in the model funding agreements which appear at Chapter 13.

There is a circular argument as to whether this clause needs to be in a Contingency Fee Agreement covering pre-issue of proceedings. By definition the Contingency Fee Agreement covers pre-issue work and if proceedings are issued, then the Conditional Fee Agreement is in place from day one.

However if the matter is settled pre-issue and costs are sought from the other side, with an additional charge to be made to the client as is usual, then it is arguable that on assessment the client could rely upon Section 74(3) in the absence of this clause being in the Contingency Fee Agreement.

The counter-argument is that it is not contentious business and Section 74(1) specifically applies only to contentious business.

It is simply not worth taking the risk. Include the wording.

Predictive Costs Regime

Road traffic accident after 6 October 2003 and before 31 July 2013 - Up to £10,000

When the accident occurred prior to 30 April 2010, it will fall to be dealt with under this scheme.

In relation to accidents occurring on or after 30 April 2010 they will have gone into the RTA Portal. If resolved in the portal then portal costs are payable.

Any such matter not resolved within the portal, but settled pre-issue is dealt with by this scheme as fixed costs outside the portal did not come in until 31 July 2013.

Any accident occurring on or after 31 July 2013 will be subject to Fixed Recoverable Costs on exiting the portal, even if proceedings are not issued as Fixed Recoverable Costs cover matters settled pre-issue and post-issue, as well as matters which go to trial.

Portal Exclusions

However there are some cases which are excluded from the portal process and where the old predictive costs regime still applies.

Costs

Costs fall in to what was often known as the Predictable, or Predictive Costs Regime and this is set out in Part II of CPR 45 and CPR 45.9(2) defines that part as applying where:-

“(a) the dispute arises from a road traffic accident occurring on or after 6 October 2003;

(b) the agreed damages include damages in respect of personal injury, damage to property, or both;

(c) the total value of the agreed damages does not exceed £10,000; and

(d) if a claim had been issued for the amount of the agreed damages, the small claims track would not have been the normal track for that claim.”

CPR 45.11 sets out the amount of those fixed costs as follows:-

“45.11

(1) Subject to paragraphs (2) and (3), the amount of fixed recoverable costs is the total of –

(a) £800;

(b) 20% of the damages agreed up to £5,000; and

(c) 15% of the damages agreed between £5,000 and £10,000.

(2) Where the claimant –

(a) lives or works in an area set out in Practice Direction 45; and

(b) instructs a legal representative who practises in that area, the fixed recoverable costs will include, in addition to the costs specified in paragraph (1), an amount equal to 12.5% of the costs allowable under that paragraph.

(3) Where appropriate, VAT may be recovered in addition to the amount of fixed recoverable costs and any reference in this Section to fixed recoverable costs is a reference to those costs net of any such VAT.”

This original predictable costs regime continues to be relevant for claims not covered by the RTA Portal, but like the portal the scheme excludes small claims. It also excludes litigants in person.

The predictive costs regime never has any application if the matter is issued. It does not then apply to pre-issue costs.

Pre 30 April 2010

Any claims arising out of an accident occurring prior to 30 April 2010 do not enter the Pre-Action Protocol for Low Value Personal Injury Claims in Road Traffic Accidents.

Given the three year limitation period in personal injury cases this situation will arise very rarely, but could apply to old cases involving children.

Pre-6 October 2003

No Fixed Costs.

Portals costs taken into account in relation to fixed costs

Any order by the court in relation to fixed costs must take into account any payment made during the portal process. The relevant rule is CPR 45.28 which reads:

"45.28. Where a claim no longer continues under the relevant Protocol the court will, when making any order as to costs including an order for fixed recoverable costs under Section II or Section IIIA of this Part, take into account the Stage 1 and Stage 2 fixed costs that have been paid by the defendant."

Costs Orders

A silent order means no costs and therefore it is vital to obtain a costs order.

"Costs" in an order means standard basis only and if a party wants indemnity costs then it is necessary to ensure that the order describes them as being such.

The word "costs" on its own in the Civil Procedure Rules gives the court discretion to order either ordinary standard costs or indemnity costs, and indemnity costs will most usually be in relation to a claimant's successful Part 36 offer, and also to disapprove of the behaviour of either party – see for example *Gulati v MGN [2015] EWHC 1482 (Ch)*, upheld on appeal.

Limitation and Staying

Where a claimant has a claim that is approaching limitation and should be a portal claim, then proceedings must be issued and a stay of those proceedings sought whilst the protocol is complied with.

The relevant paragraph of Practice Direction 8B dealing with the pre-action protocols is 16 which reads as follows:-

"Limitation

16.1. Where compliance with the relevant Protocol is not possible before the expiry of a limitation period the claimant may start proceedings in accordance with paragraph 16.2.

16.2. The claimant must –

(1) start proceedings under this Practice Direction; and

(2) state on the claim form that –

(a) the claim is for damages; and

(b) a stay of proceedings is sought in order to comply with the relevant Protocol.

16.3. The claimant must send to the defendant the claim form together with the order imposing the stay."

Practice Direction 8.2 deals with the contents of the claim form.

TABLE 6

Fixed costs in relation to the RTA Protocol			
Where the value of the claim for damages is not more than £10,000		**Where the value of the claim for damages is more than £10,000, but not more than £25,000**	
Stage 1 fixed costs	£200	Stage 1 fixed costs	£200
Stage 2 fixed costs	£300	Stage 2 fixed costs	£600
Stage 3 - Type A fixed costs	£250	Stage 3 - Type A fixed costs	£250
Stage 3 - Type B fixed costs	£250	Stage 3 - Type B fixed costs	£250
Stage 3 - Type C fixed costs	£150	Stage 3 - Type C fixed costs	£150

TABLE 6A

Fixed costs in relation to the EL/PL Protocol			
Where the value of the claim for damages is not more than £10,000		**Where the value of the claim for damages is more than £10,000, but not more than £25,000**	
Stage 1 fixed costs	£300	Stage 1 fixed costs	£300
Stage 2 fixed costs	£600	Stage 2 fixed costs	£1300
Stage 3 - Type A fixed costs	£250	Stage 3 - Type A fixed costs	£250
Stage 3 - Type B fixed costs	£250	Stage 3 - Type B fixed costs	£250
Stage 3 - Type C fixed costs	£150	Stage 3 - Type C fixed costs	£150

Chapter 28

The Statistics

STATISTICS

Here I set out the statistics in relation to the Road Traffic Accident Portal, from its inception on 30 April 2010 until 31 August 2016, and in relation to the Employers' Liability Portal and the Public Liability Portal, from its inception on 31 July 2013 until 31 August 2016.

These statistics, obtained from the portal company, contain a wealth of information to help you plan your practice and to see what happens to portal claims, that is how many drop out and for what reason etc.

These statistics are invaluable.

RTA Portal MI - 30 April 2010 - 31 August 2016 - Cumulative Total			
Portal MI		**Total**	**Total for last month**
Total number of CNFs created and sent to a Compensator		**5 073 532**	**68 932**
Total number of CNFs that left the process at the end Stage 1		**1 579 217**	**17 441**
Breakdown of	1 579 217		
i) Liability Decision Timeout		**1 067 103**	**12 172**
ii) Liability not admitted or Admitted with contributory negligence other than seatbelt		**512 114**	**5 269**
Total number of claims that have left the process at Stage 2 for reasons other than an agreed settlement		**271 378**	**7 654**
Breakdown of	271 378		
i) Interim payment of more than £1000 not agreed		**1 065**	**6**
ii) Stage 2 Settlement Pack repudiated		**2 886**	**7**
iii) Stage 2 Settlement Pack timeout/no response		**94 916**	**1 186**
iv) No agreement reached, Court Proceedings Pack completed ready for court		**172 511**	**6 455**
Total number of Stage 2 Settlement Packs where agreement has been reached		**1 364 130**	**16 727**
Total number of CNFs that left the Process using the Exit Process Function - From 29 March 2011 *		**802 677**	**15 189**
Breakdown of	802 677		
i) Incomplete CNF		**10 164**	**184**
ii) Value below £1,000		**11 449**	**204**
iii) Value of claim exceeds the upper limit		**10 193**	**94**
iv) Claim too Complex for the process		**9 937**	**82**
v) Withdrawal of claim		**19 204**	**399**
vi) Duplicate Claim		**43 955**	**798**
vii) Withdrawal of offer		**3 733**	**52**
viii) Interim Payment for a child		**414**	**11**
ix) Claim Requires further investigation		**316 216**	**6 317**
x) Other		**365 701**	**6 747**
xi) Stage 1 Costs not paid on time **		**10 242**	**261**
xii) interim payment request not answered and/or paid on time **		**1 321**	**37**
xiii) Interim Payment partial offer not accepted **		**148**	**3**

Total remaining in the system (which includes CNF's that have liability decisions outstanding)		**1 056 130**	**10 156**
* ***Note:*** *The Exit Process function was introduced in Release 1 - 29 March 2011 - and may be used at any stage of the process.*			
***** Note:*** *The reason code Stage 1 Costs not paid on time and Interim not answered or paid was introduced in Release 2 - 25 September 2012 and can only be used at the end of stage 1*			

EL (Accident only) Portal MI - 31 July 2013 - 31 August 2016 - Cumulative Total			
Portal MI		**Total**	**Total for last month**
Total number of CNFs created and sent to a Compensator via the Portal *		**142 984**	**4 396**
Total number of CNFs that left the process at the end Stage 1		**65 219**	**2 034**
Breakdown of	65 219		
i) Liability Decision Timeout		**33 349**	**1 217**
ii) Liability not admitted or Admitted with contributory negligence		**31 870**	**817**
Total number of claims that have left the process at Stage 2 for reasons other than an agreed settlement		**2 612**	**131**
Breakdown of	2 612		
i) Interim payment of more than £1000 not agreed		**31**	**0**
ii) Stage 2 Settlement Pack repudiated		**28**	**2**
iii) Stage 2 Settlement Pack timeout/no response		**1 756**	**75**
iv) No agreement reached, Court Proceedings Pack completed ready for court		**797**	**54**
Total number of Stage 2 Settlement Packs where agreement has been reached		**18 633**	**635**
Total number of CNFs that left the Process using the Exit Process Function		**32 673**	**1 033**
Breakdown of	32 673		
i) Incomplete CNF		**707**	**13**
ii) Value below £1,000		**167**	**2**
iii) Value of claim exceeds upper limit		**870**	**46**
iv) Claim too Complex for the process		**243**	**17**
v) Withdrawal of claim		**1 083**	**22**
vi) Duplicate Claim		**3 351**	**84**
vii) Withdrawal of offer		**80**	**0**
viii) Interim Payment for a child		**20**	**1**
ix) Claim Requires further investigation		**10 282**	**384**
x) Other		**13 101**	**394**

xi) Failure to acknowledge CNF on time		399	3
xii) Failure to provide adequate loss of earnings details		1 311	37
Xiii) Stage 1 costs not paid on time		821	19
XIV) Interim Payment request not answered and/or paid on time		229	10
XIV) Interim Payment partial offer not accepted		9	1
Total remaining in the system (which includes CNF's that have liability decisions outstanding)		23 847	453

* ***Note:*** *The total number of CNFs created and sent to a Compensator does not include draft copies they may have been printed and sent by Post.*

PL Portal MI - 31 July 2013 - 31 August 2016 - Cumulative Total			
Portal MI		**Total**	**Total for last month**
Total number of CNFs created and sent to a Compensator via the Portal *		**203 383**	**5 525**
Total number of CNFs that left the process at the end Stage 1		**116 719**	**3 304**
Breakdown of	116 719		
i) Liability Decision Timeout		**42 389**	**1 505**
ii) Liability not admitted or Admitted with contributory negligence		**74 330**	**1 799**
Total number of claims that have left the process at Stage 2 for reasons other than an agreed settlement		**3 071**	**137**
Breakdown of	3 071		
i) Interim payment of more than £1000 not agreed		**19**	**0**
ii) Stage 2 Settlement Pack repudiated		**90**	**3**
iii) Stage 2 Settlement Pack timeout/no response		**1 851**	**73**
iv) No agreement reached, Court Proceedings Pack completed ready for court		**1111**	**61**
Total number of Stage 2 Settlement Packs where agreement has been reached		**17 672**	**653**
Total number of CNFs that left the Process using the Exit Process Function		**39 958**	**1 123**
Breakdown of	39 958		
i) Incomplete CNF		**2 714**	**83**
ii) Value below £1,000		**208**	**1**
iii) Value of claim exceeds upper limit		**603**	**22**
iv) Claim too Complex for the process		**295**	**8**
v) Withdrawal of claim		**1 790**	**31**
vi) Duplicate Claim		**4 104**	**105**
vii) Withdrawal of offer		**116**	**4**
viii) Interim Payment for a child		**24**	**0**
ix) Claim Requires further investigation		**11 223**	**390**

x) Other		16 652	409
xi) Failure to acknowledge CNF on time		1 115	23
xii) Failure to provide adequate loss of earnings details		26	2
xiii) Stage 1 costs not paid on time		928	36
XIV) Interim Payment request not answered and/or paid on time		154	8
XV) Interim Payment partial offer not accepted		6	1
Total remaining in the system (which includes CNF's that have liability decisions outstanding)		25 963	134
* ***Note:*** *The total number of CNFs created and sent to a Compensator does not include draft copies they may have been printed and sent by Post.*			

Chapter 29

The Portal Process

THE PORTAL PROCESS

The Stages

The process consists of three stages, the first two of which are pre-action and involve no court fees.

Stage 1 involves service of the Claim Notification Form (CNF) and the defendant's response.

Stage 2 involves preparing the evidence, Settlement Pack, negotiations and possible settlement.

Stage 3 requires the issuing of proceedings under Part 8 of the Civil Procedure Rules and involves payment of a court fee.

Special provision for claims made by children

Claims made by children are not thereby excluded from the portal process, but that process is modified as follows:

- the CNF must state that the claimant is a child;

- the Statement of Truth may be signed by the child's parent or guardian as an alternative to the claimant or claimant's legal representative;

- the interim payment provisions do not apply and proceedings must be started in order to obtain the court's approval to a payment other than those made direct to treatment providers;

- court approval is necessary in relation to any proposed settlement and this is by way of a Settlement Hearing.

I deal with this in more detail elsewhere and look at the interplay between the portals and fixed costs and children's cases in chapter 39.

Practice Direction 8B, which deals with infant settlement hearings in the portals, is set out in chapter 35.

The usual rules about conflicts of interest apply and so lawyers need to check that the parent has no interest in conflict with that of the child if the parent is acting as Litigation Friend.

Stage 1

All references to "days" are to business days.

In Stage 1 the claimant completes a Claim Notification Form (CNF) on https://www.rapidclaimsettlement.org.uk/ and sends it electronically to the defendant's insurers who must respond electronically within 15 business days with a decision on liability.

A "defendant only CNF" should be sent to the defendant by first class post.

The Motor Insurers Bureau has 30 days to respond.

If liability is not admitted within that timeframe then the matter exits the portal.

If liability is admitted then the matter proceeds to Stage 2.

Although the CNF is not a claim form as such it must include a signed Statement of Truth and it stands as a letter of claim as far as the Personal Injury Pre-Action Protocol is concerned, if the matter exits the portal and proceedings are anticipated.

Thus care needs to be taken when completing the CNF and its tick box style should not be allowed to detract from its importance.

As we shall see later the very fact that a matter has ever been in the portal has significant consequences throughout the life of a case, especially in relation to costs.

Putting a matter on a portal should not be a knee-jerk reaction as soon as a personal injury claim comes in. Thought should be given as to whether it is in fact eligible for one of the portals, and whether it comes within the maximum portal limit.

Where the CNF was submitted on or after 1 June 2015, the claimant's solicitor must search the Claims and Underwriting Exchange at www.askCUE.co.uk and enter the CUE reference number on the CNF.

Failure to complete the boxes in the CNF marked as mandatory allows the defendant to exit the portal, unless the only missing information is the CUE number and the defendant has not asked the claimant to re-send the CNF with the CUE number inserted.

If the matter exits the portal due to inadequate mandatory information on the CNF, then there are adverse costs consequences for the claimant.

If judgment is subsequently entered for the claimant, the court may limit costs to portal costs only.

If the claimant has failed to provide the CUE number, having been requested to do so by the defendant, the court may not order the defendant to pay the claimant's costs and disbursements save in exceptional circumstances (CPR 45.24(2A)).

Value

RTA Matters

The RTA Protocol upper limit is:

(a) £25,000.00 where the accident occurred on or after 31 July 2013; or

(b) £10,000.00 where the accident occurred on or after 30 April 2010 and before 31 July 2013

on a full liability basis including pecuniary losses, but excluding interest and vehicle related damages.

Thus if a claim is potentially worth £40,000.00, but it is accepted from the outset that there would be at least 50% contributory negligence, reducing the maximum to £20,000.00, the matter still does not go on the portal as the value on a full liability basis exceeds the protocol upper limit.

The minimum value is more than £1,000.00, that is the small claims limit, so cases that would normally be allocated to the small claims track do not go on the portal. (Paragraph 4.1(4)).

It is not clear whether the portal process will still exclude small claims track matters as and when the small claims limit for road traffic accident work goes up to £5,000.00 and other personal injury work to £2,000 as per the government's February 2017 proposals.

Vehicle related damages

Vehicle related damages do not form part of the value of the claim for the purposes of the maximum £25,000.00 portal limit. This is achieved by a fairly clumsy combination of paragraphs 1.1(18), 1.2, 4.1 and 4.4.

Paragraph 1.1 is the definition section and paragraph 1.1(18) reads:-

"(18) 'vehicle related damages' means damages for—

(a) the pre-accident value of the vehicle;

(b) vehicle repair;

(c) vehicle insurance excess; and

(d) vehicle hire."

Thus that defines vehicle related damages.

Paragraph 1.2(1) reads:-

"1.2

(1) The 'Protocol upper limit' is—

(a) £25,000 where the accident occurred on or after 31 July 2013; or

(b) £10,000 where the accident occurred on or after 30 April 2010 and before 31 July 2013,

on a full liability basis including pecuniary losses but excluding interest."

Paragraph 4.1 sets out the scope of the portal and 4.1(3) provides that the portal applies where "the claimant values the claim at no more than the Protocol upper limit..."

After 4.1(4) the following appears in brackets:-

"(Paragraphs 1.1(18) and 4.4 state the damages that are excluded for the purposes of valuing the claim under paragraph 4.1.)"

As we have seen 1.1(18) is in fact a definition section and does not exclude anything from anything but if one then looks at 4.4 it says:-

"A claim may include vehicle related damages but these are excluded for the purposes of valuing the claim under paragraph 4.1."

The net effect of this is that vehicle related damages, however great the value, may be included in the portal claim provided that the balance of the claim does not exceed £25,000.00.

Thus if the claim, excluding vehicle related damages, is £20,000.00 and there are £80,000.00 of vehicle related damages, then that is a portal claim, even though the total is £100,000.00 and if it exits the portal it is a fixed costs claim, unless allocated to the multi-track, whereupon it ceases to be a fixed costs claim following the Court of Appeal decision in Qader *& Others v Esure Ltd & Khan v McGee [2016] EWCA Civ 1109.*

I am satisfied that all the references to vehicle related damages etc. are designed to deal with the maximum portal jurisdiction, rather than fixed costs, and that leaves open the question of precisely what fixed costs are payable if a claim exits the portal and settles for, say, £100,000.00 without being allocated to the multi-track, as in the example I have given above.

It would be open to the Claimant to argue either that *O'Beirne v Hudson* [2010] EWCA Civ 52 applies but in reverse so to speak or that the case is exceptional by reference to CPR Part 45.29J.

A further alternative to seek the 20% of costs payable on the entirety of the agreed damages (post *Qader* at first instance and pre CA decision).

The Table of Fixed Costs had a maximum pre-issue figure of £25,000.00 which suggests that the drafters never realized that there could be very much higher value claims caught by fixed costs.

The £25,000 figure is removed by Rule 8 of The Civil Procedure (Amendment) Rules 2017.

It is not clear whether this is retrospective.

That view was taken by the Court of Appeal in *Qader.*

The EL/PL Portal

This portal came into effect on 31 July 2013 and thus there has only ever been one protocol upper limit and that is £25,000.00 on a full liability basis, including pecuniary losses but excluding interest. (Paragraph 4.1(3) of the portal).

As with the RTA Portal the minimum level is more than £1,000.00, that is the small claims limit.

In February 2017 the government proposed that the non-RTA small claims limit be increased up to £2,000.

It remains to be seen whether claims up to this new small claims limit of £2,000 will be excluded from the portal.

Forms

RTA

Paragraph 1.4 of the RTA Portal reads:-

"**1.4** Subject to paragraph 1.5 the standard forms used in the process set out in this Protocol are available from Her Majesty's Courts and Tribunals Service ('HMCTS') website at www.justice.gov.uk/forms/hmcts —

(1) Claim Notification Form ('Form RTA 1' – referred to in this Protocol as 'the CNF');

(2) Defendant Only Claim Notification Form ('Form RTA 2');

(3) Medical Report Form ('Form RTA 3');

(4) Interim Settlement Pack Form ('Form RTA 4');

(5) Stage 2 Settlement Pack Form ('Form RTA 5');

(6) Court Proceedings Pack (Part A) Form ('Form RTA 6'); and

(7) Court Proceedings Pack (Part B) Form ('Form RTA 7')."

Paragraph 1.5 provides that the information required in Form RTA 3, that is the medical report form, may be provided in a different format to that set out in that form.

EL/PL

Paragraph 1.3 of the EL/PL Portal provides:-

"**1.3** Subject to paragraph 1.4 the standard forms used in the process set out in this Protocol are available from Her Majesty's Courts and Tribunals Service ('HMCTS') website at www.justice.gov.uk/forms/hmcts—

(1) Claim Notification Form ('Form EL1', 'Form ELD1' and 'Form PL1'– which are referred to in this Protocol as 'the CNF');

(2) Defendant Only Claim Notification Form ('Form EL2', 'Form ELD2' and 'Form PL2');

(3) Medical Report Form ('Form EPL3');

(4) Interim Settlement Pack Form ('Form EPL4');

(5) Stage 2 Settlement Pack Form ('Form EPL5');

(6) Court Proceedings Pack (Part A) Form ('Form EPL6'); and

(7) Court Proceedings Pack (Part B) Form ('Form EPL7')."

Paragraph 1.4 provides that the information required in Form EPL3, that is the medical report form, may be provided in a different format to that set out in that form.

Time and Limitation

The CNF starts time running under the general Pre-Action Protocol.

Completing and lodging the Claim Notification Form does not count as issuing proceedings and does not stop time running under the Limitation Act 1980.

Stage 3 of the portal does stop limitation running and there are special provisions in relation to staying an issued case to allow the portal process to be followed and I deal with this later.

Contributory negligence

Any allegation of contributory negligence, apart from the admitted failure to wear a seatbelt, causes the matter to exit the relevant portal.

Costs

RTA Portal

If the defendant admits liability, or alleges contributory negligence in relation to the claimant's admitted failure to wear a seatbelt, then the defendant must pay stage 1 fixed costs of £200.00 within 10 days of receiving the stage 2 Settlement Pack, together with, in a soft tissue injury claim, a fixed medical report fee and the cost of obtaining medical records.

Failure to do so allows the claimant to give written notice to the defendant that the claim will no longer continue in the RTA portal.

Such notice must be given within 10 days of the end of the payment period.

If no such written notice is given, or is given late, then the claim continues in the RTA portal.

This stage 1 costs procedure does not apply to cases involving a child, which I deal with elsewhere.

EL/PL Portal

The principles are the same, save that there is no provision for any case where there is an allegation of contributory negligence to remain in the portal, and so the provisions only apply if liability is admitted in full.

Exiting the portal during stage 1

I deal with exiting the portal and the consequences of doing so in detail in chapter 41.

Exit is automatic if *any* of the following occur:-

- the insurer fails to complete and return the CNF response; or
- does not admit liability; or
- alleges contributory negligence other than the admitted failure to wear a seatbelt; or
- indicates that the small claims track would be the normal track for the claim; or

- indicates that there is inadequate information on the CNF, but note the special provisions in relation to the CUE number dealt with above.

Stage 2

Stage 2 comes into play if the defendant admits liability.

Liability is defined in the portal as:

"(1) 'admission of liability' means the defendant admits that—

(a) the accident occurred;
(b) the accident was caused by the defendant's breach of duty;
(c) the defendant caused some loss to the claimant, the nature and extent of which is not admitted; and
(d) the defendant has no accrued defence to the claim under the Limitation Act 1980;"

The claimant solicitor obtains a medical report and where it is clear from the outset that an additional medical report is necessary from a medical expert in a different discipline, then a second report may be obtained from an expert in that discipline.

A stay in the process can be obtained if further medical evidence is needed.

There is no fixed timetable for obtaining medical reports.

Within 15 business days of the report being confirmed as factually accurate, the claimant solicitor must complete the Stage 2 Settlement Pack Form, which is sent electronically to the insurer, together with the medical report/s, special damages evidence and receipts and schedules and any other relevant evidence, such as photographs.

Once the report has been sent to the defendant there is no further opportunity for the claimant to challenge the facts upon which the report is based.

In claims of £10,000.00 or less, it is assumed that the medical expert will not need to see any medical records.

There are special rules in relation to medical evidence in soft tissue injury road traffic accident claims and these are dealt with in chapter 7.

The claimant must make an offer in respect of each item claimed, including general damages.

The insurer has 15 business days from receipt of the Settlement Pack to consider it and accept the claimant's offer or make a counteroffer.

Where the defendant's insurer makes a counteroffer, there is a further period of 20 business days for consultation and negotiation between the parties.

The defendant must serve counter schedules of damages and make an offer in respect of each item where the claimant's offer is not accepted.

Offers made by a defendant at Stage 2 are not to be regarded as admissions – see *Mulholland v Hughes and Conjoined Appeals, No. AP20/15, Newcastle-upon-Tyne County Court, 18 September 2015.*

Issues cannot be raised at Stage 3 if they are not set out at Stage 2 – see Mulholland above.

It is unclear whether a defendant can ask questions of the claimant's medical expert in the portal process.

There is no provision within the portal itself and therefore the answer appears to be no. However CPR 45.19(2A)(e), which applies only to the portal process, lists as a fixed medical report fee "answer to questions under Part 35: £80.00."

I think that that is an error and there is no provision within the portal process for the defendant to ask Part 35 questions of the claimant's medical expert.

Interim payments

If further reports are recommended and a stay agreed by the parties in accordance with paragraph 7.12, the claimant can request an interim payment when the Interim Settlement Pack (ISP) and initial medical reports, containing the recommendation that a subsequent medical report is required, have been sent to the defendant.

The claimant must also send evidence of pecuniary losses and disbursements.

The claimant may request:

- an interim payment of £1,000.00 in relation to general damages, and if requested the defendant must make an interim payment of £1,000.00 within 10 business days of receiving the ISP; or
- interim payments of over £1,000.00 where the claimant has specified in the ISP the amount requested, the heads of damages to which the request relates and the reason for the request.

If requested in this manner then the defendant must pay at least £1,000.00 within 15 business days from receiving the ISP and give reasons why more is not being given.

Any interim payment over £1,000.00 will relate to pecuniary losses.

Vehicle related damages may be included in a request for more than £1,000.00, but only where the claimant has already paid for them.

If an updated Compensation Recovery Unit (CRU) certificate is necessary, the defendant should apply for one as soon as possible and notify the claimant that it has done so and make an interim payment no more than 30 days after receiving the ISP.

If the defendant refuses to make an interim payment which has been properly requested, then the claimant may start Part 7 proceedings to apply to the court for an interim payment.

Likewise if a claimant is not content with the amount of the interim payment, then Part 7 proceedings may be commenced.

However if the court awards an interim payment of no more than the sum offered by the defendant, then the costs payable by the defendant are limited to stage 2 fixed costs.

In either situation the claimant must give notice to the defendant, within 10 days of the end of the payment period, that the claim will no longer continue under the portal process.

In the absence of such notice the claim continues in the portal.

No interim payment may be made if the claimant is a child and if an interim payment is reasonably required for a child, then Part 7 proceedings must be started and the claim will exit the portal.

The Settlement Pack

The stage 2 Settlement Pack (SP) must contain:-

- the stage 2 Settlement Pack form;
- any medical reports;
- any non-medical report;
- medical records/photographs;
- any witness statements;
- for soft tissue injury claims, fixed costs medical report invoice and any medical report invoice.

These documents must be sent to the defendant within 15 days of the claimant approving the final medical report and agreeing to rely on the prognosis.

Where the defendant alleges contributory negligence because of the claimant's admitted failure to wear a seatbelt, the stage 2 Settlement Pack Form must suggest a percentage reduction, which may be 0%, in the amount of damages.

The defendant has 35 days to consider the Settlement Pack and that is known as the total consideration period and is comprised of 15 days to consider it and make an offer (the "initial consideration period") and a further 20 days to negotiate a settlement (the "negotiation period").

This may be extended by agreement between the parties.

Thus a defendant has five options at this stage:-

1. to accept the claimant's proposal;
2. to make a counter proposal;
3. to withdraw the admission of causation and/or state an intention to contest liability;

4. to state that the matter is worth less than the lower financial limit, that is that the small claims track is appropriate;

5. to fail to respond in time.

Options 3, 4 and 5 cause the matter to exit the portal.

Any acceptance of the claimant's offer, or any counter offer, must be made within the initial consideration period.

If an offer is made by either party within five days of the end of the total consideration period, a further five days is allowed for consideration of that offer.

Where a defendant gives notice within the original or extended initial consideration period that it considers that the claim is a small claims track claim, or withdraws an admission of causation, or fails to respond at all, then the claim exits the portal.

If a counter offer is made then the defendant must propose an amount for each head of damages and explain why it has reduced the sum as compared with that offer.

This is designed to help the claimant when negotiating a settlement and to identify those areas still in dispute.

Any counter offer must also state the type and amount of any deductible amount where the defendant has obtained a CRU certificate.

It will be in the insurer's interest to maximize the heads of claim against which CRU recoverable benefits can be set off. This is why the portal allows for the insurer to put forward a higher sum than that proposed by the claimant under certain heads of claim.

The defendant need only explain any reduction, not any increase.

Due to the statutory ring-fencing of general damages from benefit recovery, it will generally be in the insurer's interest to maximise special damages at the expense of general damages where possible.

The claimant has until the end of the total consideration period to accept or reject the defendant's counter offer.

Late offers will extend the overall timescale.

No further counter offer is required.

Any offer to settle will automatically include stage 1 and stage 2 fixed costs and an agreement in principle to pay type C fixed costs of an advice on quantum, where such advice is justified, and also to pay disbursements in accordance with CPR 45.19.

It will include, in a soft tissue injury claim, the fixed cost of obtaining a medical report under CPR 45.19(2A)(a).

It also automatically includes any recoverable success fee but these will now be few and far between given the abolition of recoverability in relation to any Conditional Fee Agreement entered into on or after 1 April 2013, with the exception of mesothelioma claims, which do not go into the portal in any event.

For claims subject to the old RTA portal, any offer to settle will automatically include stage 2 fixed costs of £800.00 under the old CPR 45.29, together with an agreement in principle to pay disbursements and a success fee in accordance with the old CPR 45.31(1).

If an offer made in the stage 2 Settlement Pack Form is withdrawn after the total consideration period, then the claimant may start Part 7 proceedings.

Settlement achieved

Except where the claimant is a child, or an updated CRU certificate is required, where settlement is reached the defendant must pay the agreed damages, less CRU and any interim payment, any unpaid stage 1 and stage 2 fixed costs, Type C fixed costs for an additional advice on quantum, where justified, and relevant disbursements and any success fee.

Payment must be made within 10 business days of the parties agreeing a settlement.

Where no settlement is agreed, or where the claimant is a child, Part 8 proceedings are then issued in accordance with Practice Direction 8B.

I deal with the whole process of when a claimant is a child in chapter 39.

Vehicle related damages.

There are various provisions relating to the procedure concerning vehicle related damages (additional damages) and in relation to costs, depending on whether the original damages and/or the additional damages are, or are not, agreed.

Failure to reach agreement

Where the original damages, and if relevant the additional damages, are not agreed then the claimant must send the Court Proceedings Pack (Part A and Part B) Form (CPPF) to the defendant and this must contain:-

- in Part A the final schedule of the claimant's losses and the defendant's responses, together with supporting comments from both parties concerning the disputed heads of damages;
- in Part B the final offer and counter offer from the Stage 2 Settlement Pack Form and, where relevant, the offer, together with any counter offer.

The comments in the Court Proceedings Pack Part A Form must not raise anything that has not been raised in the Stage 2 Settlement Pack Form and if the defendant considers that the CPPF does not comply then it must be returned to the claimant within five business days with an explanation as to why the defendant thinks that it does not comply with the rules.

Non-settlement payment by the defendant

Except where the claimant is a child, where no settlement has been reached by the end of Stage 2, the defendant must pay the claimant the final offer made in the CPPF less recoverable benefits and any interim payment, together with any unpaid stage 1 and stage 2 fixed costs and agreed disbursements.

These payments must be made within 15 days of receiving the CPPF.

If disbursements are not agreed then the defendant must pay such sum as it considers reasonable.

If an updated CRU certificate is required the defendant should apply for one as soon as possible, in which case payment must be made within 30 days of receiving the CPPF.

Failure to pay within the time limits permits the claimant to give written notice that the claimant will no longer proceed in the portal and the claimant may then start Part 7 proceedings without costs penalties.

Where the claimant gives notice to the defendant that the claim is unsuitable for the RTA portal then the claim will no longer continue in it.

However where the court considers that the claimant acted unreasonably in exiting the portal it will only award fixed portal costs.

I deal with this extensively in chapter 41.

Should the interim payment made previously be included as part of the damages?

If the interim payment was made during the portal process then that is the end of the matter and it will not be taken into account in any subsequent Part 7 proceedings.

In *Bewicke-Copley v Ibeh Oxford County Court 029YJ613 4 June 2014*

the claimant exited the portal and issued Part 7 proceedings expecting to recover costs that follow from a matter being allocated to the fast-track.

The defendant asked the court to award the claimant judgment on the sums that had been agreed within stage 2 of the portal process, together with fixed costs that would have followed from that agreement, and to limit any further costs recoverable under the Part 7 procedure to those in the small claims track, as the outstanding balance of the claim came within that track.

The court awarded stage 2 portal costs in relation to the heads of loss that had been agreed and the remainder of the claim was allocated to the small claims track.

District Judge Vincent held that it is the intention of the portal process that individual elements of a claim may be settled within the stage 2 process and that there is no need for the whole claim to be resolved.

The heads of loss which were accepted in the portal were binding agreements and the remaining heads of loss should continue in the small claims track.

The value of the balance of any unresolved elements will determine the track allocation and therefore the costs regime; the claimant cannot add back in the resolved elements for the purposes of track allocation.

Here the claimant was injured in a road traffic accident and sustained minor soft tissue injuries from which he recovered in three months. He was a cyclist.

He issued proceedings for damages for personal injury together with a claim for the pre-accident value of his bicycle (£319.00), hire charges for a replacement bicycle (£1,278.00) and storage charges (£96.00).

The defendant argued that the personal injury claim and the pre-accident value of the bicycle had been compromised in the portal. The claimant argued that the portal does not allow a defendant to pick and choose individual items to settle and that at the time the claimant withdrew from the portal process there was no agreement in respect of the entire claim and therefore there cannot have been any settlement of any of its elements.

Here the judge upheld the defendant's submission finding not only was it possible, but indeed it was the intention of the protocol, that parties could compromise individual elements of a claim within the stage 2 process.

He found that that is what had happened in this case and therefore gave judgment in the sum of £2,319.00 plus portal fixed costs and allocated the remaining claims for credit hire and storage charges to the Small Claims Track.

The judge pointed out that the portal is specifically designed for each head of loss to be claimed separately with the defendant being required either to accept or make a counter offer, even if for zero, in respect of each head. The last column enables a running total to be kept of the amount in dispute.

The judge said:-

"I infer from this that any part of a Claimant's offer accepted by the Defendant is therefore regarded as an item 'not in dispute', thereby providing the parties a mechanism by which issues are narrowed…" (Paragraph 30)

At paragraph 31 the judge says:-

"31. If the parties have not resolved matters by the end of the stage 2 process, then stage 3 proceedings are issued. It defies logic and the aims and intentions of the protocol if at such point, all items that had previously been agreed were regarded as un-agreed. If that were the case, I would expect the protocol to state this clearly. It does not."

The judge drew an analogy with Part 36. If a Part 36 offer is accepted then that matter, or that aspect of the matter is finalised and cannot be re-litigated. Here the claimant's offers in respect of personal injury and pre-accident value were accepted and that was the end of those matters.

The judge also pointed out that the claimant had not sought to return the payments actually made by the defendant in respect of the pre-accident value of the bicycle.

It should be noted that the judge found that the reason the claimant sought to exit the portal and to insist that there had been no agreement in respect of the personal injury claim was "an attempt to manipulate the RTA Protocol Procedure in order to afford an opportunity of recovering increased costs from the Defendant."

Late payment by defendant

It is not clear what sanction, if any, applies when a defendant fails to pay settlement monies, including stage 2 costs, within 10 days of settlement as required by the rules.

My remedy would be to impose an immediate 10% uplift on all damages with a further 1% for each day the default continues.

Paragraph 7.59 reads:-

"7.59. Paragraph 7.60 applies where –

(1) the original damages are agreed; but

(2) the additional damages are not agreed."

"7.60. Where paragraph 7.59 applies –

(1) the defendant must, in relation to the original damages, pay the claimant in accordance with paragraph 7.62; and

(2) the claimant may start proceedings under Part 7 of the CPR in relation to the additional damages."

Paragraph 7.62 then sets out what must be paid but does not deal with enforcement.

What happens if "original damages" have been agreed but vehicle related damages, defined in certain circumstances in paragraph 7.51 as "the additional damages", have not been agreed?

"Original damages" include all elements of the claim in the existing stage 2 Settlement Pack. If, for example, the hire element was included in the stage 2 Settlement Pack, then the matter should proceed to stage 3.

Paragraph 6.4 reads:-

"6.4. A claim for vehicle related damages will ordinarily be dealt with outside the provisions of this Protocol under industry agreements between relevant organizations and insurers. Where there is a claim for vehicle related damages the claimant must: -

(1) state in the CNF that the claim is being dealt with by a third party; or

(2)

(a) explain in the CNF that the legal representative is dealing with the recovery of these additional costs; and

(b) attach any relevant invoices and receipts to the CNF or explain when they are likely to be sent to the defendant."

If in fact they were not, and are additional damages, then a solicitor may start proceedings under Part 7 as per paragraph 7.60.

Practice Direction 8B deals with the stage 3 procedure and, for example, paragraph 6.1(4) requires the filing of evidence of special damages.

If a solicitor withdraws a claim from the portal unreasonably then the court can restrict the costs to portal costs, whatever stage Part 7 proceedings reach. (Paragraph 7.76).

Legal Representatives only get costs

CPR 45.18 fixed costs are only recoverable where the claimant has a legal representative, and thus are not payable to Claims Management Companies. (paragraph 4.6 of RTA portal and 4.4 of EL and PL portal).

A claimant is allowed to portal in person (see Paragraph 5.10 of each portal).

Value

Where the claimant reasonably believes that the claim is valued at between £1,000.01 and the protocol upper limit, but it subsequently becomes apparent that the value of the claim is £1,000 or less, the claimant is entitled to the Stage 1 and (where relevant) the Stage 2 fixed costs. (Paragraph 5.9 of each portal).

Is it necessary to insert a figure for general damages in the interim settlement pack?

At paragraph 7.14 of the RTA Portal states: -

"7.14 The claimant must send to the defendant the Interim Settlement Pack and initial medical report(s) (including any recommendation that a subsequent medical report is justified) in order to request the interim payment."

That clearly envisages that general damages are not necessarily capable of quantification at that stage.

The Portal does require the solicitor to submit details of special damages and disbursements when submitting an Interim Settlement Pack – see RTA Portal at paragraph 7.15.

However it appears that it is not necessary to insert all of the eventual special damages and disbursements. For example one could insert loss of earnings to date but add a sentence to the effect of "reserving the right to submit details of further pecuniary losses in future…"

If indeed everything had to be included in the Interim Settlement Pack then it would not be an interim settlement pack, but rather a final settlement pack

The situation is the same in relation to the EL/PL Portal and there the relevant paragraphs are 7.13 and 7.14.

Subcontractors

A Public Liability claim is submitted through the portal but the defendant blames their subcontractors. Does the claimant need to submit a new claim against the sub-contractors through the portal, or does the denial of liability, and the possibility that there may be more than one defendant, mean that the claim automatically exits the portal?

The possibility of more than one defendant does not of itself cause the matter to drop out of the portal; that only applies in industrial disease cases- see EL/PL 4.3 (6).

If there has been a denial of liability then the matter no longer continues in the portal- see EL/PL 6.13. (3) - which provides that if the defendant does not admit liability within 40 days in a PL matter (6.11 (b)) then it no longer continues under the portal.

By virtue of EL/PL 5.11 claims which no longer continue under the Protocol cannot re-enter it.

Consequently once the matter is out of the portal it cannot go back in and must proceed in the usual way with a letter of claim against the sub-contractors and proceedings issued if appropriate.

It is an interesting point as to what costs regime then applies- Fixed Recoverable Costs or open. My view, on balance, is fixed costs.

If the solicitor decides not to proceed against the original defendant, but rather only the sub-contractor, then that seems to be a matter which should go into the portal as that particular matter would never have gone in or dropped out of the portal.

Can you charge the client a success fee when a Stage 2 interim payment is made?

No, in my view.

An interim payment is just that and if, at the Stage 3 hearing, the judge orders a lesser sum then the balance must be repaid to the defendant – see *Mulholland v Hughes and Conjoined Appeals, No. AP20/15, Newcastle-upon-Tyne County Court, 18 September 2015.*

Let us say that you get £2,000.00 in stage 2 and charge the client £500.00.

At stage 3 the judge awards £1,500.00 and therefore the maximum success fee by law – 25% of damages – is £375.00.

The client has been charged an illegal success fee.

If you operate the Underwoods Method then there is a gap between solicitor and own client costs and recovered costs, and subject to drafting the retainer carefully, you can indeed then make a charge to the client at the end of stage 2.

Are you obliged to negotiate within the 35 day period in stage 2 or can you go straight to stage 3?

Paragraph 7.35 to 7.37 of the RTA Portal reads:-

"Consideration of claim

7.35 There is a 35 day period for consideration of the Stage 2 Settlement Pack by the defendant ("the total consideration period"). This comprises a period of up to 15 days for the defendant to consider the Stage 2 Settlement Pack ("the initial consideration period") and make an offer. The remainder of the total consideration period ("the negotiation period") is for any further negotiation between the parties.

7.36 The total consideration period can be extended by the parties agreeing to extend either the initial consideration period or the negotiation period or both.

7.37 Where a party makes an offer 5 days or less before the end of the total consideration period (including any extension to this period under paragraph 7.36), there will be a further period of 5 days after the end of the total consideration period for the relevant party to consider that offer. During this period ("the further consideration period") no further offers can be made by either party."

"Will", the word used, is a mandatory word as compared with "may". Clearly even if the claimant is in receipt of a low offer s/he can counteroffer and continue the negotiations and my view is that that is what is intended and therefore a claimant cannot proceed to stage 3 before the 35 day period has expired.

Stage 2 statistics

RTA

Of the total number of claims submitted, 3,494,315 proceeded to Stage 2 and the number of claims where agreement was reached at Stage 2 was 1,364,130 which is 39.04%.

The number of claims which exited the process at this stage was 802,677 which is 22.97%.

Of those which exited the process (802,677) the reasons for exiting are as follows including the number of claims and the percentage of the total number of claims submitted to the portal.

Incomplete claim notification form	10,164	0.20%
Value below £1,000.00	11,449	0.23%
Value of claim exceeds the upper limit	10,193	0.20%
Claim too complex for the process	9,937	0.20%
Withdrawal of claim	19,204	0.38%
Duplicate claim	43,955	0.87%
Withdrawal of offer	3,733	0.07%
Interim payment for a child	414	0.01%
Claim requires further investigation	316,216	6.20%
Stage 1 costs not paid on time	10,242	0.20%
Interim payment request not answered and/or paid on time	1,321	0.03%
Other	365,701	7.21%

Employers Liability

Of the total number of claims submitted, which was 77,765 proceeded to Stage 2 and the number of claims where agreement was reached at Stage 2 was 18 633 which is 23.96%.

The number of claims which exited the process was 32,673 which is 42.02%.

Of those which exited the process (32,673) the reasons for exiting are as follows including the number of claims and the percentage of the total number of claims submitted to the portal.

Incomplete claim notification form	707	0.49%
Value below £1,000.00	167	0.12%
Value of claim exceeds the upper limit	870	0.61%
Claim too complex for the process	243	0.17%
Withdrawal of claim	1,083	0.76%
Duplicate claim	3,351	2.34%
Withdrawal of offer	80	0.06%
Interim payment for a child	20	0.01%
Claim requires further investigation	10,282	7.19%
Failure to acknowledge claim form on time	399	0.28%
Failure to provide adequate loss of earnings details	1,311	0.92%
Stage 1 costs not paid on time	821	0.57%
Interim payment request not answered and/or paid on time	229	0.16%
Other	13,101	9.16%

Public Liability

Of the total number of claims submitted, 86,664 proceeded to Stage 2 and the number of claims where agreement was reached at Stage 2 was 17,672 which is 20.39%.

The number of claims which exited the process was 39,958 which is 46.11%.

Of those which exited the process (39,958) the reasons for exiting are as follows including the number of claims and the percentage of the total number of claims submitted to the portal.

Incomplete claim notification form	2,714	1.30%
Value below £1,000.00	208	0.10%
Value of claim exceeds the upper limit	603	0.30%
Claim too complex for the process	295	0.15%
Withdrawal of claim	1,790	0.88%
Duplicate claim	4,104	2.02%
Withdrawal of offer	116	0.06%
Interim payment for a child	24	0.01%
Claim requires further investigation	11,223	5.52%
Failure to acknowledge claim form on time	1,115	0.55%
Failure to provide adequate loss of earnings details	26	0.01%
Stage 1 costs not paid on time	928	0.46%
Interim payment request not answered and/or paid on time	154	0.08%
Other	16,652	8.19%

Stage 3

Stage 3 comes into play if quantum cannot be agreed, or if the claimant is a child, and at this stage the court becomes involved and proceedings under Part 8 of the Civil Procedure Rules are issued and a court fee paid.

There is a further exchange of documents and submission of standard form documents to the court, but issues cannot be raised at stage 3 if they were not set out at stage 2.

There will be a paper only hearing unless the judge otherwise directs or either party requests an oral hearing.

The procedure for issuing Part 8 proceedings and dealing with Stage 3 is set out in Practice Direction 8B, the text of which appears at chapter 35.

The court may order any claim started under CPR Part 7 to continue under Part 8. The authority for this is Practice Direction 8B 4.1 which supplements CPR 8.1(6).

The fee for issuing Part 8 proceedings is set out in Schedule 1 of the Civil Proceedings Fees (Amendment) Order 2014. Court Fees are dealt with in chapter 19.

Practice Direction 8B, paragraph 5.2 states:

"5.2 The claim form must state –

...

(3) whether the claimant wants the claim to be determined by the court on the papers (except where a party is a child) or at a Stage 3 hearing;"

If the claimant requests, on the Claim Form, an oral Stage 3 hearing, then the court must order an oral hearing.

The position is the same if the defendant requests in the Acknowledgment of Service Form an oral Stage 3 hearing.

This is all made clear in Practice Direction 8B, paragraph 11.1:

"**11.1** The court will order that damages are to be assessed –

(1) on the papers; or

(2) at a Stage 3 hearing where –

(a) the claimant so requests on the claim form;

(b) the defendant so requests in the acknowledgment of service (Form N210B); or

(c) the court so orders,

and on a date determined by the court."

The claimant must file with the claim form:

- the Court Proceedings Pack (Part A) Form;
- the Court Proceedings Pack (Part B) Form (the claimant's and defendant's final offers) in a sealed envelope, unless the claimant is a child and the application is for a settlement hearing;
- copies of medical reports;
- evidence of special damages; and
- evidence of disbursements.

Acknowledgment of service

The defendant must file and serve an acknowledgment of service on Form N210B, not more than 14 days after service of the claim form.

A CRU Certificate which is in force should be filed and served with the acknowledgement of service or as soon after as possible.

The acknowledgment of service must also state whether the defendant wants the claim to be determined on the papers or at a stage 3 hearing and must include any objections in relation to the claim.

The acknowledgment of service may be signed and filed by the defendant's insurer.

Evidence

A claimant may only rely on evidence served on the defendant with the claim form and the defendant may only rely on evidence which has been filed and served at the same time as the acknowledgment of service.

Where the court considers that it cannot properly determine the claim without further evidence then it may order its use at the hearing.

If the court considers that further evidence must be provided and that the claim is not suitable to continue under the stage 3 procedure, then the court will order that the claim be transferred to Part 7 and will allocate the claim to a track and give directions.

Where this occurs the court will not allow stage 3 fixed costs.

The court may, of its own initiative, decide that the claim is not suitable for the stage 3 procedure.

Evidence in relation to child settlements

Where the claimant is a child and settlement has been agreed between the parties, additional documents must be filed as follows:

- a draft Consent Order;
- an advice on quantum by counsel, solicitor or other legal representative; and
- a statement verified by a Statement of Truth signed by the Litigation Friend, stating whether or not the child has recovered in line with the prognosis and stating whether there are any continuing symptoms.

Dismissal of the claim

Where the defendant opposes the claim, because the claimant has failed to follow the portal process, or has filed and served additional evidence with the claim form, the court will dismiss the claim.

Upon dismissal the claimant may start Part 7 proceedings but risks punishment in costs for failing to comply with the portal process.

There are many instances in the portals where there is no prescribed effect of default, exiting the portal will generally not be a deterrent to a claimant.

The court has a discretion to restrict the claimant to fixed CPR 45.18 costs and order the successful claimant to pay the defendant's costs of defending the matter outside the portal process, so there is a potential very real punishment in costs.

This is a deliberate sanction designed to ensure that claimants follow the portal process and to avoid unnecessary exiting of the portal and I deal with this extensively elsewhere.

Withdrawal of offers

A party may only withdraw an RTA portal offer with the court's permission, once proceedings have been started. The claim will then no longer continue under the stage 3 procedure and the court will give directions.

Permission will only be given where there is a good reason for the claim not to continue in stage 3.

In *Bostan v Royal Mail Group Ltd* (2012) Bradford Costs Court (unreported)

a settlement offer made under the Pre-action protocol for low value personal injury claims in road traffic accidents expired when the claim automatically exited the protocol after the defendant had failed either to accept the offer or make a counteroffer within the time period prescribed by the protocol.

Oral hearing

Any of the three participants, that is the claimant, the defendant or the court, can insist on an oral hearing.

Note that an oral hearing need not be physically attended by the parties. It can be a telephone hearing.

If the matter involves a child there must always be an oral hearing.

Repayment of damages

If, at the Stage 3 hearing, the judge awards a sum of damages less than has already been paid, then the court can order the claimant to repay the difference – see *Mulholland v Hughes and Conjoined Appeals, No. AP20/15, Newcastle-upon-Tyne County Court, 18 September 2015.*

Children

As well as dealing with claims where liability has been admitted, but quantum has not been agreed, stage 3 also deals with cases where a settlement has been agreed, but the claimant is a child and therefore court approval is required.

Limitation

The Part 8 procedure also applies where compliance with the relevant protocol is not possible before the expiry of the limitation period.
Practice Direction 8B, paragraph 16, sets out the procedure which allows for a claim to be issued so as to comply with the relevant limitation period, but then to be stayed so that the relevant protocol can be complied with.

Costs – all stages

Fixed costs are payable at each stage and if the matter exits the portal, then credit must be given to the paying party for portal fixed costs when costs are determined (CPR 45.28).

In other words, a claimant does not get portal costs AND fixed costs/assessed costs. Once costs are determined the amount payable is that sum less any portal costs already paid.

The starting point is that any claim exiting either of the portals is subject to Fixed Recoverable Costs.

Any *type* of claim, that is a road traffic accident claim, an employer's liability claim or a public liability claim that has been in the portal, but exits the portal, then goes, in principle, to the Fixed Recoverable Costs Scheme rather than to standard costs.

However, there is one significant exception and that is in relation to industrial disease claims.

Although such claims go onto the EL/PL portal to start with, they never go to Fixed Recoverable Costs if they exit the portal.

The authority for that statement is CPR 45.29A (2) which states:

"(2) This section does not apply to a disease claim which is started under the EL/PL Protocol."

CPR 45.29A is itself headed "Scope and Interpretation" and is the first part of Section IIIA which is headed "Section IIIA Claims Which No Longer Continue Under the RTA and EL/PL Pre-Action Protocols – Fixed Recoverable Costs".

In other words Section IIIA deals with former portal claims and CPR 45.29A sets out the scope of the Fixed Recoverable Costs Scheme and CPR 45.29A (2) specifically excludes from the scope of Fixed Recoverable Costs a disease claim which had started under the EL/PL portal.

As far as I am aware that is the only *type* of ex-portal claim that is not subject to Fixed Recoverable Costs.

However, if proceedings are issued and the matter is allocated to the multi-track, then Fixed Recoverable Costs do not apply, following the decision of the Court of Appeal in *Qader & Others v Esure Ltd & Khan v McGee [2016] EWCA Civ 1109, 16 November 2016.*

Thus the Fixed Costs Regime covers the portals, claims that have exited the portals and not been issued, and issued claims that have not been allocated to the multi-track.

Any doubts about the *Qader* decision have been ended by Rule 8.1 of The Civil Procedure (Amendment) Rules 2017, effective 6 April 2017, which provides that fixed recoverable costs only apply "for as long as the case is not allocated to the multi-track"

Disbursements

Where there is a dispute about whether an additional advice on quantum is justified, or a dispute concerning the amount or validity of any disbursement, a party may commence proceedings under CPR 45.29, so that the court may determine the issue.

Disbursements are dealt with in detail in chapter 31.

Solicitor and own client costs

None of this affects the right of the solicitor to agree ordinary solicitor and own client costs with the client and therefore to charge significantly more than recoverable costs.

In personal injury work it is almost universal for those solicitor and own client costs to be capped by reference to a percentage of damages and that is likely to be the model in higher value personal injury work and civil work generally as the Fixed Costs Regime is extended, both to other types of work, and to higher value cases.

Section 74 of the Solicitors Act 1974

Section 74(3) of the Solicitors Act 1974 provides:-

"(3) The amount which may be allowed on the assessment of any costs or bill of costs in respect of any item relating to proceedings in a county court shall not, except in so far as rules of court may otherwise provide, exceed the amount which could have been allowed in respect of that item as between party and party in those proceedings, having regard to the nature of the proceedings and the amount of the claim and of any counterclaim."

This is an important and little known provision, which on its face prevents a solicitor charging any client any element of solicitor and own client costs in any County Court matter, including small claims, fixed costs matters as well as non-fixed costs matters in both the fast-track and multi-track in the County Court.

It allows a charge on defeat, but only to the extent that between the parties recovery would have been made in the event of a win.

However Section 74(3) has the escape clause "except in so far as rules of court may provide otherwise…"

They do.

CPR 46.9 reads:-

"Basis of detailed assessment of solicitor and client costs

46.9

(1) This rule applies to every assessment of a solicitor's bill to a client except a bill which is to be paid out of the Community Legal Service Fund under the Legal Aid Act 1988 or the Access to Justice Act 1999 or by the Lord Chancellor under Part 1 of the Legal Aid, Sentencing and Punishment of Offenders Act 2012.

(2) Section 74(3) of the Solicitors Act 1974 applies unless the solicitor and client have entered into a written agreement which expressly permits payment to the solicitor of an amount of costs greater than that which the client could have recovered from another party to the proceedings.

(3) Subject to paragraph (2), costs are to be assessed on the indemnity basis but are to be presumed –

(a) to have been reasonably incurred if they were incurred with the express or implied approval of the client;

(b) to be reasonable in amount if their amount was expressly or impliedly approved by the client;

(c) to have been unreasonably incurred if –

(i) they are of an unusual nature or amount; and

(ii) the solicitor did not tell the client that as a result the costs might not be recovered from the other party.

(4) Where the court is considering a percentage increase on the application of the client, the court will have regard to all the relevant factors as they reasonably appeared to the solicitor or counsel when the conditional fee agreement was entered into or varied."

Thus the Act, read in conjunction with this rule, does allow the solicitor to charge the client more than would have been recovered, but only if there is a written agreement expressly permitting payment of a greater sum.

CPR 46.9(4) refers to Conditional Fee Agreement success fees.

The appropriate wording should go in every retainer/Client Care Letter/agreement dealing with County Court or potential County Court litigation.

I suggest the following :-

"Section 74 Solicitors Act 1974 agreement

This agreement expressly permits the solicitors to charge an amount of costs greater than that which you will recover or could have recovered from the other party to the proceedings and expressly permits payment of such sum.

This part of this agreement is made under section 74(3) of the Solicitors Act 1974 and Civil Procedure Rules 46.9 (2) and (3).

In so far as any costs or disbursements are of an unusual nature or amount these costs might not be recovered from the other party."

This law only applies to County Court matters and therefore this wording does not have to be put in matters which do not come before the County Court, for example CICA claims.

I have included it where appropriate in the model funding agreements which appear at Chapter 13.

There is a circular argument as to whether this clause needs to be in a Contingency Fee Agreement covering pre-issue of proceedings. By definition the Contingency Fee Agreement covers pre-issue work and if proceedings are issued then the Conditional Fee Agreement is in place from day one.

However if the matter is settled pre-issue and costs are sought from the other side, with an additional charge to be made to the client as is usual, then it is arguable that on assessment the client could rely upon Section 74(3) in the absence of this clause being in the Contingency Fee Agreement.

The counter-argument is that it is not contentious business and Section 74(1) specifically applies only to contentious business.

It is simply not worth taking the risk. Include the wording.

I deal in detail with the funding methods and model agreements in Part V.

I deal with the proposed extension to the Fixed Recoverable Costs Scheme in Part X.

Offers

I deal elsewhere with Part 36 in the context of the portals, but the following should be noted in relation to the portals.

Any offer to settle made at any stage by either party will automatically include, and cannot exclude –

(1) the Stage 1 and Stage 2 fixed costs;

(2) an agreement in principle to pay a sum equal to the Type C fixed costs (£150 plus VAT) of an additional advice on quantum where

such advice is justified under paragraph 7.10 of RTA portal and 7.8 EL and PL portal; (see above).

(3) an agreement in principle to pay relevant disbursements allowed in accordance with CPR 45.19; or

(4) where applicable, any success fee in accordance with CPR 45.31(1) as it was in force immediately before 1 April 2013.

(Paragraph 7.44 of RTA portal and 7.41 EL and PL portal).

There is the following transitional provision in Part 48.1 in relation to the uplift where one is recoverable

"48.1

(1) The provisions of CPR Parts 43 to 48 relating to funding arrangements, and the attendant provisions of the Costs Practice Direction, will apply in relation to a pre-commencement funding arrangement as they were in force immediately before 1 April 2013, with such modifications (if any) as may be made by a practice direction on or after that date.

(2) A reference in rule 48.2 to a rule is to that rule as it was in force immediately before 1 April 2013."

Children and costs

All civil cases of all kinds involving children are subject to special rules and I deal with the particular portal provisions in relation to children in chapter 39.

Limitation

Being in the portal process does **not** stop the limitation clock running.

Where the portal process cannot be complied with before limitation expires, then the claimant should start Part 8 proceedings and state on the claim form that the claim is for damages and that a stay of proceedings is sought so as to comply with the portal process.

Where a stay is granted, and the parties have followed the portal process, then the claimant must apply to the court to lift the stay if s/he wishes to issue proceedings.

This applies to both stage 3 proceedings issued under Part 8 and substantive proceedings issued under Part 7.

As usual, the court will then give directions.

Interest on Part 36

Part 36 is examined in detail in chapter 22 insofar as there are special rules in the portals and Fixed Recoverable Costs schemes.

However it should be noted that enhanced interest benefits on a claimant matching or beating its own Part 36 offer do not apply to stage 1 and stage 2 costs, which will have already been paid.

Thus the extra interest will be on stage 3 costs only.

This was confirmed in *Cashman v Mid Essex Hospital Services* NHS *Trust [2015] EWHC 1312 (QB).*

Rights of audience

In *McShane v Lincoln, Birkenhead County Court, unreported, case number* B11 B1440 *– 28 June 2016*

the District Judge held that a stage 3 hearing in the portal process required a qualified solicitor or barrister to appear and that no one else had rights of audience.

In my view that decision is right. Stage 3 hearings are proceedings as a court fee has been paid and the hearing is in front of the judge and it finally determines the matter.

Apart from being important in its own right, this decision confirms that a stage 3 hearing does indeed involve proceedings being issued, something which may appear to be obvious.

However the White Book apparently states otherwise.

This needs urgent clarification.

Firstly we need to know whether stage 3 proceedings under Part 8 constitute issuing for the purposes of satisfying the Limitation Act.

Secondly, in the past, whenever the small claims limit has risen the key date has been the date of issue. In other words if proceedings were issued before the limit went up, then the old costs regime applies and if they were issued after the limit went up, then the new costs regime applies.

We now know that the road traffic accident limit will go up from £1,000.00 to £5,000.00. A claim is valued at £4,000.00.

Does the issuing of stage 3 proceedings before the limit goes up mean that it remains costs bearing and if it exits the portal completely will also be costs bearing?

This is of key importance to claimant and defendant lawyers alike.

My view is that commencing stage 3 does constitute the issue of proceedings. CPR Part 7.2 defines the start of proceedings as being the issue of "a claim form" i.e. not specifically a Part 7 claim form. Part 8 proceedings generally are commenced by issuing a claim form (8.2) and the commencement of stage 3 is simply a sub-species of Part 8 generally.

Enforcement

The scenario is that a matter is settled in the portal but the insurance company have not paid the agreed damages.

There is no method of enforcement within the protocol, and therefore the issue is whether proceedings should be issued under Part 7 or Part 8.

If all matters have been agreed and it is merely the non-payment of damages and/or costs that is in issue then the matter can be dealt with under CPR 8 as the claimant is seeking "the court's decision on a question which is unlikely to involve a substantial dispute of fact" – see CPR 8.1(2)(a).

Chapter 30

Exclusions from the Portals

EXCLUSIONS FROM THE PORTALS

Here I deal with matters which are excluded from the portals, or where the issue as to whether they should be excluded is arguable. The separate, but related, issue of exiting the portals is dealt with in chapter 41.

VALUE

Small claims

Neither portal applies to a small claim, that is a claim valued at £1,000.00 or less, but note carefully how that valuation is calculated – see chapter 29.

Upper limit

Neither portal applies where the claim is valued at more than £25,000.00, but note carefully how that calculation is valued – see chapter 29.

Old upper limit

In an RTA matter where the accident occurred before 31 July 2013, the upper limit is £10,000.00 and any claim above that value is excluded completely from the portal process.

Note that the old predictive costs regime lives on and a case excluded from the RTA portals may well come within the old scheme, which I examine in chapter 37.

DATES

RTA matters

Any accident which occurred before 30 April 2010 is excluded from the portal but may be subject to the old predictive costs regime - see chapter 37.

EL/PL – except industrial disease claims

Any accident which occurred before 31 July 2013 is excluded from the portal.

Industrial disease cases

Any matter where the Letter of Claim was sent before 31 July 2013 is excluded from the portal.

If the Letter of Claim was sent on or after 31 July 2013 then the matter goes on the EL/PL portal, whatever the earliest date of the potential cause of action.

DEFINITIONS

RTA portal

A key definition in the RTA Portal is that of a road traffic accident and this is set out at paragraph 1.1(16):-

"(16) 'road traffic accident' means an accident resulting in bodily injury to any person caused by, or arising out of, the use of a motor vehicle on a road or other public place in England and Wales unless the injury was caused wholly or in part by a breach by the defendant of one or more of the relevant statutory provisions as defined by section 53 of the Health and Safety at Work etc. Act 1974;"

Thus before a claim is potentially able to go on the RTA Portal it has to come within that definition, which I will return to later.

Even if a matter does potentially come within that definition there are a whole series of exclusions.

The RTA portal does NOT apply to a claim

(1) in respect of a breach of duty owed to a road user by a person who is not a road user;

(2) made to the Motor Insurers' Bureau pursuant to the Untraced Drivers' Agreement 2003 or any subsequent or supplementary Untraced Drivers' Agreements;

(3) where the claimant or defendant acts as personal representative of a deceased person;

(4) where the claimant or defendant is a protected party as defined in CPR 21.1(2);

(5) where the claimant is bankrupt;

(6) where the defendant's vehicle is registered outside the United Kingdom;

(7) where there is not bodily injury, that is in the case of psychological injury only.

Note that the portal DOES apply to MIB uninsured driver claims. (Paragraph 4.5), and does apply to children, but not to cases involving protected parties.

Breach of duty

Note that the RTA portal does NOT apply to a claim in respect of a breach of duty owed to a road user by a person who is **not** a road user.

Thus although an injury allegedly caused by, for example, defective road repairs is a road traffic accident it does not enter the road traffic accident portal.

It is arguable that it does not enter the new Employers' Liability/Public Liability portal either as that portal excludes claims

"for damages arising out of a road traffic accident (as defined in paragraph 1.1(16) of the Pre-Action Protocol for Low Value Personal Injury Claims in Road Traffic Accidents.)"

As we have seen paragraph 1.1(16) reads:-

"(16) 'road traffic accident' means an accident resulting in bodily injury to any person caused by, or arising out of, the use of a motor vehicle on a road or other public place in England and Wales unless the injury was caused wholly or in part by a breach by the defendant of one or more of the relevant statutory provisions as defined by section 53 of the Health and Safety at Work etc Act 1974;"

and thus does not take matters any further.

A case not going into either portal cannot go into Fixed Recoverable Costs as that regime only applies if the matter has been in the portal. This is because Fixed Recoverable Costs only apply to matters "which no longer continue" under the portals.

Thus it is a pre-condition of Fixed Recoverable Costs that the matter has been in, and has come out of, one of the portals.

A matter not going into Fixed Recoverable Costs will either go straight to open standard costs or, in certain instances, the old predictive costs regime.

For example, a claimant is involved in a car crash which occurs as a result of a fault with the vehicle and brings a claim against the dealer who sold the car.

This does not fall within RTA protocol, as this is a breach of duty owed to a road user by a person who is not a road user. It is also excluded from the Employers' Liability/Public Liability protocol as it falls *within* the definition of a road traffic accident under the RTA protocol.

Clearly such a scenario is a road traffic accident within the meaning of CPR 45.9(4).

However this claim does not necessarily go straight to open standard costs and my view is that if the claim is settled for £10,000.00 or less pre-issue, then it goes to the old predictive costs regime.

The RTA/EL-PL conundrum in relation to road traffic accidents

The EL/PL portal excludes claims:-

"for damages arising out of a road traffic accident (as defined in paragraph 1.1(16) of the Pre-Action Protocol for Low Value Personal Injury Claims and Road Traffic Accidents)."

It is presumed that that exclusion from the EL/PL Portal was to stop road traffic matters being brought in that portal where fees are higher, but that begs the question as to whether there can be road traffic accidents which are therefore excluded from both portals.

That could be determined either way.

However the exclusion from the EL/PL Portal specifically refers to the definition of a road traffic accident in the Road Traffic Accident Portal and therefore if the matter is not a road traffic accident within the meaning of paragraph 1.1(16) of the Road Traffic Accident Portal then it appears not to be excluded from the EL/PL Portal.

Accidents arising out of the use of a motor vehicle on a road satisfy that part of the definition but then appear to be excluded by the words:-

"unless the injury was caused wholly or in part by a breach by the defendant of one or more of the relevant statutory provisions as defined by section 53 of the Health and Safety at Work etc. Act 1974;"

Thus if the matter does not come within paragraph 1.1(16), for whatever reason, then my view is that it is not excluded from the EL/PL Protocol and thus would appear to be a public liability claim which is not caught by paragraph 1.1(16).

I admit to having changed my mind on this one.

The wording is very clumsy, but on public policy grounds, and on a purposive construction of the will of Parliament it would be absurd if such a claim was subject to open costs and the wording can certainly be interpreted in the way that I have set out above, that is that the only road traffic related exclusions from the EL/PL Portal are if the matter comes within the definition in the Road Traffic Accident Portal.

Obviously if it does come within the RTA Portal definition then it goes into that portal, and if it does not go into that RTA Portal, then it is not excluded from the EL/PL Portal.

Road Traffic Acts

There is considerable case law in the context of the Road Traffic Act 1988 and its predecessors in connection with matters such as what constitutes "use" of a motor vehicle, what is "a road or other public place", what is an "accident" etc.

Detailed consideration of such matters is beyond the scope of this book, but the case law developed under the Road Traffic Act 1988 is relevant when considering the scope of, and therefore potential exclusions from, the RTA portal.

I do deal with below as to whether trams and invalid carriages are motor vehicles within the meaning of the portal.

Section 53 of Health and Safety at Work etc. Act 1974

As seen in the portal definition above, an accident is not classed as a road traffic accident if "the injury was caused wholly or in part by a breach by the defendant of one or more of the relevant statutory provisions as defined by Section 53 of the Health and Safety at Work etc. Act 1974"

Those statutory provisions are:-

Control of Substances Hazardous to Health Regulations 2002, SI 2002/2677;

Lifting Operations and Lifting Equipment Regulations 1998, SI 1998/2307;

Management of Health and Safety at Work Regulations 1999, SI 1999/3242;

Manual Handling Operations Regulations 1992, SI 1992/2793;

Personal Protective Equipment at Work Regulations 1992, SI 1992/2966;

Provision and Use of Work Equipment Regulations 1998, SI 1998/2306;

Work at Height Regulations 2005, SI 2005/ 735;

Workplace (Health, Safety and Welfare) Regulations 1992 SI 1992/3004;

The Construction (Design and Management) Regulations 2007, SI 2007/320."

This provision was drafted and came into force before the Enterprise and Regulatory Reform Act 2013 which expressly states that breaches of these Regulations no longer give rise to a civil cause of action per se from 1 October 2013.

Protected parties

A protected party is a person who lacks mental capacity to conduct his or her own proceedings within the meaning of the Mental Capacity Act 2005.

Claims involving a child, either as a claimant or defendant, are not excluded from the portals.

Bankrupts

Neither portal applies where the claimant is bankrupt (RTA portal, paragraph 4.5(5), EL/PL portal, paragraph 4.3(4)).

However as there are major issues for lawyers acting for bankrupts in any type of personal injury case, whether it will be a portal claim or not, I deal with this whole subject separately in chapter 27.

Death and the portals

Neither portal applies where either the claimant or defendant acts as personal representative of a deceased person (RTA portal, paragraph 4.5(3), EL/PL portal, paragraph 4.3(1)).

It is not clear what happens when a claimant or defendant dies after a CNF has been submitted.

There is no provision that in such circumstances the matter automatically exits the portal.

However presumably a person then "acts as personal representative…" and thus the matter cannot remain in the portal.

A client dying during a case causes considerable problems for lawyers, as well as of course for the client.

Consequently I deal with this whole subject separately in chapter 24.

Litigants in Person

CPR 45.9(3) excludes the application of that section where the claimant is a litigant in person or section III or section III A of this Part applies.

Section III is the portals, technically the pre-action protocols for low value personal injury claims in road traffic accidents and low value personal injury (employers' liability and public liability) claims and section III A deals with claims which no longer continue under the RTA and EL/PL Pre-Action Protocols – Fixed Recoverable Costs.

As CPR 45.9(3) only excludes fixed costs for litigants in person in matters which are in, or have been in, one of the portals, it does not exclude such a claim from the old predictive costs regime applies, where appropriate.

Psychological injury only

A person suffers psychological injuries only following a road traffic accident. The injuries are clearly less than £25,000.00 and on the face of it the matter is suitable for the Pre-Action Protocol for Low Value Personal Injury Claims in Road Traffic Accidents, but does that protocol in fact apply?

Paragraph 1.1(16) of that protocol provides:-

"(16) 'road traffic accident' means an accident resulting in bodily injury to any person caused by, or arising out of, the use of a motor vehicle on a road or other public place in England and Wales unless the injury was caused wholly or in part by a breach by the defendant of one or more of the relevant statutory provisions as defined by section 53 of the Health and Safety at Work etc. Act 1974;"

If the claimant has suffered psychological injuries only then they are not bodily injuries and therefore the matter does not appear to come within the terms of the portal.

Paragraph 1.1(16A) is significant in its definition of a "soft tissue injury claim" as a "claim brought by an occupant of a motor vehicle where the significant physical injury caused is a soft tissue injury and includes claims where there is a minor psychological injury secondary in significance to the physical injury;"

The significance of that is that, in a slightly different context, it requires the physical injury to be the main injury.

The scope of the protocol is dealt with in paragraph 4.1 and although 4.1(2) requires the claim to include damages in respect of personal injury, which clearly psychological injuries are, it also needs to satisfy paragraph 4.1(1) in that it must be a claim for damages which "arises from a road traffic accident" and one is then thrown back on the definition of "road traffic accident" in paragraph 1.1(16).

The Shorter Oxford English Dictionary has, as the relevant definition of "bodily":-

"Of, belonging to, or affecting the human body or physical nature."

The relevant definition of "psychological" is:-

"Of or pertaining to the functioning of the mind, mental, affecting or pertaining to the mental and emotional state of a person; having a mental not a physical cause."

As far as I am aware there is no case law on this point.

Let us assume that there was a bodily injury and thus on the face of it the matter is brought within the portal.

What about a situation where a drunken pedestrian is entirely responsible for the accident and the car was stationary and the claim is by the driver or a passenger in the car?

Is that an accident "caused by" the use of a motor vehicle on a road etc.? Is it an accident "arising out of" the use of a motor vehicle on a road etc.?

Again I am unaware of any case law on the point but it seems to me that the mere fact that a motor vehicle is on the road does not of itself mean that an accident is inevitably "caused by" or "arises out of" the use of a motor vehicle on a road.

In one case under the old Portal, a delivery driver was unloading a wheeled trolley/cage from the back of a lorry which became stuck on the tail lift of the lorry. The Claimant went to assist, and the trolley/cage fell on her causing injury. That was held by a DJ to be a road traffic accident for the purposes of the old Portal.

Trams

An accident involving a tram is clearly a road traffic accident and could also be an employers' liability case, for example where the injured person is an employee, or a public liability case.

However section 4.3(11) of the Employers' Liability and Public Liability Protocol provides that that portal does not apply to a claim

"for damages arising out of a road traffic accident (as defined in paragraph 1.1(16) of the Pre-Action Protocol for Low Value Personal Injury Claims in Road Traffic Accidents)."

The scope of the RTA Protocol is defined as follows:-

"4.1. This Protocol applies where—

(1) a claim for damages arises from a road traffic accident where the CNF is submitted on or after 31 July 2013"

A key question is whether an accident involving a tram is a road traffic accident. The definitions under the protocol read:-

"1.1. In this Protocol—

(13) 'motor vehicle' means a mechanically propelled vehicle intended for use on roads…

(15) 'road' means any highway and any other road to which the public has access and includes bridges over which a road passes;

(16) 'road traffic accident' means an accident resulting in bodily injury to any person caused by, or arising out of, the use of a motor vehicle on a road or other public place in England and Wales unless the injury was caused wholly or in part by a breach by the defendant of one or more of the relevant statutory provisions as defined by section 53 of the Health and Safety at Work etc. Act 1974;"

An RTA is therefore an accident resulting in bodily injury to any person caused by, or arising out of, the use of a motor vehicle on a road or other public place in England and Wales.

Is a tram a motor vehicle?

The definition of motor vehicle under the protocol is limited but the Road Traffic Act 1988 specifically defines both motor vehicle and tram car.

Section 185 of that Act defines a motor vehicle as:-

""'motor car" means a mechanically propelled vehicle, not being a motor cycle or an invalid carriage, which is constructed itself to carry a load or passengers and the weight of which unladen—

(a) if it is constructed solely for the carriage of passengers and their effects, is adapted to carry not more than seven passengers exclusive of the driver and is fitted with tyres of such type as may be specified in regulations made by the Secretary of State, does not exceed 3050 kilograms,

(b) if it is constructed or adapted for use for the conveyance of goods or burden of any description, does not exceed 3050 kilograms, or 3500 kilograms if the vehicle carries a container or containers for holding for the purposes of its propulsion any fuel which is wholly gaseous at 17.5 degrees Celsius under a pressure of 1.013 bar or plant and materials for producing such fuel,

(c) does not exceed 2540 kilograms in a case not falling within sub-paragraph (a) or (b) above,"

It is true that that is the definition of a motor car whereas the Road Traffic Accident Protocol refers to a motor vehicle and clearly that includes all sorts of motor vehicles which are not cars.

However Section 192 of the Road Traffic Act 1988 specifically defines a tram car:-

"""tramcar" includes any carriage used on any road by virtue of an order under the Light Railways Act 1896, and

"trolley vehicle" means a mechanically propelled vehicle adapted for use on roads without rails power transmitted to it from some external source."

Given this separate definition I do not believe that a tram falls under the RTA Protocol definition of a motor vehicle. The RTA Portal Claim Notification Form does not lend itself to a claim involving a tram; what would one put as the vehicle registration number for example?

The Pre-Action Protocol for Low Value Personal Injury (Employers' Liability and Public Liability) claims defines a public liability claim as:-

"(18) 'public liability claim'—

(a) means a claim for damages for personal injuries arising out of a breach of a statutory or common law duty of care made against—

(i) a person other than the claimant's employer…"

Thus a claim involving a tram car and a member of the public would fall under this broad definition, but if the claim was by a driver or conductor or member of staff on the tram car, then it would fall under the Employers' Liability provision.

Actions for damages arising out of a road traffic accident, as defined in paragraph 1.1(16) of the Pre-Action Protocol for Low Value Personal Injury Claims in Road Traffic Accidents, are specifically excluded from the Employers' Liability and Public Liability Portal, presumably to stop road traffic accidents attracting the higher fees in that portal.

However, as set out above, my view is that a tram car is not a motor vehicle and therefore does not come within the definition in paragraph 1.1(16) and so is not excluded from the Employers' Liability and Public Liability Portal.

Consequently a tram car accident cannot go into the Road Traffic Accident Portal but can, in appropriate circumstances, go into the Employers' Liability and Public Liability Portal.

Invalid carriages

Sections 143 and 185 of the Road Traffic Act 1988 specifically exclude invalid carriages from the provisions, but there is no such exclusion in the RTA portal.

Thus an accident caused by a mobility scooter may be subject to the RTA portal, even though insurance does not have to be maintained for such a vehicle.

Certain mobility scooters are approved for use on roads and are subject to a maximum speed of eight miles per hour.

If such a scooter had an accident, even in a pedestrian area, then it appears to come within the portal process, just like any other motor vehicle within the portal definition.

Air accidents

A person is walking down the steps whilst getting off of an aeroplane in England and an accident occurs.

Let us assume that the matter is covered by the Montreal Convention. Is this covered by the Public Liability Portal and therefore Fixed Costs?

It is an accident occurring in England and Wales and on the face of it is a public liability claim for less than £25,000.00 and is not positively excluded.

Therefore my view is that it is indeed covered.

However, does it involve a breach of the duty of care, or a breach of statutory duty as required by the portal?

On the face of it, the situation gives rise to a public liability claim in England and Wales which is not specifically excluded from the portal process. Although my instincts tell me it should not be covered I cannot think of any good reason to back up that view.

Paragraph 7.59 gives a general right to the claimant to give notice to the defendant that the claim is unsuitable for the portal and gives an example as there being complex issues of fact or law. That comes with a major health warning which is that "where the court considers that the claimant acted unreasonably in giving such notice it will award no more than the fixed costs in Rule 45.18."

My advice is to issue in the portal and see what the defendant's response is. I appreciate that that means that if the matter is resolved quickly in the portal one would only get limited costs, but if it is indeed resolved with little work and little fuss solicitor and client should both be happy.

Having said that paragraph 1.1(18) – the definition section says

"(18) "public liability claim" –

(a) means a claim for damages for personal injuries arising out of a breach of a statutory or common law duty of care….."

The Montreal Convention is incorporated in to the law of England and Wales by the Carriage By Air Act 1961, as amended. Thus there is no breach of a common law duty of care. That leaves the issue of whether there is a breach of a statutory duty of care. On the face of it there is, as the governing law is an Act of Parliament.

That also raises an additional problem. If in fact the potentially disputed facts of the case mean that the Montreal Convention does not apply, then clearly the claim is a public liability claim covered by the portal and one would be at risk of only getting portal costs by following the conventional court route.

This reinforces my advice to issue in the portal. To issue and exit the portal involves no cost risk; to not enter the portal poses a very significant costs risk.

Small claims

Matters which would be allocated to the small claims track are excluded from the portal process and I deal with the whole subject of small claims, and what is a small claim, in Part IV, Chapter 8 to 12 inclusive.

Paragraph 4.1 of the RTA Portal reads:-

"**Scope**

4.1 This Protocol applies where—

…

(4) if proceedings were started the small claims track would not be the normal track for that claim."

Note that although a claim may include vehicle related damages these are excluded for the purposes of valuing the claim under paragraph 4.1. This is a little misleading as in fact it only applies to the valuation under paragraph 4.1(3), that is that the protocol applies where the claimant values claim at no more than the protocol upper limit, which is £25,000.00.

Thus if non-vehicle related damages are £20,000.00 and vehicle related damages are £40,000.00, then those vehicle related damages are ignored for the purposes of valuation and thus although the claim is for £65,000.00 the matter nevertheless goes into the portal.

It does not work the other way round in relation to the exclusion of small claims. Thus if non-vehicle related damages are £800.00 and vehicle related damages are £11,000.00, the matter still goes into the portal as it would not have been allocated to the small claims track as the court on allocation under CPR 26 does not exclude vehicle related damages.

I deal later with what are vehicle related damages.

Paragraph 5.9 of the RTA portal provides that where the claimant reasonably believes that the claim is valued at between £1,000.00 and the protocol upper limit, £25,000.00, but it subsequently becomes apparent that the value of the claim is less than £1,000.00 then the claimant is entitled to the Stage 1 and (where relevant) the Stage 2 fixed costs.

Claims above £25,000.00

The RTA portal upper limit is £25,000.00 but vehicle related damages do not form part of the claim for the purposes of this maximum.

This applies where the accident occurred on or after 31 July 2013 and in relation to accidents that occurred on or after 30 April 2010 and before 31 July 2013 the upper limit is £10,000.00.

Given the limitation period of three years in personal injury matters there will be few cases caught by the old limit, but there will be some, for example cases involving children as the three year time limit does not run until the child achieves its majority.

The calculation is made on a full liability basis including pecuniary losses, but excluding interest and, as we have seen, excluding vehicle related damage.

Thus a claim for £30,000.00 where there is agreed contributory negligence of 50%, reducing the claim to £15,000.00, nevertheless does not go into the portal as on a full liability basis the portal upper limit is exceeded.

By Paragraph 4.3 of the RTA Portal:

"This Protocol ceases to apply to a claim where, at any stage, the claimant notifies the defendant that the claim has now been revalued at more than the Protocol upper limit."

Paragraph 4.2 of the EL/PL portal is in identical terms.

Paragraph 7.76 allows the claimant to give notice to the defendant that the claim is unsuitable for the portal and gives an example of there being complex issues of fact or law. However the reason could be that the claimant now values the matter at above the upper limit.

In those circumstances the claim no longer continues under the portal, but if the court considers that the claimant acted unreasonably in giving such notice it will award only portal costs under CPR 45.18.

Thus considerable care needs to be taken in valuing the claim.

If a matter settles for below £25,000.00 in circumstances where it was never put on the portal, then it is likely that only portal costs, and not even Fixed Recoverable Costs, will be awarded.

CPR 45.24(2)(ii) provides that the court may order the defendant to pay no more than the fixed costs in Rule 45.18 – that is portal costs – if the claimant valued the claim at more than £25,000.00, so that the claimant did not need to comply with the relevant protocol.

Portal costs and Fixed Recoverable Costs are automatic and the indemnity principle does not apply – see *Nizami v Butt.*

However a claim settled pre-issue, which has not been in the portal, is subject to the indemnity principle and on the face of it there is no entitlement to any costs, absent contractual agreement with the defendant.

If the matter is put on the portal and then removed under paragraph 7.76 but ultimately settles for £25,000.00 or less then the court is likely to consider that the claimant acted unreasonably in exiting the portal and will award portal costs only.

I deal with exiting the portal in chapter 41.

Portals and vehicle related damages

Vehicle related damages do not form part of the value of the claim for the purposes of the maximum £25,000.00 portal limit. This is achieved by a fairly clumsy combination of paragraphs 1.1(18), 1.2, 4.1 and 4.4.

Paragraph 1.1 is the definition section and paragraph 1.1(18) reads:-

"(18) 'vehicle related damages' means damages for—

(a) the pre-accident value of the vehicle;

(b) vehicle repair;

(c) vehicle insurance excess; and

(d) vehicle hire."

Thus that defines vehicle related damages.

Paragraph 1.2(1) reads:-

"1.2

(1) The 'Protocol upper limit' is—

(a) £25,000 where the accident occurred on or after 31 July 2013; or

(b) £10,000 where the accident occurred on or after 30 April 2010 and before 31 July 2013,

on a full liability basis including pecuniary losses but excluding interest."

Paragraph 4.1 sets out the scope of the portal and 4.1(3) provides that the portal applies where "the claimant values the claim at no more than the Protocol upper limit…"

After 4.1(4) the following appears in brackets:-

"(Paragraphs 1.1(18) and 4.4 state the damages that are excluded for the purposes of valuing the claim under paragraph 4.1.)"

As we have seen 1.1(18) is in fact a definition section and does not exclude anything from anything but if one then looks at 4.4 it says:-

"A claim may include vehicle related damages but these are excluded for the purposes of valuing the claim under paragraph 4.1."

The net effect of this is that vehicle related damages, however great the value, may be included in the portal claim provided that the balance of the claim does not exceed £25,000.00.

Thus if the claim, excluding vehicle related damages, is £20,000.00 and there are £80,000.00 of vehicle related damages, then that is a portal claim, even though the total is £100,000.00 and if it exits the portal it is a fixed costs claim, provided that it is not allocated to the multi-track.

I am satisfied that all the references to vehicle related damages etc. are designed to deal with the maximum portal jurisdiction, rather than to affect fixed costs and that does leave open the question of precisely what fixed costs are payable if a claim exits the portal and settles for say £100,000.00 in the example I have given above.

The Table of Fixed Costs had a maximum pre-issue band of £25,000.00, which suggests that the drafters never realized that there could be very much higher value claims caught by fixed costs.

The £25,000 figure is removed by Rule 8 of The Civil Procedure (Amendment) Rules 2017 effective 6 April 2017.

It is not clear whether this is retrospective.

EL & PL Portals exclusions

Exclusions

Paragraph 4.3 lists 11 exclusions from the portal and thus the EL and PL portal does NOT apply:-

(1) where the claimant or defendant acts as personal representative of a deceased person;

(2) where the claimant or defendant is a protected party as defined in CPR 21.1(2);

(3) in the case of a public liability claim, where the defendant is an individual ('individual' does not include a defendant who is sued in their business capacity or in their capacity as an office holder);

(4) where the claimant is bankrupt;

(5) where the defendant is insolvent and there is no identifiable insurer;

(6) in the case of a disease claim, where there is more than one employer defendant;

(7) for personal injury arising from an accident or alleged breach of duty occurring outside England and Wales;

(8) for damages in relation to harm, abuse or neglect of or by children or vulnerable adults;

(9) which includes a claim for clinical negligence;

(10) for mesothelioma;

(11) for damages arising out of a road traffic accident (as defined in paragraph 1.1(16) of the Pre-Action Protocol for Low Value Personal Injury Claims in Road Traffic Accidents).

Key points to note are that mesothelioma, clinical negligence and road traffic accidents are excluded, with road traffic accidents entering a separate portal. Cases involving children, but not those involving protected parties, go in the portal.

Paragraph 6.1(2) of the Employers' Liability and Public Liability protocol provides that if the insurer's identity is not known or the defendant is known not to hold insurance cover, then the CNF must be sent to the defendant's registered office or principle place of business and a Defendant Only CNF is not required.

6.1(3) provides that were the insurer's identity is not known, the claimant must make a reasonable attempt to identify the insurer and, in an Employers' Liability claim, the claimant must have carried out a database search through the Employers' Liability Tracing Office.

In a disease claim the CNF should be sent to the insurer identified as the insurer identified as the insurer last on risk for the employer for the material period of employment (6.1(4)).

Note however that in a public liability claim where the defendant is an individual the matter does not go onto the portal. Thus a public liability matter involving a child as a defendant would not go on to the PL portal, because a child must be an individual, so the reason is because the defendant is an individual, not because he or she is a child.

An individual does not include a defendant who is sued in their business capacity or in their capacity in an office - holder, unlikely but theoretically possible, for a child.

Vulnerable Adult

The concept of a vulnerable adult is dealt with only in the Employers' Liability and Public Liability Portal and not in the Road Traffic Act Portal.

By paragraph 1.1(20) of the EL/PL Portal this is defined as follows:-

"(20) "Vulnerable adult" has the same meaning as in paragraph 3(5) of Schedule 1 to the Legal Aid, Sentencing and Punishment of Offenders Act 2012.

By that provision "vulnerable adult" means a person aged 18 or over whose ability to protect himself or herself from abuse is significantly impaired through physical or mental disability or illness, through old age or otherwise."

Employers' Liability and Public Liability

What is a disease?

The EL and PL protocol, in the definition section at 1.1(12) states that "disease claim" means a claim within sub-paragraph (14)(b), that is:-

"a disease that the claimant is alleged to have contracted as a consequence of the employer's breach of statutory or common law duties of care in the course of the employee's employment, other than a physical or psychological injury caused by an accident or other single event;"

As disease claims go straight from the portal to open, standard costs, rather than entering the Fixed Recoverable Costs scheme, the definition is important.

There have already been a number of relevant cases as the question is also important in relation to the old fixed success fee scheme, which lives on in relation to conditional fee agreements entered in to on or before 31 March 2013.

In *Patterson v Ministry of Defence* [2012] EWHC 2767 (QB) [2012 All ER (D) 127 (Oct)

the Queen's Bench Division of the High Court held that symptoms arising from exposure to cold weather did not constitute a disease, but rather an ordinary employers' liability claim.

Mr Justice Males states that to use the dictionary definitions of "disease":

"would be to expand the concept so far that the exception ("disease" within Section V of CPR 45) would leave far too little scope for the basic rule in Section IV to operate. That cannot be right." (Paragraph 33).

Mr Justice Males goes on to state that the definition of "disease" in paragraph 2.2 of the Pre-Action Protocol for Personal Injury Claims does not apply as this definition was there for the draftsman of CPR Part 45 to use but they did not.

Such injuries are known as non-freezing cold injuries. The court's reasoning was that as such injuries were not caused by any virus, bacteria, noxious agent or parasite, they were not a disease.

In *Fountain v Volker Rail Limited,* 24 August 2012, Central London County Court

His Honour Judge Mitchell, sitting with Master Hurst of the Senior Courts' Costs Office, held that exacerbation of a pre-existing condition was an injury and not a disease.

This was an appeal from the first instance decision of Master Haworth of the Senior Courts' Costs Office.

Modern medical opinion means that Noise-Induced Hearing Loss, traditionally treated by the law as a disease, may in fact be an injury.

The same is true in relation to Hand/Arm Vibration Syndrome.

For an interesting article on this issue see Andrew Hogan's blog NIHL and HAVS: Not diseases after all?

In *Dalton v British Telecommunications plc* [2015] EWHC 616 (QB) the High Court defined disease as follows:-

"In my judgment consideration of the legislative history in this case strongly indicates that Parliament intended the term 'disease' in sections IV and V of CPR 45 to include any illness (whether physical or physiological), disorder, ailment, affliction, complaint, malady or derangement other than a physical or physiological injury solely caused by an accident or other similar single event. The provisions of section IV are therefore restricted to injuries caused by accidents (or other single events), preserving the long-established distinction."

Simon Gibbs has pointed out on his blog that under this definition symptoms caused by a single accident or event are an injury, whereas symptoms caused by more than one accident or event are a disease, meaning that if a person hits his thumb with a hammer he has suffered an injury but if he bangs it a second time then he is suffering from a disease. He has described that as nonsense.

The legal problem arises from the fact that there is a complete failure in the Civil Procedure Rules to define disease. The High Court in 2012 took a different view from the High Court in the case of Dalton v British Telecommunications plc. In *Patterson v Ministry of Defence* [2012] EWHC 2767 the High Court held:-

"Notwithstanding the objective of CPR 45 to provide a clear and certain test for the award of success fees, inevitably questions may arise as to whether particular conditions are to be characterised as "diseases". When that occurs, and when the answer is not obvious, there is in my judgment no single test or definition which can be applied. In circumstances where the Rule itself provides no definition of "disease", and where the dictionaries do not assist, it would not be practicable or sensible for the court to attempt to supply its own definition."

The problem of definition is arising in noise induced hearing loss cases. Simon Gibbs again:-

"If my hearing is damaged as a result of an explosion in a factory, that appears to be clearly an injury. If my hearing is damaged as a result of a single acoustic shock caused by defective electrical equipment, that would also appear to be an injury I have suffered. Does it really become a disease if the hearing loss follows a number of minor acoustic shocks or exposure to a high level of noise over a prolonged period?"

Exclusions

In *Broni and Others v Ministry of Defence* [2015] EWHC 66 (QB) 20 January 2015

the Queen's Bench Division of the High Court held that the pre 1 April 2013 Fixed Recoverable Success Fee Scheme, contained in CPR 45 Section IV, did not apply to claims brought by members of the Armed Forces in respect of injuries suffered in the course of service.

The High Court thus allowed appeals against three decisions of Masters in the Senior Courts Costs Office who had held that the regime did apply as the claimants were employees within the meaning of CPR 45.20(1)(a), which states that:-

"This section applies where… the dispute is between an employee and his employer".

CPR 45.20(3)(b) states that employee has the meaning given to it by section 2(1) of the Employer's Liability (Compulsory Insurance) Act 1969 which states:-

"For the purposes of this Act the term "employee" means an individual who has entered into or works under a contract of service or apprenticeship with an employer whether by way of manual labour, clerical work or otherwise, whether such contract is expressed or implied, oral or in writing."

The claimants argued that serving members of the Armed Forces did not work under a contract of service and thus were not employees. They relied on the judgment in *Quinn v Ministry of Defence* [1998] PIQR 387 where the court said:-

"For my part, I would have no doubt at all that when Mr Quinn enlisted in the Royal Navy pursuant to the King's Regulations neither he nor the Crown had any intention to create legal relations. Further, as a matter of public policy… there is binding authority that there is no such contract. In relation to members of the Armed Forces, as with Police Officers, I can see no reason to find that those long-standing public policy considerations should be changed."

The High Court accepted that this argument whilst recognising that there could be a considerable number of groups outside the Fixed Recoverable Success Fee Scheme, such as Police Officers, Civil Servants and Members of the Judiciary.

By Paragraph 1.1(13) of the Employers' Liability Portal "employee" has the meaning given to it by section 2(1) of the Employers' Liability (Compulsory Insurance) Act 1969".

Consequently this decision excludes all of those types of workers from the Employers' Liability portal and they move into the Public Liability portal. This is because paragraph 1.1(18) says:

(18) "Public Liability claim"

(a) means a claim for damages for personal injuries arising out of a breach of a statutory or common law duty of care made against –

(i) a person other than the claimant's employer; or

(ii) the claimant's employer in respect of matters arising other than in the course of the claimant's employment; but

(b) does not include a claim for damages arising from a disease that the claimant is alleged to have contracted as a consequence of breach of statutory or common law duties of care, other than a physical or psychological injury caused by an accident or other single event;

As the Employers' Liability and Public Liability portal is one and the same this makes virtually no difference within the portal.

However once outside the portal it does make a significant difference. Pre-issue for claims between £1,000 and £5,000 the fixed recoverable costs are the same, but for all other matters public liability fixed recoverable costs are lower than Employers' Liability fixed recoverable costs.

When a defendant is not registered on the claims portal

Paragraph 6.1 of the RTA portal states:-

"6.1 The claimant must complete and send—

(1) the CNF to the defendant's insurer; and

(2) the 'Defendant Only CNF' to the defendant by first class post, except where the defendant is a self-insurer in which case the CNF must be sent to the defendant as insurer and no 'Defendant Only CNF' is required."

However paragraph 5, titled "Communication between the parties" states:-

"Communication between the parties

5.1 Subject to paragraph 6.1(2), where the Protocol requires information to be sent to a party it **must be sent via** www.claimsportal.org.uk (or any other Portal address that may be prescribed from time to time). The claimant will give an e-mail address for contact in the Claim Notification Form ('CNF'). All written communications not required by the Protocol must be sent by e-mail.

5.2 Where the claimant has sent the CNF to the wrong defendant, the claimant may, in this circumstance only, send the CNF to the correct defendant. The period in paragraph 6.11 or 6.13 starts from the date the CNF was sent to the correct defendant."

(My emphasis)

Questions and Answers are provided by the workshop run by The Claims Portal which can be found here –

https://view.officeapps.live.com/op/view.aspx?src=http%3A%2F%2Fwww.claimsportal.org.uk%2Fmedia%2F73967%2FIntroductory-talk-Q-As-issue.doc

"Question

What is the process if the defendant is not registered on the portal?

Answer:

The first step would appear to be to contact the defendant direct. Particularly in relation to a PL claim they may be dealing with the claim, or they may have a claims handler, if there is a deductible or excess on any insurance cover. If they do not have a delegated authority and need to register, direct them to the Helpdesk - helpdesk@rapidclaimsettlement.org.uk"

The insurer should register on the Claims Portal as all communications between the parties must be done via the portal in accordance with paragraph 5 of the portal.

There is no fee to register and thus even the smallest insurer should register so as to comply with the portal.

The claims portal maintains a spreadsheet of all of the RTA compensators and insurers that are registered on the claims portal.

The current version is version 177 and is up to date as at January 2017 and this is updated at http://www.claimsportal.org.uk/en/developers/rta-insurer-index-table/

There are currently 418 different companies.

False imprisonment and wrongful detention

Claims for damages for false imprisonment and/or wrongful detention are likely to be against the police, but that will not always be the case. For example there have been a number of cases where shops have wrongly detained alleged shoplifters and thus in those circumstances the claim will be against the business.

If there is injury involved, either physical or psychological, do such claims go on the EL/PL Portal as public liability claims?

Paragraph 1.1(18) defines a public liability claim in the following terms:-

"(18) 'public liability claim' –

(a) means a claim for damages for personal injuries arising out of a breach of a statutory or common law duty of care made against—

 (i) a person other than the claimant's employer; or

 (ii) the claimant's employer in respect of matters arising other than in the course the claimant's employment; but

(b) does not include a claim for damages arising from a disease that the claimant is alleged to have contracted as a consequence of breach of statutory or common law duties of care, other than a physical or psychological injury caused by an accident or other single event;"

The exclusions are contained in paragraph 4.3 of the protocol.

Consequently my view is that if there are physical injuries arising from wrongful arrest/assault by the police then that is indeed a public liability claim which goes into the portal, subject to matters such as the value of the claim etc.

Note that paragraph 4.3(8) of the portal excludes claims "for damages in relation to harm, abuse or neglect of or by children or vulnerable adults;".

Paragraph 1.1(20) of the portal defines a vulnerable adult as follows:-

"(20) 'vulnerable adult' has the same meaning as in paragraph 3(5) of Schedule 1 to the Legal Aid, Sentencing and Punishment of Offenders Act 2012"

By that provision "vulnerable adult" means a person aged 18 or over whose ability to protect himself or herself from abuse is significantly impaired through physical or mental disability or illness, through old age or otherwise.

I am unaware of any case law on this point in relation to the portals but I could clearly see circumstances in which the "or otherwise" provision would mean that a person in custody falls within the definition of a vulnerable adult.

Subject to that point, my view, as stated above, is that physical injuries in such circumstances do come within the Pre-Action Protocol for Low Value Personal Injury (Employers' Liability and Public Liability) Claims.

As to where there is only psychological injury, that is an interesting point.

The Road Traffic Accident Portal specifically defines a road traffic accident as meaning "an accident resulting in bodily injury to any person…"

I deal with this definition under the heading **Psychological injury only** in dealing with the exclusions from the RTA Portal above.

However there is no such restriction in the EL/PL Portal and indeed the wording quoted above from paragraph 1.1(18)(b) indicates that a psychological injury only does come within the portal. Note the reference to "a physical or psychological injury".

Thus my view is that even where there is only psychological injury, the matter does potentially come within the EL/PL Portal.

Housing disrepair

Can a housing disrepair claim which includes a claim for damages for a specific accident/illness linked to the housing disrepair go onto the EL/PL portal?

As we have seen the issue of whether a portal injury matter goes into a portal is determined by the nature of the claim, not the injury, that is whether or not it is an RTA, EL or PL claim.

Hybrid matters can go in and therefore the fact that the main claim is for housing disrepair does not exclude the claim from the portal process.

An illness linked to housing disrepair is excluded as paragraph 1.1(18)(ii)(b) of the EL/PL portal states that a public liability claim:-

"does not include a claim for damages arising from a disease that the claimant is alleged to have contracted as a consequence of breach of statutory or common law duties of care, other than a physical or psychological injury caused by an accident or other single event;"

Section 4 of the Defective Premises Act 1972 places a statutory duty on the landlord to take such care as is reasonable in all the circumstances to see that visitors are reasonably safe from personal injury.

Section 4(1) reads:-

"4(1) Where premises are let under a tenancy which puts on the landlord an obligation to the tenant for the maintenance or repair of the premises, the landlord owes to all persons who might reasonably be expected to be affected by defects in the state of the premises a duty to take such care as is reasonable in all the circumstances to see that they are reasonably safe from personal injury or from damage to their property caused by a relevant defect."

Thus an injured visitor's claim would be a public liability claim which would go on the portal.

Multiple claimants where one claim exceeds jurisdiction

Supposing that two people have claims arising from the same accident and one claim is clearly within the portal limit and one is clearly outside the limit.

Does that mean that one claim goes into the portal and one does not, rather than the claims being dealt with together?

Yes, in my view. There is nothing in the portals or the Pre-Action Protocol re personal injury claims generally to suggest otherwise.

Nor is there any reason why there should be. If the portal matter is resolved within the portal, then well and good. If not then it can be joined with the non-portal claim when Part 7 proceedings are issued.

It may then well be that the claims are allocated to the multi-track and therefore fixed costs will not apply following the decision of the Court of Appeal in *Qader & Others v Esure Ltd & Khan v McGee [2016] EWCA Civ 1109, 16 November 2016*.

The considerations are no different to a situation where one of a number of claims is settled and one is not.

If, for example, a husband and wife were involved in a road traffic accident in which the wife suffered severe injuries such as brain damage and paralysis, while the husband escaped with a few weeks of mild whiplash, there is no need or reason for the claims to be dealt with together on quantum.

Of course if liability is an issue then the matters do not remain in the portal process anyway.

It will be sensible to indicate the position to the defendant and its insurer – that there is a related claim not proceeding through the portal.

Does an EL/PL claim go on the portal if the defendant is not insured?

There are different provisions within the Pre-Action Protocol for Low Value Personal Injury (Employers' Liability and Public Liability) Claims, depending on whether it is in fact an employers' liability or public liability claim.

It is always the claimant, not the defendant, who begins the portal process.

Under paragraph 1.1(11) "defendant" includes, where the context indicates, the defendant's insurer or legal representative.

Under paragraph 4.3 the protocol does not apply to a claim –

"(1) where the claimant or defendant acts as personal representative of a deceased person;

(2) where the claimant or defendant is a protected party as defined in rule 21.1(2);

(3) in the case of a public liability claim, where the defendant is an individual ('individual' does not include a defendant who is sued in their business capacity or in their capacity as an office holder);

…

(5) where the defendant is insolvent and there is no identifiable insurer;."

Thus if the defendant is both insolvent **and** there is no identifiable insurer then the matter does not go in the protocol. However if the defendant is insolvent **but** there is an identifiable insurer, then it does go in the protocol and it also goes into the protocol if there is no identifiable insurer but the defendant is not insolvent.

Thus there needs to be both insolvency and no identifiable insurer for the matter to be excluded from the portal process.

Paragraph 6.1(2) specifically deals with the situation where the insurer's identity is not known. That is a slightly different situation as compared with there being an uninsured defendant, but nevertheless, as will be seen, it is relevant.

Paragraph 6.1(2) reads:-

"(2) If—

(a) the insurer's identity is not known; or

(b) the defendant is known not to hold insurance cover,

the CNF must be sent to the defendant's registered office or principal place of business and no Defendant Only CNF is required."

Under paragraph 6.1(3) where the insurer's identity is not known, the claimant must make a reasonable attempt to identify the insurer and, in an employers' liability claim only, the claimant must have carried out a database search through the Employers' Liability Tracing Office.

In a disease claim, the CNF should be sent to the insurer identified as the insurer last on risk for the employer for the material period of employment. (6.1(4)).

If the CNF or Defendant Only CNF cannot be sent to the defendant via the prescribed portal address, it must be sent via first class post and this must be done, in a case where the CNF is sent to the insurer, at the same time or as soon as practicable after the CNF is sent. (Paragraph 6.2).

Chapter 31

Disbursements

DISBURSEMENTS

This chapter contains Public Sector information licensed under the Open Government Licence V3.0.

EXPERTS REPORTS

Road Traffic Accident Matters

General

Soft Tissue Injuries

Soft tissue injury road traffic accident claims are subject to a separate regime in relation to expert evidence and this is dealt with in detail in Chapter 5 – Soft Tissue Injury Claims – and Chapter 6 – Fixed Cost Medical Reports and MedCo.

It is expected that in most road traffic accident matters, whether soft tissue injuries or not, where the value is no more than £10,000.00, the medical expert will not need to see any medical records. (Paragraph 7.5 of the RTA Portal).

In most cases, whatever the value, a report from a non-medical expert will not be required, but a report may be obtained where it is reasonably required to value the claim. (Paragraph 7.9(1) of RTA portal).

Employers' Liability and Public Liability Portal

It is expected that most claimants will obtain a medical report from one expert but additional medical reports may be obtained from other experts where the injuries require reports from more than one medical discipline (Paragraph 7.2 EL and PL portal).

Any subsequent medical report from an expert who has already reported must be justified and a report may be justified where –

(1) the first medical report recommends that further time is required before prognosis of the claimant's injuries can be determined; or

(2) the claimant is receiving continuing treatment; or

(3) the claimant has not recovered as expected in the original prognosis.

(Paragraph 7.6 of EL and PL portal).

Non-medical reports – EL and PL

Paragraph 7.7 of EL and PL portal provides that in most cases a report from a non-medical expert will not be required, but a report may be obtained where it is reasonably required to value the claim.

Except in relation to soft tissue injury claims in road traffic matters, disbursements, including experts' reports, are not subject to the Fixed Costs Regime, either in the portal or if the matter exits to Fixed Recoverable Costs.

Any dispute over disbursements is dealt with under CPR 45.19.

Anything required by the expert to assist in the preparation of evidence is a disbursement, whereas anything required for treatment purposes is special damages.

It may be the case that something that was required for treatment, and therefore forms part of special damages, does end up being used to assist in relation to the medical evidence. Assistance may be gained by asking the question:-

"Would this have been obtained if there was no legal claim ongoing?"

Generally this should be less of a problem now as the person preparing the report should have nothing to do with the treatment. Thus there should be a clear division between an expense incurred in relation to treatment and by a separate medical person in relation to a report for legal proceedings.

Effectively, a claimant can have two bites at the cherry. If an item of special damages is successfully challenged by the paying party on the ground that it is costs, then it can be claimed as costs.

Matters are not always that simple in that a global offer, or an overall offer in respect of special damages, may be made and accepted without it being clear which items, if any, were being challenged.

There are potential problems in those cases where there are fixed costs in relation to specified medical reports and obtaining records etc. If the actual cost is higher than the recoverable fixed cost, then the solicitor or client will end up paying it and thus will want that item as one of special damages, which are not capped.

In *Charman v John Reilly (Civil Engineers) Ltd [2013]* the court dealt with the reasonableness of medical report fees in portal claims and held that a reasonable fee for a medical report is no more than £240.00, broken down as to:-

- £50.00 plus VAT for the agency element of the claim; and
- £150.00 plus VAT for the expert's fee.

On 11 November 2016 the Judicial Office announced that Lord Justice Jackson would be carrying out a review of Fixed Recoverable Costs, with a view to extending them to other types of civil litigation and to higher value claims.

Lord Justice Jackson has specifically asked for suggestions as to how disbursements should be dealt with within an expanded Fixed Recoverable Costs Regime.

Counsel / Specialist Solicitor – all portals

The self-explanatory Paragraph 7.10 of RTA portal and 7.8 of EL and PL portal reads-

"In most cases under this Protocol, it is expected that the claimant's legal representative will be able to value the claim. In some cases with a value of more than £10,000 (excluding vehicle related damages), an additional advice from a specialist solicitor or from counsel may be justified where it is reasonably required to value the claim."

Paragraph 7.44 of RTA portal refers to "a sum equal to the Type C fixed costs of an additional advice on quantum of damages where such advice is justified under paragraph 7.10." Exactly the same principle is set out in the EL and PL portal (Paragraph 7.41).

Paragraph 1.1(17) of RTA portal and 1.1(19) of EL and PL portal in the definition section states:-

"""Type C fixed Costs" has the same meaning as in rule 45.18(2) of the Civil Procedure Rules 1998."

CPR 45.18(2) sets Type C fixed costs at £150.00 (plus VAT).

Other issues

It will be seen from the text of CPR 45.19, which appears at the end of this chapter, that the court's powers to allow disbursements are limited in portal matters.

CPR 45.19(1) provides that subject to (2A) to (2E) the court may allow a claim for a disbursement of a type mentioned in paragraphs (2) or (3), but will not allow a claim for any other type of disbursement.

Those disbursements which may be allowed in a portal matters are:-

(a) the cost of obtaining –

(i) medical records;

(ii) a medical report or reports or non-medical expert reports as provided for in the relevant Protocol;

(aa) Driver Vehicle Licensing Authority;

(bb) Motor Insurance Database;

(b) court fees as a result of Part 21 being applicable;

(c) court fees payable where proceedings are started as a result of a limitation period that is about to expire;

(d) court fees in respect of the Stage 3 Procedure; and

(e) any other disbursement that has arisen due to a particular feature of the dispute.

Part 21 is a reference to children and those under a disability. Matters involving those under a disability do not go in either portal and therefore that is a reference to the court fee in relation to an infant approval hearing.

It will be noted that CPR 45.19(2)(e) makes provision for payment of "any other disbursement that has arisen due to a particular feature of the dispute."

I will return to that later.

CPR 45.19(2A) imposes fixed costs – and note that they are fixed and not capped – in relation to medical reports in soft tissue injury claims under the RTA Portal.

Note that fixed medical report fees do **not** apply to soft tissue injuries in the EL/PL portal.

CPR 45.19(2D) provides that VAT may be added to all of the figures for medical reports and records.

CPR 45.19(2C) provides that if a report from an expert not listed in CPR 45.19(2A) (bb) is required, then the cost is not fixed, but the use of that expert and the cost must be justified.

That provision applies only to soft tissue injury claims in the RTA Portal and the wording refers to "a further report from an expert not listed in paragraph (2A) (b)".

That does not mean a further report from that expert. What is means is a report over and above the initial one obtained from an expert under CPR 45.19(2A) (a), which is fixed at £180.00 plus VAT, whoever it is obtained from.

Thus the structure of what is a clumsily worded provision is that in RTA Portal soft tissue injury matters only, the first report, whoever it is from, has a fixed cost of £180.00 plus VAT.

If a further report is obtained from experts within the disciplines mentioned in CPR 45.19(2A)(b)(i) to (iv) then the costs are fixed as stated in that rule.

However if a report, that is not the first report, is obtained from an expert not listed in that paragraph then the cost is not fixed.

CPR 45.19(2B) provides that save in exceptional circumstances, which are nowhere defined, and have not been subject to any case law, no fee may be allowed for the cost of obtaining a report from a medical expert who –

(a) has provided treatment to the claimant;

(b) is associated with any person who has provided treatment; or

(c) proposes or recommends treatment that they or an associate provide treatment.

Note that this provision applies to all medical experts in all types of work and whether or not the matter started in the portal and whether or not it is subject to Fixed Recoverable Costs.

Thus it would apply to a small claim that does not go into the portal and a £10 million catastrophic loss claim.

CPR 45.19(2E) provides that "associate", "associated with", "fixed costs medical report" and "soft tissue injury claim" have the same meaning as in paragraphs 1.1(1A), (10A) and (16A) respectively, of the RTA Portal.

I deal with this in detail in Chapter 6 but it is important to note that, whatever the value of the claim, this rule applies and therefore even if you are only dealing with high value claims you need familiarity with the portals.

CPR 45.19(3) allows further disbursements in the case of RTA Portal, but **not** EL/PL matters, namely:-

(a) an engineer's report; and

(b) a search of the records of the—

(i) Driver Vehicle Licensing Authority; and

(ii) Motor Insurance Database.

In fact the items listed in (3)(b) already appear at CPR 45.19(2)(aa) and (bb) and do not need to be repeated here, but they are.

"As provided for in the relevant protocol"

It will be noted that CPR 45.19(2)(ii) provides for recovery of the cost of a medical report or reports or non-medical expert reports "as provided for in the relevant protocol", for which read Portals.

Road Traffic Accident Portal

The cost of expert medical and non-medical reports and specialist legal advice obtained is dealt with at paragraph 7.31 of the RTA Portal which reads as follows:-

"Costs of expert medical and non-medical reports and specialist legal advice obtained

7.31

(1) Where the claimant obtains more than one expert report or an advice from a specialist solicitor or counsel—

(a) the defendant at the end of Stage 2 may refuse to pay; or

(b) the court at Stage 3 may refuse to allow,

the costs of any report or advice not reasonably required.

(2) Therefore, where the claimant obtains more than one expert report or obtains an advice from a specialist solicitor or counsel—

(a) the claimant should explain in the Stage 2 Settlement Pack why they obtained a further report or such advice; and

(b) if relevant, the defendant should in the Stage 2 Settlement Pack identify the report or reports or advice for which they will not pay and explain why they will not pay for that report or reports or advice."

Thus the cost of additional medical reports, or any report from a non-medical expert or advice from a specialist solicitor or counsel, is within the discretion of the court.

Paragraph 7.32A provides that in a soft tissue injury claim, the Stage 2 Settlement Pack is of no effect unless the medical report is a fixed cost medical report.

I deal with the portal procedure elsewhere but that is the provision which makes it compulsory to use a fixed cost medical report in a soft tissue injury claim.

Paragraph 7.32(4) provides that the Stage 2 Settlement Pack must include "evidence of disbursements (for example the cost of any medical report)".

Paragraph 7.44 provides that any offer to settle made at any stage by either party will automatically include, and cannot exclude…

"(3) an agreement in principle to pay relevant disbursements allowed in accordance with rule 45.19;

…"

Paragraph 7.45 provides that where there is a dispute about whether an additional advice on quantum of damages is justified or about the amount or validity of any disbursement, the parties may use the procedure set out in CPR 45.29.

That rule provides that where the parties to a dispute have a written agreement on all issues but have failed to agree the amount of costs, they may start proceedings under that rule so that the court can determine the amount of those costs.

Paragraph 7.47 provides that except where the claimant is a child, or where a CRU certificate has not been obtained, the defendant must pay the relevant disbursements allowed in accordance with rule 45.19, including any disbursements fixed under Rule 45.19(2A) - paragraph 7.47(5) of the RTA Portal.

Paragraph 7.62(5) makes similar provisions in relation to settlement after a claim for additional damages.

In relation to the non-settlement payment by the defendant at the end of Stage 2, the defendant must pay the disbursements in Rule 45.19 that have been agreed, including any disbursements fixed under Rule 45.19(2A) (paragraph 7.70 of the portal), and where the amount of a disbursement is not agreed, the defendant must pay such an amount for the disbursement as the defendant considers reasonable. (Paragraph 7.71).

In an appropriate case, that allows the defendant to pay nothing if it considers that that is the reasonable amount for a disbursement, because it believes the disbursement to have been unnecessary.

The EL/PL Portal in relation to these matters is in identical terms and the relevant provision is 7.29 of the Pre-Action Protocol for Low Value Personal Injury (Employers' Liability and Public Liability) Claims which reads:-

"Costs of expert medical and non-medical reports and specialist legal advice obtained

7.29

(1) Where the claimant obtains more than one expert report or an advice from a specialist solicitor or counsel—

(a) the defendant at the end of Stage 2 may refuse to pay; or

(b) the court at Stage 3 may refuse to allow,

the costs of any report or advice not reasonably required.

(2) Therefore, where the claimant obtains more than one expert report or obtains an advice from a specialist solicitor or counsel—

(a) the claimant should explain in the Stage 2 Settlement Pack why they obtained a further report or such advice; and

(b) if relevant, the defendant should in the Stage 2 Settlement Pack identify the report or reports or advice for which they will not pay and explain why they will not pay for that report or reports or advice."

CPR 45.29 reads:-

"Costs-only application after a claim is started under Part 8 in accordance with Practice Direction 8B

45.29

(1) This rule sets out the procedure where –

(a) the parties to a dispute have reached an agreement on all issues (including which party is to pay the costs) which is made or confirmed in writing; but

(b) they have failed to agree the amount of those costs; and

(c) proceedings have been started under Part 8 in accordance with Practice Direction 8B.

(2) Either party may make an application for the court to determine the costs.

(3) Where an application is made under this rule the court will assess the costs in accordance with rule 45.22 or rule 45.25.

(4) Rule 44.5 (amount of costs where costs are payable pursuant to a contract) does not apply to an application under this rule."

Interpreter's fees needed during a medical examination

It is arguable that if an interpreter is required during a client's medical examination then that is part of the cost of obtaining a medical report in CPR 45.19(2) (a) (ii).

If the court agrees then there is no need to look further, although due to the fixed costs in soft tissue matters the claimant may want a finding that the interpreter's fee does not come within the cost of obtaining a medical report.

If the court does not agree that an interpreter's fee comes within the cost of obtaining a medical report, then CPR 45.19(2) (e) comes into play and that allows the recoverability of "any other disbursement that has arisen due to a particular feature of the dispute."

The dictionary definition of "feature" is:-

"a distinctive or characteristic part of a thing; some part of which arrests the attention by its conspicuousness or prominence."

Roget's Thesaurus gives the following alternatives for "feature":-

"Attribute, quality, property, trait, mark, hallmark, trademark; aspect, facet, side, point, detail, factor, ingredient, component, constituent, element, theme; peculiarity, idiosyncrasy, quirk, oddity."

In my view something which satisfies this description in relation to the claimant may be a particular feature of the dispute. After all the dispute is simply that which is in disagreement between the claimant and the defendant and to separate it out and say that something which is particular and peculiar to the claimant is not "a particular feature of the dispute" would not make sense.

For those firms who have a significant non-English speaking clientele this is an important point.

There is also a potential human rights issue under the European Convention on Human Rights in that a failure to even give the court a discretion to add on interpreter's fees is potentially discriminatory on the grounds of race or ethnic origin.

There is also an argument that is breaches European Union law in not allowing parity for all European Union citizens.

There are conflicting, non-binding, decisions in relation to this issue.

In *Gao v Enterprise Rent-a-Car, Oldham County Court, 21 May 2009, case number: 80L01799* the District Judge made that distinction, stating that the need for an interpreter was due to a particular feature of the claimant and not a particular feature of the dispute, a line of reasoning followed in *Olesiejuk v Maple Industries*, Liverpool County Court, 4 January 2012, where the matter was determined by a Circuit Judge.

However in Madej v Maciszyn, Senior Courts Costs Office, 29 November 2013, Case No CC 1206761

Master Campbell allowed an interpreter's fee in a fixed costs case where, again the key issue was whether a characteristic of the claimant, rather than the case, could amount to "a particular feature of the dispute."

He held that it could and gave other examples, such as a claimant with a mobility problem who requires a carer to be present at the medical examination for the medical report, or at court.

Master Campbell rejected the suggestion that a particular feature of the claimant could not be a particular feature of the dispute.

He also rejected the idea that consideration of such extra disbursements undermined the "fixed" element of fixed costs, pointing out that it was a deliberate policy decision to fix costs, but not disbursements and that the very rule itself envisaged disbursements not specifically listed.

The issue was not whether court had power to award the cost of extra disbursements in a particular case, but whether an interpreter's fee came within the definition in the rule giving the court such discretion.

The Human Rights issue was raised in this case but in view of the court's finding that did not fall to be considered.

The Master granted leave to appeal.

"Mr Williams [Benjamin Williams QC] tells me that there have been conflicting decisions and that whatever the outcome, this is an appropriate case in which permission to appeal should be given so that the matter can be resolved by a Judge of the High Court. In my view, that is a compelling reason why permission should be granted under CPR 52. If the parties would draft an appropriate order for approval the matter can go forward for resolution at a higher level should the Defendant wish to follow that course."

That did not happen and I am unaware of any binding authorities on that point.

Such issues will assume much greater importance as fixed costs spread to all types of civil work in relation to claims of much greater value and to multi-track claims potentially of much greater complexity.

All of these matter are currently being considered by Lord Justice Jackson who is due to report by 31 July 2017.

Guidance would be welcome.

That leaves open the question of whether a court has the discretion to exercise the "escape" clause allowing for the recovery of legal costs over and above Fixed Recoverable Costs. The problem is that that provision relates to legal costs, rather than disbursements, and on the face of it an interpreter's fee is a disbursement and not legal costs.

The relevant provision is CPR 45.29J which reads:-

Claims for an amount of costs exceeding fixed recoverable costs

"45.29J

(1) If it considers that there are exceptional circumstances making it appropriate to do so, the court will consider a claim for an amount of costs (excluding disbursements) which is greater than the fixed recoverable costs referred to in rules 45.29B to 45.29H.

(2) If the court considers such a claim to be appropriate, it may—

(a) summarily assess the costs; or

(b) make an order for the costs to be subject to detailed assessment.

(3) If the court does not consider the claim to be appropriate, it will make an order—

(a) if the claim is made by the claimant, for the fixed recoverable costs; or

(b) if the claim is made by the defendant, for a sum which has regard to, but which does not exceed the fixed recoverable costs,

and any permitted disbursements only."

Counsel's fees

No separate fee is recoverable in relation to counsel drafting pleadings, holding a conference or indeed generally anything else. The starting point is that any portal or FRC matter does not require the involvement of counsel.

Counsel's fees as such are not recoverable in Fixed Recoverable Costs cases – it is assumed that the solicitor will deal with all matters in such cases. You are free to instruct counsel but you do not get a separate fee as it is part of the legal spend. If it were otherwise you could take the fixed costs and get counsel to do everything and charge all of counsel's fees as a disbursement.

Advocacy fees, for trial, are recoverable as per the Tables and the fee is the same whoever the advocate is, barrister or solicitor, and irrespective of seniority or expertise.

No advocacy fee is recoverable if the matter settles before the day of trial. Clearly the solicitor gets the benefit of a higher fee the further the matter progresses through the Fixed Costs Matrix. Counsel does not.

Advice

RTA 7.10 reads:-

"In most cases under this Protocol, it is expected that the claimant's legal representative will be able to value the claim. In some cases with a value of more than £10,000 (excluding vehicle related damages), an additional advice from a specialist solicitor or from counsel may be justified where it is reasonably required to value the claim."

EL/PL 7.8 is in similar terms.

That this applies only to an advice on quantum is confirmed by RTA 7.47(4) and EL/PL 7.44(4) which read:-

"…where an additional advice on quantum of damages is justified under paragraph 7.10 [7.8 in EL/PL], a sum equal to the Type C fixed costs to cover the cost of that advice."

Type C costs are £150.00 plus VAT.

It is unclear as to whether you can instruct a specialist solicitor in your own firm and get the extra fee.

Given these claims will be handled by lower grade fee earners I see no reason why the specialist solicitor should not be a grade A fee earner within the same firm. Equally, one could now employ a barrister in a solicitor's firm and claim it as Counsel's fee even though it is in-house Counsel providing the advice.

The CPR specifically deal with other work by counsel.

CPR 45.23B reads:-

"Where—

(a) the value of the claim for damages is more than £10,000;

(b) an additional advice has been obtained from a specialist solicitor or from counsel;

(c) that advice is reasonably required to value the claim,

the fixed costs may include an additional amount equivalent to the Stage 3 Type C fixed costs."

Type C fixed costs are £150.00 plus VAT.

CPR 45.29I reads:-

"(1) Subject to paragraphs (2A) to (2E), the court—

(a) may allow a claim for a disbursement of a type mentioned in paragraphs (2) or (3); but

(b) will not allow a claim for any other type of disbursement.

(2) In a claim started under either the RTA Protocol or the EL/PL Protocol, the disbursements referred to in paragraph (1) are—

...

(c) the cost of any advice from a specialist solicitor or counsel as provided for in the relevant Protocol;"

The EL/PL protocol makes clear that advice from counsel MAY be justified where reasonably required to value the claim:

"7.8. In most cases under this Protocol, it is expected that the claimant's legal representative will be able to value the claim. In some cases with a value of more than £10,000, an additional advice from a specialist solicitor or from counsel may be justified where it is reasonably required to value the claim."

CPR 45.29I (1) (h) allows the recovery of "any other disbursement reasonably incurred due to a particular feature of the dispute."

I know that some courts have allowed counsel's fees in those circumstances. My view is that that is wrong given that this same rule specifically sets out the circumstances in which counsel's fees may be claimed, but I appreciate that there is another view in relation to that.

Additionally, I am aware of some courts (by no means all) allowing a fee for a conference with Counsel especially in cases where fundamental dishonesty is raised expressly or implicitly and the case remains on the fast track.

CPR 45.29H (1) deals with interim applications and reads:-

"(1) Where the court makes an order for costs of an interim application to be paid by one party in a case to which this Section applies, the order shall be for a sum equivalent to one half of the applicable Type A and Type B costs in Table 6 or 6A."

CPR 45.29H (3) reads:-

"(3) If an order for costs is made pursuant to this rule, the party in whose favour the order is made is entitled to disbursements in accordance with rule 45.29I."

Thus even if a costs order is made, one is thrown back on the CPR 45.29I definition.

It would be rare on a Case Management Conference for the court to order one party to pay the costs, absent particularly bad conduct by the paying party.

The relevant Type A & B costs are £250.00 and therefore a sum equivalent to one half of those costs is £125.00.

My starting point is that you receive nothing as this is just part of running the case.

However in light of *Sharp v Leeds City Council*, 1 February 2017, [2017] EWCA Civ 33a CMC or allocation hearing likely to be treated as an interim application for costs purposes?

Children & Disbursements

CPR 45.12(2)(b) provides that the court may allow court fees payable on an application to the court and fees payable for instructing counsel where they are necessarily incurred by reason of one or more of the claimants being a child or protected party as defined in Part 21.

Thus counsel's fees are recoverable as a disbursement under that rule, but there is no additional fee if the solicitor prepares the advice herself or himself.

This reflects how badly the rules are written. In fact if you look at CPR 45.12(2)(b) what it actually says is that the court can allow fees payable for instructing counsel or court fees payable on an application to the court. Clearly the word "or" should be "and" and on a literal reading of that rule you either get counsel's fees or the court fees, but you cannot get both.

There are other similar confusions.

RTA Portal 7.10 reads:-

"7.10 In most cases under this Protocol, it is expected that the claimant's legal representative will be able to value the claim. In some cases with a value of more than £10,000 (excluding vehicle related damages), an additional advice from a specialist solicitor or from counsel may be justified where it is reasonably required to value the claim."

EL/PL 7.8 is in similar terms.

Thus it is unclear as to whether you can instruct a specialist solicitor in your own firm and get the extra fee in those circumstances.

That paragraph specifically states that it is expected that the claimant's legal representative, rather than counsel, will be able to value the claim and yet CPR 45.12 allows for the recovery of counsel's fees, but allows no extra cost for the solicitor, even though it is expected that the solicitor will be able to value the claim!

Thus the position in relation to children, in precisely the same case is:-

Settled in the portal: £150.00 extra fee payable to counsel or specialist solicitor;

Settled out of the portal pre-issue: no extra fee payable;

Settled after proceedings issued: £150.00 fee for counsel but no fee if the solicitor does the work.

I deal with the whole issue of cases involving children in detail in Chapter 39.

After the Event Insurance Premiums and Success Fees

Mesothelioma

In the context of personal injury the success fee and after-the-event insurance premium remain recoverable in full in mesothelioma cases. Currently such cases are not covered by the EL/PL portal as they are specifically excluded by paragraph 4.3(10).

A matter which could not have gone into a portal cannot be subject to fixed costs.

Thus mesothelioma cases are subject neither to the portal process nor fixed recoverable costs.

Clinical Negligence

Success fees in clinical negligence cases are not recoverable.

However, to a limited extent, after the event insurance premiums are still recoverable in clinical negligence cases.

Recoverability relates to that element of any after the event insurance policy covering the risk of incurring a liability to pay for an expert report or reports relating to liability or causation in respect of clinical negligence (or against that risk and other risks).

Is the premium recoverable if in fact a report is not obtained, maybe because liability and causation are admitted after the policy is incepted but before the report is obtained?

The relevant regulations, are the Recovery of Costs Insurance Premiums in Clinical Negligence Proceedings (No 2) Regulations 2013 which state:

"3. (1) A costs order made in favour of a party to clinical negligence proceedings who has taken out a costs insurance policy may include provision requiring the payment of an amount in respect of all or part of the premium of that policy if—

(a) the financial value of the claim for damages in respect of clinical negligence is more than £1,000; and

(b) the costs insurance policy insures against the risk of incurring a liability to pay for an expert report or reports relating to liability or causation in respect of clinical negligence (or against that risk and other risks).

(2) The amount of the premium that may be required to be paid under the costs order shall not exceed that part of the premium which relates to the risk of incurring liability to pay for an expert report or reports relating to liability or causation in respect of clinical negligence in connection with the proceedings."

Thus Regulation 3(1) (b) makes it clear that the costs insurance policy does indeed insure against the *risk* of incurring a liability to pay for an expert report in respect of clinical negligence and there is no need for a report actually to have been purchased. This argument is further strengthened by the text of the original Statutory Instrument, SI 2013/92, which was declared ultra vires by the Parliamentary Committee which examines such matters.

Regulation 2 read as follows:

"2. (1) Subject to paragraph (2), a costs order made in favour of a party to clinical negligence proceedings may include provision requiring the payment of an amount in respect of the relevant part of the premium of a costs insurance policy taken out by that party which insures against the risk of incurring liability to pay for one or more expert reports in connection with the proceedings (or against that risk and other risks).

(2) A costs order may not require the payment of an amount in respect of the relevant part of the premium which relates to the liability to pay for any expert report if—

(a) the report was not in the event obtained;

(b) the report did not relate to liability or causation; or

(c) the cost of the report is not allowed under the costs order."

Consequently under Regulation 2(2) (a) one was not able to obtain a costs order in relation to any part of the premium if the report was not in the event obtained.

Although Parliament had to pass a fresh Statutory Instrument in any event, because the original one was ultra vires, Parliament has chosen to alter extensively the provisions of the original Statutory Instrument and that is one of the key restrictions that has been removed.

It is settled law that if Parliament changes any Act of Parliament or Statutory Instrument then it intends something by that change.

This is in contrast when there has been no change, where it is not necessary the case that Parliament has addressed the particular point.

Here Parliament has clearly made a deliberate decision to remove the provision that there is no recoverability of the after-the-event insurance premium if the report was not in the event obtained and to replace it with the provision set out above whereby it is indeed the risk of incurring a liability which is the relevant point.

Note that at present clinical negligence cases are not covered by the portals, and therefore cannot be the subject of fixed recoverable costs.

Extension of Fixed Costs

Clinical negligence claims are likely to be covered by fixed costs following Lord Justice Jackson's review. LJ Jackson's report is due out by 31 July 2013.

Disbursements

45.19

(1) Subject to paragraphs (2A) to (2E), the court –

(a) may allow a claim for a disbursement of a type mentioned in paragraphs (2) or (3); but

(b) will not allow a claim for any other type of disbursement.

(2) In a claim to which either the RTA Protocol or EL/PL Protocol applies, the disbursements referred to in paragraph (1) are –

(a) the cost of obtaining –

(i) medical records;

(ii) a medical report or reports or non-medical expert reports as provided for in the relevant Protocol;

(aa) Driver Vehicle Licensing Authority;

(bb) Motor Insurance Database;

(b) court fees as a result of Part 21 being applicable;

(c) court fees payable where proceedings are started as a result of a limitation period that is about to expire;

(d) court fees in respect of the Stage 3 Procedure; and

(e) any other disbursement that has arisen due to a particular feature of the dispute.

(2A) In a soft tissue injury claim to which the RTA Protocol applies, the only sums (exclusive of VAT) that are recoverable in respect of the cost of obtaining a fixed cost medical report or medical records are as follows—

(a) obtaining the first report from an accredited medical expert selected via the MedCo Portal: £180;

(b) obtaining a further report where justified from an expert from one of the following disciplines—

(i) Consultant Orthopaedic Surgeon (inclusive of a review of medical records where applicable): £420;

(ii) Consultant in Accident and Emergency Medicine: £360;

(iii) General Practitioner registered with the General Medical Council: £180; or

(iv) Physiotherapist registered with the Health and Care Professions Council: £180;

(c) obtaining medical records: no more than £30 plus the direct cost from the holder of the records, and limited to £80 in total for each set of records required. Where relevant records are required from more than one holder of records, the fixed fee applies to each set of records required;

(d) addendum report on medical records (except by Consultant Orthopaedic Surgeon): £50; and

(e) answer to questions under Part 35: £80.

(2B) Save in exceptional circumstances, no fee may be allowed for the cost of obtaining a report to which paragraph (2A) applies where the medical expert—

(a) has provided treatment to the claimant;

(b) is associated with any person who has provided treatment; or

(c) proposes or recommends treatment that they or an associate then provide.

(2C) The cost of obtaining a further report from an expert not listed in paragraph (2A)(b) is not fixed, but the use of that expert and the cost must be justified.

(2D) Where appropriate, VAT may be recovered in addition to the cost of obtaining a fixed cost medical report or medical records.

(2E) In this rule, 'accredited medical expert', 'associate', 'associated with', 'fixed cost medical report' 'MedCo' and 'soft tissue injury claim' have the same meaning as in paragraph 1.1(A1), (1A), (10A), (12A), and (16A), respectively, of the RTA Protocol.

(3) In a claim to which the RTA Protocol applies, the disbursements referred to in paragraph (1) are also the cost of—

(a) an engineer's report; and

(b) a search of the records of the—

(i) Driver Vehicle Licensing Authority; and

(ii) Motor Insurance Database.

Chapter 32

Case Law

CASE LAW

The courts will not look kindly on claimant lawyers seeking to have cases dealt with outside the portals, and both portals contain express provisions that where a court considers that the claimant acted unreasonably in exiting the portal it will award no more than CPR 45.18 fixed portal costs.

Please also see Chapter 41 for further consideration of cases exiting the portal.

This is highlighted in the case of *Ilahi v Usman*, Manchester County Court 29 November 2012

where the court held that the claimant had behaved unreasonably in withdrawing its stage 2 portal offer and thus causing the matter to exit the portal and consequently should only get portal costs.

Although this is only a County Court decision by a Circuit Judge leave to appeal to the Court of Appeal was refused by Lord Justice Jackson who gave brief reasons as follows:-

"I agree with the analysis of the provisions of the Pre-action Protocol for Low Value PI Claims in RTAs made by Judge Platts. I also agree with the judge's application of those provisions to the facts of this case."

Of course this is not a Court of Appeal decision but it is a decision with which Lord Justice Jackson has specifically agreed.

Throughout I refer to the wording of the portal at the relevant time.

Paragraph 7.55 of the portal at the time provided that if agreement was not reached during stage 2 then the claimant "must" send to the defendant a Court Proceedings Pack thus initiating the stage 3 procedure and under paragraph 7.61 the defendant must pay to the claimant its final offer of damages (in this case £2,400.00).

Instead the claimant withdrew its offer without explanation thus causing the matter to exit the portal under 7.39. At the time that paragraph read:-

"7.39 Where a party withdraws an offer made in the Stage 2 Settlement Pack Form after the total consideration period or further consideration period, the claim will no longer continue under this Protocol and the claimant may start proceedings under Part 7 of the CPR."

The matter went to a disposal hearing.

The District Judge awarded the claimant costs on the standard, open basis.

The District Judge failed to consider CPR 45.36 which provided:-

"(1) This rule applies where the claimant –

(a) does not comply with the process set out in the RTA Protocol; or

(b) elects not to continue with that process,

and starts proceedings under Part 7.

(2) Where a judgment is given in favour of the claimant but –

(a) the court determines that the defendant did not proceed with the process set out in the RTA Protocol because the claimant provided insufficient information on the Claim Notification Form;

(b) the court considers that the claimant acted unreasonably –

(i) by discontinuing the process set out in the RTA Protocol and starting proceedings under Part 7;

(ii) by valuing the claim at more than £10,000, so that the claimant did not need to comply with the RTA Protocol; or

(iii) except for paragraph (2)(a), in any other way caused the process in the RTA Protocol to be discontinued; or

(c) the claimant did not comply with the RTA Protocol at all despite the claim falling within the scope of the RTA Protocol;

the court may order the defendant to pay no more than the fixed costs in rule 45.29 together with the disbursements allowed in accordance with rule 45.30 and success fee in accordance with rule 45.31(3)."

On appeal the Judge held that by taking a step – withdrawing the offer – which would cause the matter automatically to exit the portal, the claimant was electing not to continue with the portal and therefore CPR 45.36 was engaged, and that all that should be awarded was fixed portal costs.

The Appeal Judge went on to hold that the claimant had acted unreasonably in withdrawing her offer and that her reason for doing so was to get much higher costs and that that was against "the spirit if not the letter of the Protocol".

In the alternative the same considerations should have applied if the court had exercised its discretion under CPR 44.3.

CPR 44.3 gives courts a very wide discretion in relation to costs and specifically provides that the court must have regard to all circumstances including the conduct of all the parties and that includes conduct before, as well as during, the proceedings and in particular the extent to which the parties followed the Practice Direction (Pre-Action Conduct) or any relevant Pre-Action Protocol.

The Appeal Judge held that the principles set out by the Court of Appeal in

Voice and Script International Ltd v Alghafar [2003] EWCA Civ 736

applied here. In that decision the Court of Appeal said that the court was free to impose small claims costs even if the matter had not been allocated and even if that approach was not expressly stated in the CPR "it follows from two essential principles, first, the discretionary nature of costs orders and second, the overriding requirement of proportionality in civil litigation generally".

His Honour Judge Platts stated at paragraphs 30 and 31 of his judgment:-

> "30.I am forced to the conclusion that the real reason for the claimant withdrawing her offer was to take advantage of the costs implications of bringing a Part 7 claim. Those advantages are, first, that a defendant will be under more pressure to settle since it might face a higher costs

> liability if he does not make an offer which the claimant accepts or fails to beat at hearing; and, second, that if the matter does go to a hearing the claimant's solicitors will potentially recover more in costs than they otherwise would have done…
>
> 31. In my judgment to manipulate the RTA Protocol procedure to take the claim away from stage 3 and into part 7 because of the costs implications is contrary to the spirit if not the letter of the Protocol and wholly contrary to the overriding objective. The court has developed the RTA Protocol in order to provide a speedy, certain and cost effective way of dealing with these claims."

In *Nicole Chapman v Tameside Hospital NHS Foundation Trust, Bolton County Court, 15 June 2016, Case number B74YM281*

the defendant was ordered to pay all of the claimant's costs where the claimant discontinued shortly before trial following disclosure by the defendant of documents which it should have disclosed during the portal process.

The matter was an Occupiers' Liability slipping case. The defendant denied liability and stated that it had no documents to disclose.

Proceedings were issued. The defendant then disclosed documents showing that it had a reasonable cleaning and inspection system.

The claimant discontinued.

The claimant was awarded fixed costs up to the post-listing, pre-trial stage less the fixed recoverable costs sum applicable had the matter settled pre-issue.

The court described the defendant's conduct as "entirely unacceptable" and was critical of the National Health Service Litigation Authority.

The Pre-Action Protocol for Personal Injury Claims provides that:-

"The Defendant should also enclose with the response, documents in their possession which are material to the issues between the parties, and which would be likely to be ordered to be disclosed by the court, either on an application for pre-action disclosure, or on disclosure during proceedings."

CPR 44.2(1) provides:-

"(1) The court has a discretion as to –

- whether costs are payable by one party to another;
- the amount of those costs; and
- when they are to be paid."

CPR 44.2(4) states:-

"(4) In deciding what order (if any) to make about costs, the court will have regard to all the circumstances, including –

- the conduct of all the parties;"

CPR 44.2(5) says:-

"(5) The conduct of the parties includes –

- conduct before, as well as during, the proceedings and in particular the extent to which the parties followed the Practice Direction – Pre-Action Conduct or any relevant pre-action protocol;
- whether it was reasonable for a party to raise, pursue or contest a particular allegation or issue;
- the manner in which a party has pursued or defended its case or a particular allegation or issue; and
- whether a claimant who has succeeded in the claim, in whole or in part, exaggerated its claim.

The court awarded costs on the basis of the stage costs of £3,790.00 without the added 20% of damages as no damages were recovered.

It then set-off the portal costs of £950.00 which the claimant would have incurred anyway, representing the point where the matter would have been stopped had the NHSLA disclosed its evidence when it should have done so.

Consequently the defendant was ordered to pay the claimant £2,840.00 plus VAT and disbursements.

Of course in a Conditional Fee Agreement case, as this was, a claimant would normally be prevented from recovering costs due to the indemnity principle. However that principle does not apply in fixed costs cases – see *Nizami v Butt [2006] EWHC 159 (QB).*

The court also recognized the extra danger involved of defendants behaving badly in fixed costs cases:-

"15. The Defendant's behaviour in the conduct of this litigation was entirely unacceptable. It's exactly the type of conduct which Part 44.2 is designed to address. Under the modern costs provisions, of course, the costs sanctions become increasingly important. The Claimant's solicitors are pursuing these matters, PI claims, and at the end of the claim are recovering costs which are fixed and which are not by any stretch of the imagination, generous. There is a danger of — I am not saying it has happened in this case — this is a pure inadequacy of approach by the Litigation Authority and the Trust, but there is a danger that defendants and their representatives will cause difficulties in the course of litigation, so as to run up the work which claimant's solicitors are having to do in the knowledge that those solicitors cannot recover costs reflecting that work. And of course, it always has to be borne in mind the provisions of CPR 1.3, that the parties to litigation have an obligation to assist the Court to further the overriding objective. The overriding objective firstly being to try and avoid costs and the issue of proceedings if at all possible, which is the whole purpose of the pre-action protocol, of course and secondly, when such claims are brought that they be dealt with in an efficient manner, in a proper manner so as to avoid excessive costs, involving public resources, delay and so on."

The court rejected any suggestion that CPR 44.2 did not apply to fixed costs cases:-

"18. I am satisfied that the provisions of Rule 44.2 can be applied. It would be a nonsensical situation if the rules which are provided by Rule 44.2 to give the Court the power to impose sanctions to penalise those who abuse the system, and clearly there has been abuse here by the Trust and possibly by the Litigation Authority initially representing them. I am certainly not suggesting that Weightmans have been dealing with it improperly, they are obviously having to deal with what information they are supplied. But it would be a nonsensical situation if the rules, in an appropriate case where the fixed costs regime did apply, precluded the Court from imposing the sanctions provided under Rule 44.2 and 44.2, of course, gives the Court an unqualified discretion. I do not accept that I am bound by the Part 45 scales, but I clearly have to bear them in mind. It would be nonsensical if the Claimant's solicitors could achieve a windfall and recover more costs than they would have done had the matter gone to trial or settled in favour of the Claimant at the stage that it was discontinued. That would be absolutely nonsensical."

Comment

Although this is a first instance decision it is of considerable importance as this type of scenario is not uncommon. The whole issue will become of much greater importance as and when fixed costs spread to much higher value claims and also to non-personal injury claims.

This could apply where the wrong insurers are shown in the MID search.

Track Allocation

In *Bewicke-Copley v Ibeh* Oxford County Court 029YJ613 4 June 2014

District Judge Vincent held that it is the intention of the portal process that individual elements of a claim may be settled within the stage 2 process and that there is no need for the whole claim to be resolved.

The value of the balance of any unresolved elements will determine the track allocation and therefore the costs regime; the claimant cannot add back in the resolved elements for the purposes of track allocations.

Here the claimant was injured in a road traffic accident and sustained minor soft tissue injuries from which he recovered in three months. He was a cyclist.

He issued proceedings for damages for personal injury together with a claim for the pre-accident value of his bicycle (£319.00), higher charges for a replacement bicycle (£1,278.00) and storage charges (£96.00).

The defendant argued that the personal injury claim and the pre-accident value of the bicycle had been compromised in the portal. The claimant argued that the portal does not allow a defendant to pick and choose individual items to settle and that at the time the claimant withdrew from the portal process there was no agreement in respect of the entire claim and therefore there cannot have been any settlement of any of its elements.

The defendant asked the court to award the claimant judgment on the sums it said had been agreed within stage 2 of the portal process, together with the fixed costs that would have followed from that agreement, then to limit any further costs recoverable under the Part 7 procedure to small claims track costs as the balance of the claim would have been a small claim.

Here the judge upheld the defendant's submission finding that it was not only was it possible, but indeed it was the intention of the protocol that parties could compromise individual elements of a claim within the stage 2 process.

He found that that is what had happened in this case and therefore gave judgment in the sum of £2,319.00 plus portal fixed costs and allocated the remaining claims for credit hire and storage charges to the Small Claims Track.

The judge pointed out that the portal is specifically designed for each head of loss to be claimed separately with the defendant being required either to accept or make a counterclaim offer, even if for zero, in respect of each head. The last column enables a running total to be kept of the amount in dispute.

The judge said:-

"I infer from this that any part of a Claimant's offer accepted by the Defendant is therefore regarded as an item 'not in dispute', thereby providing the parties a mechanism by which issues are narrowed…" (Paragraph 30)

At paragraph 31 the judge says:-

"31. If the parties have not resolved matters by the end of the stage 2 process, then stage 3 proceedings are issued. It defies logic and the aims and intentions of the protocol if at such point, all items that had previously been agreed were regarded as un-agreed. If that were the case, I would expect the protocol to state this clearly. It does not."

The judge drew an analogy with Part 36. If a Part 36 offer is accepted then that matter, or that aspect of the matter is finalised and cannot be re-litigated. Here the claimant's offers in respect of personal injury and pre-accident value were accepted and that was the end of those matters.

The judge also pointed out that the claimant had not sought to return the payments actually made by the defendant in respect of the pre-accident value of the bicycle.

It should be noted that the judge found that the reason the claimant sought to exit the portal and to insist that there had been no agreement in respect of the personal injury claim was "an attempt to manipulate the RTA Protocol Procedure in order to afford an opportunity of recovering increased costs from the Defendant."

Track allocation was also addressed in

Akhtar v Boland [2014] EWCA Civ 872

where the Court of Appeal gave guidance on the relevant considerations in deciding whether a matter should be allocated to the fast track or the small claims track.

The facts of the matter are complicated due to what the court described as an incoherent defence.

However the key point is that if an admission of a clear and certain sum reduces the amount in dispute so as to bring it within the small claims jurisdiction rather than the fast-track jurisdiction, then it should indeed be allocated to the small claims track.

CPR 26.7 and 26.8 provide

"26.7

(1) In considering whether to allocate a claim to the normal track for that claim under rule 26.6, the court will have regard to the matters mentioned in rule 26.8(1).

(2) ……

26.8

(1) When deciding the track for a claim, the maters to which the court shall have regard include –

(a) the financial value, if any, of the claim;

(b) ………

(c) the likely complexity of the facts, law or evidence………

(2) It is for the court to assess the financial value of a claim and in doing so it will disregard –

(a) any amount not in dispute;"

This is supported by Practice Direction 26A.

"**7.2** The object of this paragraph is to explain what will be the court's general approach to some of the matters set out in rule 26.8.

'the financial value of the claim'

7.3

(1) Rule 26.8(2) provides that it is for the court to assess the financial value of a claim.

(2) Where the court believes that the amount the claimant is seeking exceeds what he may reasonably be expected to recover it may make an order under rule 26.5(3) directing the claimant to justify the amount.

'any amount not in dispute'

7.4 In deciding, for the purposes of rule 26.8(2), whether an amount is in dispute the court will apply the following general principles:

(1) Any amount for which the defendant does not admit liability is in dispute,

(2) Any sum in respect of an item forming part of the claim for which judgment has been entered (for example a summary judgment) is not in dispute,

(3) Any specific sum claimed as a distinct item and which the defendant admits he is liable to pay is not in dispute,

(4) Any sum offered by the defendant which has been accepted by the claimant in satisfaction of any item which forms a distinct part of the claim is not in dispute.

It follows from these provisions that if, in relation to a claim the value of which is above the small claims track limit of £10,000, the defendant makes, before allocation, an admission that reduces the amount in dispute to a figure below £10,000 (see CPR Part 14), the normal track for the claim will be the small claims track. As to recovery of pre-allocation costs, the claimant can, before allocation, apply for judgment with costs on the amount of the claim that has been admitted (see CPR rule 14.3 but see also paragraph 7.1(3) of Practice Direction 46 under which the court has a discretion to allow pre-allocation costs)."

The Court of Appeal gave helpful guidance as to the correct approach to ambiguous or qualified admissions.

"16. Where an allegation made by one party in proceedings is admitted by the other party in unqualified terms, that other party must not, seek to adduce evidence or raise arguments to the effect that that admission is not binding on him. The court has no jurisdiction to investigate a fact that has been admitted, unless the party making the admission obtains the permission of the court under CPR 14.1(5) to withdraw the admission and does so.

17. This principle applies even more strongly to a judgment for all or part of a claim. Neither party may adduce evidence or make submissions that if accepted would lead to decisions or findings inconsistent with the judgment, unless there is a successful application to set the judgment aside.

18. Where a defendant admits part, and not the whole, of an unliquidated damages claim, the claimant is entitled to

judgment on that admission, and to pursue the proceedings to seek and obtain judgment for the balance. Contrary to the claimant's submission, such a judgment does not extinguish the claimant's cause of action.

19. Where an admission is equivocal, or inconsistent with other allegations in the defence, the claimant may, and should, seek further information or clarification of the defendant's case under CPR 18.1. If the claimant fails to do so, and the court considers that it is uncertain what are the issues between the parties that fall to be determined at trial, it may itself make an order for clarification, and in an extreme case, where the defence is truly incoherent, the court may strike it out. On an application such as that heard by DJ Fox, if the court is uncertain as to whether an admission is unqualified, or as to its effect, I would expect the court to seek and to obtain clarification from the defendant at the hearing, and for that clarification to be made or confirmed in writing (under CPR 18.1 or in an amended defence).

20. In the present case, it is clear that DJ Fox interpreted the defence as including an unqualified admission that the claimant was entitled to the sum of £2,496: hence he entered judgment for that sum. We have the transcript of the argument before the Judge, from which it is clear that initially the claimant made no application to set the judgment aside, and that the defendant accepted that at trial the claimant could not recover less than the admitted sums totalling £2,496. It follows that at trial the allegations in the defence that were inconsistent with the admissions in paragraphs 1 to 5 would be disregarded, and could indeed have been struck out. However, in the discussion after judgment, Mr Dawes, for the claimant, accepted that if the allocation of the claim was changed the judgment would have to be set aside.

21. It follows from this that at trial the defendant could not, for example, challenge the entitlement of the claimant to damages for loss of use of his vehicle, or the reasonable need of the claimant to hire a replacement vehicle for a reasonable time and at a reasonable hire charge: for the defendant to do so would be inconsistent with the admission in paragraph 2 (as well as with the judgment). The rate of the hire charge and its duration beyond 21 days would be in issue.

22. CPR 26 fell to be applied to the proceedings after the claimant had obtained his judgment. CPR 26.7 and 26.8 provide, so far as relevant:

> "**26.7**
>
> (1) In considering whether to allocate a claim to the normal track for that claim under rule 26.6, the court will have regard to the matters mentioned in rule 26.8(1).
>
> (2) …
>
> *Matters relevant to allocation to a track*
>
> **26.8**
>
> (1) When deciding the track for a claim, the matters to which the court shall have regard include –
>
> (a) the financial value, if any, of the claim;
>
> (b) …
>
> (c) the likely complexity of the facts, law or evidence.
>
> …."
>
> (2) It is for the court to assess the financial value of a claim and in doing so it will disregard –
>
> (a) any amount not in dispute;
>
> …"

23. Once the court had determined that the defendant accepted that the claimant was entitled to judgment in the sum of £2,496, the only sum in dispute was the balance of the claim, which was less than £5,000. This is confirmed by paragraph 7.4(2) of CPR PD 26A. The relevant parts of that PD are as follows:

"**7.2** The object of this paragraph is to explain what will be the court's general approach to some of the matters set out in rule 26.8.

'The financial value of the claim'

7.3

(1) Rule 26.8(2) provides that it is for the court to assess the financial value of a claim.

(2) Where the court believes that the amount the claimant is seeking exceeds what he may reasonably be expected to recover it may make an order under rule 26.5(3) directing the claimant to justify the amount.

'any amount not in dispute'

7.4 In deciding, for the purposes of rule 26.8(2), whether an amount is in dispute the court will apply the following general principles:

(1) Any amount for which the defendant does not admit liability is in dispute,

(2) Any sum in respect of an item forming part of the claim for which judgment has been entered (for example a summary judgment) is not in dispute,

(3) Any specific sum claimed as a distinct item and which the defendant admits he is liable to pay is not in dispute,

(4) Any sum offered by the defendant which has been accepted by the claimant in satisfaction of any item which forms a distinct part of the claim is not in dispute.

It follows from these provisions that if, in relation to a claim the value of which is above the small claims track limit of £10,000, the defendant makes, before allocation, an admission that reduces the amount in dispute to a figure below £10,000 (see CPR Part 14), the normal track for the claim will be the small claims track. As to recovery of pre-allocation costs, the claimant can, before allocation, apply for judgment with costs on the amount of the claim that has been admitted (see CPR rule 14.3 but see also paragraph 7.1(3) of Practice Direction 46 under which the court has a discretion to allow pre-allocation costs)."

24. In my judgment, in the circumstances before him, in which the claimant retained the judgment for £2,496, the Judge was entitled to allocate the claim to the small claims track, since the sum remaining in dispute was less than £5,000.

25. Mr Weir pointed out that this result meant that many, if not most, of the issues in the case would be those that would have to be decided if the claim had remained in the fast track. That may be so, but it would equally be so if the claim had been for less than £5,000 from the beginning. If a case is too complex for the small claims track, the court may allocate it to another track: see CPR 26.8(1)(c). The present case is not such a case, and it has never been suggested that it is."

In *Singh v Ajaz, Bristol County Court, 27 September 2016*

His Honour Judge Denyer QC held, on appeal, that the Fixed Recoverable Costs Regime under CPR 45.29A applied to the costs of a claim properly begun under the RTA Protocol and which was subsequently allocated to the small claims track.

Thus as the law stands a defendant in a personal injury claim will not be able to achieve a costs saving by making a partial admission to bring the matter within the small claims track, a view supported by Rule 8.1 of The Civil Procedure (Amendment) Rules 2017 which provides that fixed recoverable costs only apply "for as long as the case is not allocates to the multi-track."

Factually complicated claims, or those that will require legal arguments, will not generally be suitable for the small claims track, regardless of their financial value. The need for a number of witnesses or significant expert evidence may indicate that the facts are too complicated for the matter to be in the small claim track.

Assessment on Standard Basis

In *Davies and Others v Greenway,* Senior Courts Costs Office, 30 October 2013, Case No JMS 1205590 the SCCO held that an order for assessment on the standard basis prevented the court from simply restricting the claimants' costs to road traffic accident protocol amounts.

However the court was entitled to decide that those protocol amounts were the proportionate and reasonable sums without conducting a line by line assessment.

Here the claims were settled for less than £10,000 and would have been subject to RTA protocol fixed costs, but the claimants' solicitors sent them to the wrong insurer and failed to re-submit them to the correct insurer, who had admitted liability.

Correspondence with the correct insurer produced a limited response and proceedings were issued and judgment entered with quantum to be assessed and the claims were then settled by consent, and the Consent Order provided:

"The Defendant to pay the Claimants' costs of this action on the standard basis to be assessed if not agreed".

The claimants' solicitors served a bill totalling £17,430.11. The defendant served Points of Dispute arguing that the claimant had unreasonably failed to comply and/or elected not to continue with the RTA process and its fixed costs scheme and that costs should be limited to "an amount commensurate with the costs under CPR 45 of Section VI pursuant to the express power in CPR 45.36".

In *O'Beirne v Hudson* [2011] 1 WLR 17171 the Court of Appeal held that where there was a consent order for assessment on a standard basis the court could not limit the costs to those that are fixed costs for the small claims track.

The defendant argued that the same difficulty does not arise in the RTA protocol as CPR 45.36 expressly provides that the court can limit costs to RTA protocol amounts.

The claimants argued that the consent order was binding and that the defendants were seeking to re-write it, and that pursuant to

Solomon v Cromwell [2011] EWCA Civ 1584

an award of fixed costs cannot constitute a standard basis of assessment.

The court held that CPR 45.36 did not apply; the defendant had consented to an order for detailed assessment on the standard basis and that is a contract that the court had no power to vary. The Master said that even if he was wrong about that he bore in mind that the power set out in CPR 45.36 is discretionary and not mandatory.

At the detailed assessment the Costs Judge is obliged to have regard to all the circumstances in deciding whether the costs were proportionately and reasonable incurred or were proportionate and reasonable in amount. The Costs Judge must also have regard to the conduct of the parties including in particular the efforts made, if any, before and during the proceedings in order to try and resolve the dispute.

The Costs Master then quoted at length from the Cambridge County Court decision of 13 January 2011 in *Smith v Wyatt.*

In that case the claimants sought permission to appeal to the Court of Appeal and at a permission hearing [2011] EWCA Civ 941, Lord Justice Moore-Bick stated:

"10. It is the function of the Costs Judge to determine whether costs have been reasonably and necessarily incurred and if he can see that a particular course of conduct has led to a group of costs being incurred unnecessarily , he is entitled to say that and need not to consider each item individually. In my view the argument to the contrary is not really sustainable".

The original Cambridge County Court judgment, approved by the Court of Appeal, contained the following passage, quoted by the Costs Master here:

"13. The essential test that emerges from *O'Beirne and Drew* appears to me to have two elements, one of substance and one of process.

(a) In substantive terms, the test to be applied on a detailed assessment when this problem arises is:

whether it is reasonable for the paying party to pay more than would have been recoverable had the relevant alternative regime applied.

(b) In process terms, what is important is that the Costs Judge always bears in mind that he is both conducting a detailed assessment and applying the test at (a) above. If he does so, and having done so concludes that it was not reasonable to take the case out of the alternative regime and hence not unreasonable to incur the extra costs that flow from that unreasonable decision, he will have remained within his proper discretion. If he does not do so, but simply concludes that the case ought really to have been (say) a small claim and therefore that the regime automatically and comprehensively applies, regardless of reasonableness one way or

> the other, he will have stepped outside of his discretion and in effect re-written the costs order he is supposed to be applying".

The Costs Master here said "…..it is important that I form a view on the issue of proportionality". That view was that the costs were disproportionate.

Furthermore the claimants' failure to comply with the RTA protocol led to disproportionate costs being unreasonably and unnecessarily incurred.

Having found disproportionality the Costs Master said that it was open to him to go through the bill on an item by item basis but that, following *Smith v Wyatt*, he was not obliged to do so.

Had the claimants acted reasonably by re-serving the CNF on the correct insurer they would only have been able to recover RTA protocol costs. It would be unjust to allow them to recover more and thus benefit from their unreasonable conduct.

Thus although the consent order required the court to carry out a detailed assessment the court was entitled, in that detailed assessment, to limit costs to RTA protocol costs and that was the order of the Costs Master.

In *Abdul Qaiyum v Ocado Ltd* (2013) CC (Shoreditch)

District Judge Cooper held that the claimant's solicitors in a vehicle related damages claim following a road traffic accident had been guilty of misconduct in issuing the claim prematurely and in attempting to ensure that the claim was dealt with outside the portal for an ulterior purpose outside the interests of justice between the parties to the claim.

The claimant had brought claims for personal injury and vehicle-related damages against the defendant following a road traffic accident.

Three days after the date of the accident the claimant's solicitors asked for confirmation that the vehicle damage claim would not be dealt with under the protocol.

The defendant replied that they had not received documentary evidence in respect of the vehicle related damages and refused to confirm that the vehicle related damages fell outside the protocol.

The defendant submitted that two sets of costs were being run up and that the case should have proceeded within the protocol. The defendant also argued that the vehicle related damages claim had been deliberately kept outside the protocol by the claimant's solicitors.

It was held:

(1) All claims arising out of the same facts should ideally be heard in the same proceedings. If they were not, a defence of abuse of process or estoppel might be raised.

The claims should have been dealt with within the same protocol. Contrary to the claimant's solicitors assertion the protocol did not say that where the same representative was dealing with both the vehicle related claim and the personal injury clam, the vehicle damage would normally be dealt with outside the protocol.

It only fell outside the protocol if it was being dealt with under an industry agreement between relevant organisers and insurers. That was not the case. If it was dealt with by the same legal representative, as it was in the instant case, then it was within the protocol (see paragraphs 14-17 of judgment).

(2) The claimant's solicitors request for confirmation that the case did not fall within the protocol was premature. The defendant had not had time to consider the quantum of the claim or whether it could be negotiated.

The claimant's solicitors had issued the claim prematurely to avoid the changes in the CPR that were due to take effect, whereby the value of the small claims track cases increased from £5000 to £10,000.

The claimant's solicitors had therefore issued the claim prematurely for an ulterior purpose outside the interests of justice between the parties to the claim, in a way in which they might benefit from the costs regime in force at the time.

The claimant's solicitors had been guilty of misconduct. In splitting the claim in two, the claimant's solicitors had ensured that the costs that were outside the protocol became costs of litigation.

The litigation was started by the claimant's solicitors issuing the claim. That was done not only without using the protocol, but prematurely in terms of issuing the claim before quantum had been sent to the defendant with the relevant documentation.

The claimant's solicitors were not entitled to any more costs.

An order for indemnity costs in the defendant's behaviour was appropriate because of the manipulation of the protocol and because of the premature issue of the claim (paragraphs 18-23).

In *Phillips v Willis [2016] EWCA Civ 401*

the Court of Appeal said that the starting point should be that any matter that has started in the portal should stay within it and not be transferred to the Small Claims Track, or any other track, unless absolutely necessary and the decision here to transfer the matter to the Small Claims Track was wrong in law and irrational.

"Once a case is within the RTA protocol, it does not automatically exit when the personal injury claim is settled. On the contrary, the RTA process is carefully designed to whittle down the disputes between the parties as the case passes through the various stages. It is to be expected that the sum in issue between the parties will be much smaller when the case reaches Stage 3 than it was back in Stage 1. The mere fact that the personal injury claim has been resolved is not specified as being a reason to exit from the RTA process."

Here the claimant was injured in a road traffic accident and liability was admitted and general damages for personal injury, together with other losses, were agreed and the only issue remaining in dispute related to car hire charges.

The matter proceeded to Stage 3 of the portal by virtue of the claimant issuing a claim under Part 8 of the Civil Procedure Rules.

However when the parties attended the hearing the District Judge transferred the matter to the Small Claims Track and made directions and this was on the basis that the only issue remaining was car hire charges and that the matter should proceed under Part 7.

The claimant appealed to the Circuit Judge who upheld the decision of the District Judge.

However the Court of Appeal overturned the District Judge's decision. The Court of Appeal was critical of the District Judge saying that he had caused the parties to incur substantial extra costs as a result of the order which he made of his own motion in circumstances where both parties were happy to have the matter dealt with within Stage 3 of the portal.

The Court of Appeal said:-

"29. The costs which the district judge caused the parties to incur were totally disproportionate to the sum at stake. First, the parties would have to pay a further court fee of £335.00 as a result of the district judge's order. Secondly, the parties would incur the costs of complying with the district judge's elaborate directions."

The Court of Appeal then set out those extensive directions and pointed out that the remaining sum in dispute was just £462.00.

The Court of Appeal went on to say:-

"30. I dread to think what doing all that would have cost, but that was not the end of the matter. Both parties would need to instruct representatives to attend the further hearing. They would also have to write off the costs of the 9 April hearing [the Stage 3 Portal Hearing]. At the end of all that, the winning party would recover virtually no costs, because the case was now proceeding on the small claims track.

31. In my view, the district judge's decision taken on 9 April 2014 that further evidence was necessary to resolve the outstanding dispute between the parties was irrational. The district judge was not entitled to reach that conclusion."

The Court of Appeal recognized that the issue in the appeal is how courts should deal with low value road traffic accident claims where the personal injury element has been resolved and only a modest dispute about car hire charges remains.

Although this case involved the pre-31 July 2013 portal, the principle applies to the current portals.

The Court of Appeal gives a helpful summary of the Stage 1 and Stage 2 portal procedure and says that if the matter is not settled by the end of Stage 2, the "case then proceeds to Stage 3, which is litigation."

The Court of Appeal then went on to say:-

"9. At this point, Practice Direction 8B takes centre stage. PD 8B requires the claimant to issue proceedings in the County Court under CPR Part 8. The practice direction substantially modifies the Part 8 procedure so as to make it suitable for low value RTA claims where only quantum is in dispute. This modified procedure is designed to minimise the expenditure of further costs and in the process to deliver fairly rough justice. This is justified because the sums in issue are usually small, and it is not appropriate to hold a full blown trial. The evidence which the parties can rely upon at Stage 3 is limited to that which is contained in the court proceedings pack. A court assesses the items of damages which remain in dispute, either on paper or at a single "Stage 3 hearing"."

The Court of Appeal stated that the provision which was of key importance to the present case is paragraph 7 of Practice Direction 8B, relating to the Stage 3 process, which reads:-

"7.1. The parties may not rely upon evidence unless –

(1) it has been served in accordance with paragraph 6.4;

(2) it has been filed in accordance with paragraph 8.2 and 11.3; or

(3) (where the court considers that it cannot properly determine the claim without it), the court orders otherwise and gives directions.

7.2. Where the court considers that –

(1) further evidence must be provided by any party; and

(2) the claim is not suitable to continue under the Stage 3 procedure,

the court will order that the claim will continue under Part 7, allocate the claim to a track and give directions.

7.3. Where paragraph 7.2 applies the court will not allow stage 3 fixed costs."

The Court of Appeal dismissed as irrelevant the fact that the personal injury element of the claim had been settled and that that personal injury element was the gateway to the portal.

The court held that the District Judge had no power under paragraph 7.2 of Practice Direction 8B to direct that the case should proceed under Part 7, rather than Part 8.

As to when that paragraph could ever apply the Court of Appeal suggested that there might be cases involving complex issue of law or fact which are not suitable for resolution at a Stage 3 hearing.

The Court of Appeal also considered CPR 8.1(3) which provides:-

"The court may at any stage order the claim to continue as if the claimant had not used the Part 8 procedure and, if it does so, the court may give any directions it considers appropriate."

The Court of Appeal accepted that the language of that rule is wider than that in paragraph 7.2 of the Practice Direction but said that "CPR 8.1(3) cannot be used to subvert the protocol process".

The Court of Appeal said that in any event the District Judge here was relying upon paragraph 7.2 of the Practice Direction, and not CPR 8.1(3) but if they were wrong in that view then it would have been an impermissible exercise of the power under CPR 8.1(3) to transfer this particular case out of Part 8 and into Part 7 of the CPR.

I am grateful to Steven Turner, Counsel for the Respondent, for background information in relation to this matter.

Further guidance, interim payments and admissions

In *Mulholland v Hughes and Conjoined Appeals, No. AP20/15, Newcastle-upon-Tyne County Court, 18 September 2015*

the court held that a defendant cannot raise an issue at a stage 3 hearing that had not been set out in the Response Pack at stage 2.

The court also held that it can order a claimant to repay money if, at the stage 3 hearing, it is found that the damages due are less than the sums already paid.

Here the judge was hearing four appeals in relation to the interpretation of the RTA portal.

In three of the cases the defendant had not raised at stage 2 a point in relation to the need for a hire vehicle, but raised the point at the stage 3 hearing.

The judge rejected an argument that offers made by a defendant at stage 2 should be regarded as admissions but said that it was not open to a defendant to raise something at a stage 3 hearing that had not been raised at stage 2.

The court said that the Settlement Pack and Response are not pleadings but they do require the parties to set out their case and it is incumbent on a defendant to set out clearly the precise nature of the defence, that is what is agreed and what is disputed and why it is disputed.

The court referred to paragraph 7.41 of the Protocol:-

"The defendant must also explain in the counter-offer why a particular head of damage has been reduced. The explanation will assist the claimant when negotiating a settlement and will allow both parties to focus on those areas of the claim that remain in dispute."

"It follows that it is the intention of the Protocol that if a defendant wishes to raise an issue such as the need for hire, that is to be done at the time of the making of the counter-offer. To allow a defendant to raise the issue of need at Stage 3 runs entirely contrary to the notion that at the end of Stage 2 the parties should have clarity as to what remains in dispute."

The court also held that requiring the claimant to prove need for car hire in every case was inconsistent with paragraph 7.11 which provides that in most cases witness statements will not be required and this indicates that witness statements will only be needed where hire, or for example the need for care, is formally raised by the defendant at stage 2.

"Irrespective of the above, I regard it as inequitable and unfair for a defendant, for the first time, to raise the issue of need at the Stage 3 hearing. It seems to me that it is tantamount to trial 'by ambush'. It hardly needs to be said that to litigate in that way runs entirely contrary to the spirit of the Protocol, the expected behaviour of the parties and the intended collaborative approach."

"Finally, in relation to this ground of appeal, even if it were permissible for a defendant to raise the question of need at a Part 8 hearing, given the absence of any forewarning, in my judgment, the proper course would have been to adjourn to enable the claimant to file evidence to demonstrate need: this is permitted by paragraph 7.1(3) and paragraph 7.2 of the practice direction. As I have made clear, however, in my opinion, the defendant should be estopped from raising need at this very late stage."

Repayment of sums paid

The court held that there was nothing to prevent the court from ordering repayment of monies already paid under the protocol.

In the fourth appeal, what was in issue was the amount of general damages for pain, suffering and loss of amenity and the judge had awarded a sum less than that offered by the defendant at stage 2 and ordered repayment of the difference and that decision was upheld in this appeal.

"It cannot be just or equitable that a claimant is entitled to retain a sum in excess of that which is awarded by the court at the end of a hearing. That would be, in my view, manifestly unfair to the defendant. I do not think that such was the intention of the Protocol. If the claimant chooses to go to a Stage 3 hearing, he must accept the risk that a court will award less than the non-settlement payment and that he will have to refund the difference."

"In the final analysis, a Protocol offer is, in essence, what is now generally referred to as a 'Part 36 offer'. It is, after all, governed by CPR Part 36. Its purpose is the same, principally to obtain protection in costs. There is a difference in that under the usual provisions of Part 36, no money is in fact paid to the claimant but it seems to me that the same principles should apply."

"Arguably, the closest analogy is a 'Payment into Court' pursuant to RSC Ord. 22 and CCR Ord. 11 which were largely superseded by Part 36. (Although there is still provision for payments into Court by virtue of CPR Part 37.) Under the old regime, if a Claimant (Plaintiff) did not recover more than the sum paid into Court, the Defendant was entitled to have the balance returned to him."

"Accordingly, my view is that the non-settlement payment should be treated as an interim payment and, therefore, governed by CPR Part 25."

"The claimant should send the Stage 2 Settlement Pack to the defendant within 15 days of the claimant approving —

(1) the *final* medical report and agreeing to rely on the prognosis in that report; or

(2) any non-medical expert report,

whichever is later." (My italics)

I realise that that is in the context of a second or subsequent report from the same expert, for the reasons set out in paragraph 7.8, but the use of the word "final" in paragraph 7.33 strongly suggests that one cannot submit further medical evidence once the Stage 2 Settlement Pack has been sent to the defendant.

I am reinforced in that by paragraph 7.66 which provides:-

"Comments in the Court Proceedings Pack (Part A) Form must not raise anything that has not been raised in the Stage 2 Settlement Pack Form."

One can see the logic of having a cut-off point. It could happen that the medical evidence was obtained after the case had been to court, or had been settled by acceptance of a Part 36 offer or whatever. In those circumstances one would not have been able to reopen the case.

What about a new report dealing with fresh symptoms or unexpected medical developments?

If the new report is relevant and admissible then it should be paid for by the defendant if the case is won. If it is not admissible then obviously the defendant does not have to pay for it.

I am presuming that any additional injury does not take the claim above the portal limit of £25,000.00. If it does there is no problem as that is a reason for exiting the portal.

However that still leaves open the question of whether any evidence not produced by the end of Stage 2 is ever admissible in subsequent Part 7 proceedings. To allow that would effectively allow a claimant to bypass the decision in Phillips v Willis by exiting the portal, issuing Part 7 proceedings and getting the new evidence in that way.

Paragraph 7.76 gives the claimant an unfettered right to exit the portal. The problem is that "where the court considers that the claimant acted unreasonably in giving such notice it will award no more than the fixed costs in rule 45.18."

Exiting the portal to try and get such fresh evidence in is likely to result in the court finding that the claimant has acted unreasonably. In those circumstances the court is likely to order the claimant to pay all of the defendant's costs for dealing with the matter out of the portal, even though the claimant wins the case.

The cost of an admissible report is recoverable. There is no prohibition in obtaining a second medical report and one would not need to show that it was a disbursement reasonably incurred due to a particular feature of the dispute under CPR 45.29I (2) (h).

Even in a soft tissue injury claim paragraph 7.8B makes provision for a further medical report in certain circumstances.

Paragraph 7.2 of the portal states:-

"It is expected that most claimants will obtain a medical report from one expert, but additional medical reports may be obtained from other experts where the injuries require reports from more than one medical discipline."

The limitation in paragraph 7.8 is in relation to a subsequent medical report from an expert who has already reported and does not deal with obtaining a medical report from a second or subsequent expert.

Paragraph 7.12 under the heading "Stay of Process" provides:-

"7.12. Where the claimant needs to obtain a subsequent expert medical report or a non-medical report, the parties should agree to stay the process in this Protocol for a suitable period. The claimant may then request an interim payment in accordance with paragraphs 7.13 to 7.16."

Although that does not specify the stage of the proceedings reached where there can be a stay for this reason it does refer to interim payment and that is of course a pre-stage 2 issue and paragraph 7.12 appears amongst other pre-stage 2 matters.

If further medical evidence could be provided after the Stage 2 Settlement Pack has been sent, one would expect that to appear in paragraphs 7.32 onwards dealing with the Stage 2 Settlement Pack and subsequent events.

At paragraph 19 of *Mulholland v Hughes and Conjoined Appeals, No. AP20/15, Newcastle-upon-Tyne County Court, 18 September 2015* the judge says:-

"It is important to understand the difference between Part A of the Court Proceedings Pack and Part B. Whereas the former is essentially a final schedule and counter-schedule with comments from both parties supporting their positions, the latter is confined to the claimant's final offer and the defendant's final offer expressed in global terms (the 'Protocol offer'). It is specifically recorded on the Part B Form that the offer inserted in Part B may differ from the total of the separate heads of claims listed in Part A. There would therefore appear to be three options: for each party to make a final offer which is the sum of the heads of damage set out on the Part B Form, to make a final offer which is less than the aggregate of the heads of damage on the Part A Form or which is more than the aggregate of the amount of the heads of damage on the Part A Form. On the face of it, it would be surprising if the defendant's final offer was less than the aggregate of the heads of damage on the Part A Form and, equally, surprising if the claimant's final offer was more than the aggregate of the heads of damage on the Part A Form. The requirement of the Part B Form is that it should be submitted to the court in a sealed envelope, only to be opened at the conclusion of the hearing when the Court considers costs (CPR 36.28)."

That means that in Part B both the claimant and the defendant get the opportunity to make a further offer each as their "final offers".

Permission of the court to include a witness statement from the claimant which was not included at stage 2 - Practice Direction 8B 7.1(3) is clear:-

"The parties may not rely upon evidence unless –

(3) (where the court considers that it cannot properly determine the claim without it), the court orders otherwise and gives directions."

At paragraph 22 of the Mulholland judgment the judge said:-

"Paragraph 7.1 of PD8 stipulates that no additional documents or evidence may be submitted without the permission of the court. Unless a further order of the court is made, the claim is therefore determined, whether on paper or at a hearing, based upon the documents submitted with the claim form and the acknowledgement of service."

As to including emails exchanged after stage 2, my view is that this cannot be done. Paragraph 7.66 is clear:-

"7.66. Comments in the Court Proceedings Pack (Part A) Form must not raise anything that has not been raised in the Stage 2 Settlement Pack Form."

One can include within Part A any emails that are relevant to Part A as governed by paragraph 7.64(2)(a) which provides that the form must contain:-

"(a) in Part A, the final schedule of the claimant's losses and the defendant's responses comprising only the figures specified in subparagraphs (1) and (2) above, together with supporting comments and evidence from both parties on any disputed heads of damage;"

Thus emails that are comments or evidence on quantum can be included.

Paragraph 7.64(2)(b) and 7.66 are somewhat confusing but I am satisfied that both parties do indeed get the opportunity to make further offers as their final offers and those final offers are kept from the judge whereas the Part A offers are not.

A request for a Stage 3 hearing must be started by a claim form under Part 8

Paragraph 5.2 of Practice Direction 8B states:

> "5.2 The claim form must state –
>
> (3) whether the claimant wants the claim to be determined by the court on the papers (except where a party is a child) or at a Stage 3 hearing"

If the Claimant has requested an oral hearing for the Stage 3 hearing on the Claim Form then the court will order an oral hearing. This is made clear in paragraph 11.1 of Practice Direction 8B, which states

11.1 The court will order that damages are to be assessed –

(1) on the papers; or

(2) at a Stage 3 hearing where –

(a) the claimant so requests on the claim form;

(b) the defendant so requests in the acknowledgment of service (Form N210B); or

(c) the court so orders,

and on a date determined by the court.'

Paragraph 11.1(2)(a) states that a Stage 3 hearing will be ordered where the Claimant has requested this on the Claim Form.

Paragraph 11.1 means that if either of the parties to the claim request an oral hearing, whether in the Claim Form or in the Acknowledgement of Service, the court will order an oral hearing.

Where an offer has been made and settlement is reached after the issue of the claim but before the trial commences, fixed recoverable costs of £250 apply.

The agreed damages and fixed costs must be paid within ten days of settlement.

Chapter 33

The RTA Portal: the text

THE RTA PORTAL – THE TEXT

This chapter contains Public Sector information licensed under the Open Government Licence V3.0.

The April 2010 Pre-Action Protocol for Low Value Personal Injury Claims and Road Traffic Accidents

This protocol was replaced on 31 July 2013 by the current protocol, the full text of which is set out below.

Paragraph 4.2 of the new protocol provides that the April 2010 Pre-Action Protocol will continue to apply, as it stood immediately before 31 July 2013, to all claims where the CNF was submitted before 31 July 2013.

There will be few cases continuing under the old protocol and therefore I have not set out the full text here.

However it can be accessed by going to References and Sources on the blog accompanying this book and clicking on Pre-Action Protocol for Low Value Personal Injury Claims and Road Traffic Accidents – the 2010 Scheme.

To access the blog go to www.kerryunderwood.wordpress.com.

You can subscribe to the blog by visiting the above address and scrolling down to the bottom of the archive posts list on the right hand side of the page where it says email subscriptions.

Type your email address and click subscribe; once you receive the email click the link in the email and you have subscribed.

That gives you constant free access to all of the posts and each new post will be emailed to you.

Below is set out the full text of the Pre-Action Protocol for Low Value Personal Injury Claims in Road Traffic Accidents from 31 July 2013.

Pre-Action Protocol for Low Value Personal Injury Claims in Road Traffic Accidents from 31 July 2013

Contents

SECTION I - INTRODUCTION

Definitions

1.1 In this Protocol—

(A1) 'accredited medical expert' means a medical expert who—

(a) prepares a fixed cost medical report pursuant to paragraph 7.8A(1) before 1 June 2016 and, on the date that they are instructed, the expert is registered with MedCo as a provider of reports for soft tissue injury claims; or

(b) prepares a fixed cost medical report pursuant to paragraph 7.8A(1) on or after 1 June 2016 and, on the date that they are instructed, the expert is accredited by MedCo to provide reports for soft tissue injury claims;

(1) 'admission of liability' means the defendant admits that—

(a) the accident occurred;

(b) the accident was caused by the defendant's breach of duty;

(c) the defendant caused some loss to the claimant, the nature and extent of which is not admitted; and

(d) the defendant has no accrued defence to the claim under the Limitation Act 1980;

(1A) 'associate' means, in respect of a medical expert, a colleague, partner, director, employer or employee in the same practice and 'associated with' has the equivalent meaning;

(2) 'bank holiday' means a bank holiday under the Banking and Financial Dealings Act 1971;

(3) 'business day' means any day except Saturday, Sunday, a bank holiday, Good Friday or Christmas Day;

(4) 'certificate of recoverable benefits' has the same meaning as in rule 36.22(1)(e)(i) of the Civil Procedure Rules 1998.

(5) 'child' means a person under 18;

(6) 'claim' means a claim, prior to the start of proceedings, for payment of damages under the process set out in this Protocol;

(7) 'claimant' means a person starting a claim under this Protocol unless the context indicates that it means the claimant's legal representative;

(8) 'CNF' means a Claim Notification Form;

(9) 'deductible amount' has the same meaning as in rule 36.22(1)(d) of the Civil Procedure Rules 1998;

(10) 'defendant' means the insurer of the person who is subject to the claim under this Protocol, unless the context indicates that it means—

(a) the person who is subject to the claim;

(b) the defendant's legal representative;

(c) the Motor Insurers' Bureau ('MIB'); or

(d) a person falling within the exceptions in section 144 of the Road Traffic Act 1988 (a "self-insurer");

(10A) 'fixed cost medical report' means a report in a soft tissue injury claim which is from a medical expert who, save in exceptional circumstances —

(a) has not provided treatment to the claimant;

(b) is not associated with any person who has provided treatment; and

(c) does not propose or recommend treatment that they or an associate then provide;

(11) 'legal representative' has the same meaning as in rule 2.3(1) of the Civil Procedure Rules 1998;

(12) 'medical expert' means a person who is—

(a) registered with the General Medical Council;

(b) registered with the General Dental Council; or

(c) a Psychologist or Physiotherapist registered with the Health Care Professions Council;

(12A) 'MedCo' means MedCo Registration Solutions;

(13) 'motor vehicle' means a mechanically propelled vehicle intended for use on roads;

(14) 'pecuniary losses' means past and future expenses and losses;

(15) 'road' means any highway and any other road to which the public has access and includes bridges over which a road passes;

(16) 'road traffic accident' means an accident resulting in bodily injury to any person caused by, or arising out of, the use of a motor vehicle on a road or other public place in England and Wales unless the injury was caused wholly or in part by a breach by the defendant of one or more of the relevant statutory provisions[1] as defined by section 53 of the Health and Safety at Work etc Act 1974;

(16A) 'soft tissue injury claim' means a claim brought by an occupant of a motor vehicle where the significant physical injury caused is a soft tissue injury and includes claims where there is a minor psychological injury secondary in significance to the physical injury;

(17) 'Type C fixed costs' has the same meaning as in rule 45.18(2) of the Civil Procedure Rules 1998; and

(18) 'vehicle related damages' means damages for—

(a) the pre-accident value of the vehicle;

(b) vehicle repair;

(c) vehicle insurance excess; and

(d) vehicle hire.

1.2

(1) The 'Protocol upper limit' is—

(a) £25,000 where the accident occurred on or after 31 July 2013; or

(b) £10,000 where the accident occurred on or after 30 April 2010 and before 31July 2013,

on a full liability basis including pecuniary losses but excluding interest.

(2) Any reference in this Protocol to a claim which is, or damages which are, valued at no more than the Protocol upper limit, or between £1,000 and the Protocol upper limit, is to be read in accordance with subparagraph (1).

1.3 A reference to a rule or practice direction, unless otherwise defined, is a reference to a rule in the Civil Procedure Rules 1998 ('CPR') or a practice direction supplementing them.

1.4 Subject to paragraph 1.5 the standard forms used in the process set out in this Protocol are available from Her Majesty's Courts and Tribunals Service ('HMCTS') website at www.justice.gov.uk/forms/hmcts —

(1) Claim Notification Form ('Form RTA 1' – referred to in this Protocol as 'the CNF');

(2) Defendant Only Claim Notification Form ('Form RTA 2');

(3) Medical Report Form ('Form RTA 3');

(4) Interim Settlement Pack Form ('Form RTA 4');

(5) Stage 2 Settlement Pack Form ('Form RTA 5');

(6) Court Proceedings Pack (Part A) Form ('Form RTA 6'); and

(7) Court Proceedings Pack (Part B) Form ('Form RTA 7').

1.5 The information required in Form RTA 3 may be provided in a different format to that set out in that Form.

Preamble

2.1 This Protocol describes the behaviour the court expects of the parties prior to the start of proceedings where a claimant claims damages valued at no more than the Protocol upper limit as a result of a personal injury sustained by that person in a road traffic accident. The Civil Procedure Rules 1998 enable the court to impose costs sanctions where it is not followed.

Aims

3.1 The aim of this Protocol is to ensure that—

(1) the defendant pays damages and costs using the process set out in the Protocol without the need for the claimant to start proceedings;

(2) damages are paid within a reasonable time; and

(3) the claimant's legal representative receives the fixed costs at each appropriate stage.

3.2 In soft tissue injury claims, the additional aim of this Protocol is to ensure that -

(1) the use and cost of medical reports is controlled;

(2) in most cases only one medical report is obtained;

(3) the medical expert is normally independent of any medical treatment; and

(4) offers are made only after a fixed cost medical report has been obtained and disclosed.

Scope

4.1 This Protocol applies where—

(1) a claim for damages arises from a road traffic accident where the CNF is submitted on or after 31st July 2013;

(2) the claim includes damages in respect of personal injury;

(3) the claimant values the claim at no more than the Protocol upper limit; and

(4) if proceedings were started the small claims track would not be the normal track for that claim.

(Paragraphs 1.1(18) and 4.4 state the damages that are excluded for the purposes of valuing the claim under paragraph 4.1.)

(Rule 26.6 provides that the small claims track is not the normal track where the value of any claim for damages for personal injuries (defined as compensation for pain, suffering and loss of amenity) is more than £1,000.)

4.2 The Pre-Action Protocol for Low Value Personal Injury Claims in Road Traffic Accidents which commenced on 30th April 2010 will continue to apply (as it stood immediately before 31 July 2013) to all claims where the CNF was submitted before 31 July 2013.

4.3 This Protocol ceases to apply to a claim where, at any stage, the claimant notifies the defendant that the claim has now been revalued at more than the Protocol upper limit.

4.4 A claim may include vehicle related damages but these are excluded for the purposes of valuing the claim under paragraph 4.1.

4.5 This Protocol does not apply to a claim—

(1) in respect of a breach of duty owed to a road user by a person who is not a road user;

(2) made to the MIB pursuant to the Untraced Drivers' Agreement 2003 or any subsequent or supplementary Untraced Drivers' Agreements;

(3) where the claimant or defendant acts as personal representative of a deceased person;

(4) where the claimant or defendant is a protected party as defined in rule 21.1(2);

(5) where the claimant is bankrupt; or

(6) where the defendant's vehicle is registered outside the United Kingdom.

4.6 The fixed costs in rule 45.18 apply in relation to a claimant only where a claimant has a legal representative.

4.7

(1) Subject to subparagraph (2), provisions for soft tissue injury claims, and in particular the requirement that the first report from a medical expert must be a fixed cost medical report, apply to any such claim for damages which arises from a road traffic accident where the CNF is submitted on or after 1 October 2014.

(2) The provisions, in respect of soft tissue injury claims, for accredited medical experts and the MedCo Portal, and the provisions, in respect of all claims, for searches of ask.CUEPI.com, identified in the first column (and specified
in the corresponding second column) below, apply to claims for damages which arise from a road traffic accident where the CNF is submitted on or after the corresponding date specified in the third column—

Column 1	Column 2	Column 3
Accredited medical experts	Paragraph 1.1(A1)	6 April 2015
In a soft tissue injury claim, the requirement that the first medical report must be a fixed cost medical report from an accredited medical expert selected via the MedCo Portal	Paragraphs 1.1(12A), 7.8A(1), 7.8B(3) and 7.32A	6 April 2015
Searches of askCUEPI.com	Paragraphs 5.10(3), 5.10A, 6.3A 6.8(2) and 6.9	1 June 2015

(3) In a soft tissue injury claim, where a medical expert is instructed to provide the first fixed cost medical report before 6 April 2015, but the CNF is submitted on or after that date, that report shall be treated as a fixed cost medical report obtained from an accredited medical expert selected via the MedCo Portal.

SECTION II – GENERAL PROVISIONS

Communication between the parties

5.1 Subject to paragraph 6.1(2), where the Protocol requires information to be sent to a party it must be sent via www.claimsportal.org.uk (or any other Portal address that may be prescribed from time to time). The claimant will give an e-mail address for contact in the Claim Notification Form ('CNF'). All written communications not required by the Protocol must be sent by e-mail.

5.2 Where the claimant has sent the CNF to the wrong defendant, the claimant may, in this circumstance only, send the CNF to the correct defendant. The period in paragraph 6.11 or 6.13 starts from the date the CNF was sent to the correct defendant.

Time periods

5.3 A reference to a fixed number of days is a reference to business days as defined in paragraph 1.1(3).

5.4 Where a party should respond within a fixed number of days, the period for response starts the first business day after the information was sent to that party.

5.5 All time periods, except those stated in—

(1) paragraph 6.11 (the insurer's response);

(2) paragraph 6.13 (MIB's response); and

(3) paragraph 7.37 (the further consideration period),

may be varied by agreement between the parties.

5.6 Where this Protocol requires the defendant to pay an amount within a fixed number of days the claimant must receive the cheque or the transfer of the amount from the defendant before the end of the period specified in the relevant provision.

Limitation period

5.7 Where compliance with this Protocol is not possible before the expiry of the limitation period the claimant may start proceedings and apply to the court for an order to stay (i.e. suspend) the proceedings while the parties take steps to follow this Protocol. Where proceedings are started in a case to which this paragraph applies the claimant should use the procedure set out under Part 8 in accordance with Practice Direction 8B ("the Stage 3 Procedure").

5.8 Where the parties are then unable to reach a settlement at the end of Stage 2 of this Protocol the claimant must, in order to proceed to Stage 3, apply to lift the stay and request directions in the existing proceedings.

Claimant's reasonable belief of the value of the claim

5.9 Where the claimant reasonably believes that the claim is valued at between £1,000 and the Protocol upper limit, but it subsequently becomes apparent that the value of the claim is less than £1,000, the claimant is entitled to the Stage 1 and (where relevant) the Stage 2 fixed costs.

Claimants without a legal representative

5.10 Where the claimant does not have a legal representative, on receipt of the CNF the defendant must—

(1) explain the period within which a response is required;

(2) explain that the claimant may obtain independent legal advice; and

(3) undertake a search of askCUEPI (website at: www.askCUE.co.uk) or an equivalent search system for defendants.

5.10A Where the claimant does not have a legal representative, paragraph 6.3A does not apply.

Discontinuing the Protocol process

5.11 Claims which no longer continue under this Protocol cannot subsequently re-enter the process.

SECTION III – THE STAGES OF THE PROCESS

Stage 1

Completion of the Claim Notification Form

6.1 The claimant must complete and send—

(1) the CNF to the defendant's insurer; and

(2) the 'Defendant Only CNF' to the defendant by first class post, except where the defendant is a self-insurer in which case the CNF must be sent to the defendant as insurer and no 'Defendant Only CNF' is required.

6.2 The 'Defendant Only CNF' must be sent at the same time or as soon as practicable after the CNF is sent.

6.3 All boxes in the CNF that are marked as mandatory must be completed before it is sent. The claimant must make a reasonable attempt to complete those boxes that are not marked as mandatory.

6.3A

(1) Before the CNF is sent to the defendant pursuant to paragraph 6.1, the claimant's legal representative must undertake a search of askCUEPI (website at: www.askCUE.co.uk) and must enter in the additional information box in the CNF the unique reference number generated by that search.

(2) Where the claimant has sent the CNF without the unique reference number required by subparagraph (1), the defendant may require the claimant to resend the CNF with the reference number inserted. The period in paragraph 6.11 or 6.13 starts from the date the CNF was sent with the unique reference number.

(3) Where the claimant has sent the CNF without the unique reference number required by subparagraph (1) and the defendant does not require the claimant to resend the CNF pursuant to subparagraph (2), the defendant must respond in accordance with paragraph 6.11 or 6.13.

6.4 A claim for vehicle related damages will ordinarily be dealt with outside the provisions of this Protocol under industry agreements between relevant organisations and insurers. Where there is a claim for vehicle related damages the claimant must—

(1) state in the CNF that the claim is being dealt with by a third party; or

(2)

(a) explain in the CNF that the legal representative is dealing with the recovery of these additional amounts; and

(b) attach any relevant invoices and receipts to the CNF or explain when they are likely to be sent to the defendant.

6.5 Where the claimant is a child, this must be noted in the relevant section of the CNF.

6.6 The statement of truth in the CNF must be signed either by the claimant or by the claimant's legal representative where the claimant has authorised the legal representative to do so and the legal representative can produce written evidence of that authorisation. Where the claimant is a child the statement of truth may be signed by the parent or guardian. On the electronically completed CNF the person may enter their name in the signature box to satisfy this requirement.

Rehabilitation

6.7 The claimant must set out details of rehabilitation in the CNF. The parties should at all stages consider the Rehabilitation Code which may be found at: http://www.iua.co.uk/IUA_Member/Publications

Failure to complete the Claim Notification Form

6.8

(1) Subject to subparagraph (2) and paragraph 6.3A(2), where the defendant considers that inadequate mandatory information has been provided in the CNF, that shall be a valid reason for the defendant to decide that the claim should no longer continue under this Protocol.

(2) Where the claimant has sent the CNF to the defendant without the unique reference number required by paragraph 6.3A(1), but the defendant does not

require the claimant to resend the CNF with the reference number inserted pursuant to paragraph 6.3A(2), the fact that the claimant has not provided this information shall not be a valid reason for the defendant to decide that the claim should no longer continue under this Protocol.

6.9 Rule 45.24(2) and (2A) sets out the sanctions available to the court where it considers that the claimant provided inadequate information in the CNF.

Response from insurer

6.10 The defendant must send to the claimant an electronic acknowledgment the next day after receipt of the CNF.

6.11 The defendant must complete the 'Insurer Response' section of the CNF ("the CNF response") and send it to the claimant within 15 days.

Application for a certificate of recoverable benefits

6.12 The defendant must, before the end of Stage 1, apply to the Compensation Recovery Unit (CRU) for a certificate of recoverable benefits.

Motor Insurers' Bureau

6.13 Where no insurer is identified and the claim falls to be dealt with by the MIB or its agents the CNF response must be completed and sent to the claimant within 30 days.

6.14 Where the MIB passes the claim to an insurer to act on its behalf, that insurer must notify the claimant of that fact. There is no extension to the time period in paragraph 6.13.

Contributory negligence, liability not admitted or failure to respond

6.15 The claim will no longer continue under this Protocol where the defendant, within the period in paragraph 6.11 or 6.13—

(1) makes an admission of liability but alleges contributory negligence (other than in relation to the claimant's admitted failure to wear a seat belt);

(2) does not complete and send the CNF response;

(3) does not admit liability; or

(4) notifies the claimant that the defendant considers that—

(a) there is inadequate mandatory information in the CNF; or

(b) if proceedings were issued, the small claims track would be the normal track for that claim.

6.16 Where the defendant does not admit liability under paragraph 6.15(3), the defendant must give brief reasons in the CNF response.

6.17 Where paragraph 6.15 applies the claim will proceed under the Pre-Action Protocol for Personal Injury Claims starting at paragraph 6.3 of that Protocol (which allows a maximum of three months for the defendant to investigate the claim) except that where paragraph 6.15(4)(a) applies the claim will proceed under paragraph 5.1 of that Protocol.

(For admissions made in the course of the process under this Protocol, see rule 14.1B.)

(Paragraph 2.10A of the Pre-Action Protocol on Personal Injury provides that the CNF can be used as the letter of claim except where the claim no longer continues under this Protocol because the CNF contained inadequate information.)

Stage 1 fixed costs

6.18 Except where the claimant is a child, the defendant must pay the Stage 1 fixed costs in rule 45.18 and, in a soft tissue injury claim, the cost of obtaining the fixed cost medical report and any cost for obtaining medical records in rule 45.19(2A) (collectively the "Stage 1 fixed recoverable costs") where—

(1) liability is admitted; or

(2) liability is admitted and contributory negligence is alleged only in relation to the claimant's admitted failure to wear a seat belt, within 10 days after

receiving the Stage 2 Settlement Pack, provided that invoices for the cost of obtaining the medical report and any medical records in a soft tissue injury claim have been included in the Stage 2 Settlement Pack.

6.19 Where the defendant fails to pay the Stage 1 fixed recoverable costs within the period specified in paragraph 6.18 the claimant may give written notice that the claim will no longer continue under this Protocol. Unless the claimant's notice is sent to the defendant within 10 days after the expiry of the period in paragraph 6.18 the claim will continue under this Protocol.

Defendant's account of the accident in soft tissue injury claims

6.19A Where liability is admitted in a soft tissue injury claim, it is expected that in most cases the defendant's account will not be relevant to the procedure in Stage 2. In the limited cases where it is considered appropriate, the defendant may send their account to the claimant electronically at the same time as the CNF response. The defendant's insurer must have the defendant's written authority to provide this account and, in sending it, is certifying that it has that authority. For the purposes of this paragraph, the defendant's written authority may be provided electronically.

6.19B The procedure in paragraph 6.19A applies to the MIB, save that the MIB is certifying that the defendant user of the vehicle has provided such authority.

Stage 2

Medical Reports – all claims

7.1 The claimant should obtain a medical report, if one has not already been obtained.

7.2 It is expected that most claimants will obtain a medical report from one expert, but additional medical reports may be obtained from other experts where the injuries require reports from more than one medical discipline.

7.3 The claimant must check the factual accuracy of any medical report before it is sent to the defendant. There will be no further opportunity for the claimant to challenge the factual accuracy of a medical report after it has been sent to the defendant.

7.4

(1) The medical expert should identify within the report—

(a) the medical records that have been reviewed; and

(b) the medical records considered relevant to the claim.

(2) The claimant must disclose with any medical report sent to the defendant any medical records which the expert considers relevant.

7.5 In most claims with a value of no more than £10,000, it is expected that the medical expert will not need to see any medical records.

7.6 Any relevant photograph(s) of the claimant's injuries upon which the claimant intends to rely should also be disclosed with the medical report.

7.7 Where the claimant was not wearing a seat belt the medical report must contain sufficient information to enable the defendant to calculate the appropriate reduction of damages in accordance with principles set out in existing case law.

All claims other than soft tissue injury claims – subsequent medical reports

7.8 A subsequent medical report from an expert who has already reported must be justified. A report may be justified where—

(1) the first medical report recommends that further time is required before a prognosis of the claimant's injuries can be determined; or

(2) the claimant is receiving continuing treatment; or

(3) the claimant has not recovered as expected in the original prognosis.

Soft tissue injury claims – medical reports

7.8A In addition to paragraphs 7.1 to 7.7, and subject to paragraph 7.8B, in a soft tissue injury claim—

(1) the first report must be a fixed cost medical report from an accredited medical expert selected for the claim via the MedCo Portal (website at: www.medco.org.uk); and

(2) where the defendant provides a different account under paragraph 6.19A, the claimant must provide this as part of the instructions to the medical expert for the sole purpose of asking the expert to comment on the impact, if any, on diagnosis and prognosis if—

(a) the claimant's account is found to be true; or

(b) the defendant's account is found to be true.

7.8B In a soft tissue injury claim—

(1) it is expected that only one medical report will be required;

(2) a further medical report, whether from the first expert instructed or from an expert in another discipline, will only be justified where—

(a) it is recommended in the first expert's report; and

(b) that report has first been disclosed to the defendant; and

(3) where the claimant obtains more than one medical report, the first report must be a fixed cost medical report from an accredited medical expert selected via the MedCo Portal and any further report from an expert in any of the following disciplines must also be a fixed cost medical report—

(a) Consultant Orthopaedic Surgeon;

(b) Consultant in Accident and Emergency Medicine;

(c) General Practitioner registered with the General Medical Council;

(d) Physiotherapist registered with the Health and Care Professions Council.

Non-medical expert reports

7.9

(1) In most cases, a report from a non-medical expert will not be required, but a report may be obtained where it is reasonably required to value the claim.

(2) Paragraph 7.3 applies to non-medical expert reports as it applies to expert medical reports.

Specialist legal advice

7.10 In most cases under this Protocol, it is expected that the claimant's legal representative will be able to value the claim. In some cases with a value of more than £10,000 (excluding vehicle related damages), an additional advice from a specialist solicitor or from counsel may be justified where it is reasonably required to value the claim.

Witness statements

7.11 In most cases, witness statements, whether from the claimant or otherwise, will not be, required. One or more statements may, however, be provided where reasonably required to value the claim.

Stay of process

7.12 Where the claimant needs to obtain a subsequent expert medical report or a non-medical report, the parties should agree to stay the process in this Protocol for a suitable period. The claimant may then request an interim payment in accordance with paragraphs 7.13 to 7.16.

Request for an interim payment

7.13 Where the claimant requests an interim payment of £1,000, the defendant should make an interim payment to the claimant in accordance with paragraph 7.18.

7.14 The claimant must send to the defendant the Interim Settlement Pack and initial medical report(s) (including any recommendation that a subsequent medical report is justified) in order to request the interim payment.

7.15 The claimant must also send evidence of pecuniary losses and disbursements. This will assist the defendant in considering whether to make an offer to settle the claim.

7.16 Where an interim payment of more than £1,000 is requested the claimant must specify in the Interim Settlement Pack the amount requested, the heads of damage which are the subject of the request and the reasons for the request.

7.17 Unless the parties agree otherwise—

(a) the interim payment of £1,000 is only in relation to general damages; and

(b) where more than £1,000 is requested by the claimant, the amount in excess of £1,000 is only in relation to pecuniary losses.

Interim payment of £1,000

7.18 Where paragraph 7.13 applies the defendant must pay £1,000 within 10 days of receiving the Interim Settlement Pack.

Interim payment of more than £1,000

7.19 Subject to paragraphs 7.24 and 7.25, where the claimant has requested an interim payment of more than £1,000 the defendant must pay—

(1) the full amount requested less any deductible amount which is payable to the CRU;

(2) the amount of £1,000; or

(3) some other amount of more than £1,000 but less than the amount requested by the claimant,
within 15 days of receiving the Interim Settlement Pack.

7.20 Where a payment is made under paragraphs 7.19(2) or (3) the defendant must briefly explain in the Interim Settlement Pack why the full amount requested by the claimant is not agreed.

7.21 Where the claim is valued at more than £10,000 the claimant may use the procedure at paragraphs 7.13 to 7.20 to request more than one interim payment.

7.22 Nothing in this Protocol is intended to affect the provisions contained in the Rehabilitation Code.

Vehicle related damages – interim payments

7.23 Claims for vehicle related damages will ordinarily be dealt with outside the provisions of this Protocol under industry agreements between relevant organisations and insurers. However, where the claimant has paid for the vehicle related damages, the sum may be included in a request for an interim payment under paragraph 7.16.

Application for a certificate of recoverable benefits

7.24 Paragraph 7.25 applies where the defendant agrees to make a payment in accordance with paragraph 7.19(1) or (3) but does not yet have a certificate of recoverable benefits or does not have one that will remain in force for at least 10 days from the date of receiving the Interim Settlement Pack.

7.25 The defendant should apply for a certificate of recoverable benefits as soon as possible, notify the claimant that it has done so and must make the interim payment under paragraph 7.19(1) or (3) no more than 30 days from the date of receiving the Interim Settlement Pack.

Request for an interim payment where the claimant is a child

7.26 The interim payment provisions in this Protocol do not apply where the claimant is a child. Where the claimant is a child and an interim payment is reasonably required proceedings must be started under Part 7 of the CPR and an application for an interim payment can be made within those proceedings.

(Rule 21.10 provides that no payment, which relates to a claim by a child, is valid without the approval of the court.)

7.27 Paragraph 7.26 does not prevent a defendant from making a payment direct to a treatment provider.

Interim payment – supplementary provisions

7.28 Where the defendant does not comply with paragraphs 7.18 or 7.19 the claimant may start proceedings under Part 7 of the CPR and apply to the court for an interim payment in those proceedings.

7.29 Where the defendant does comply with paragraph 7.19(2) or (3) but the claimant is not content with the amount paid, the claimant may still start proceedings. However, the court will order the defendant to pay no more than the Stage 2 fixed costs where the court awards an interim payment of no more than the amount offered by the defendant or the court makes no award.

7.30 Where paragraph 7.28 or 7.29 applies the claimant must give notice to the defendant that the claim will no longer continue under this Protocol. Unless the claimant's notice is sent to the defendant within 10 days after the expiry of the period in paragraphs 7.18, 7.19 or 7.25 as appropriate, the claim will continue under this Protocol.

Costs of expert medical and non-medical reports and specialist legal advice obtained

7.31

(1) Where the claimant obtains more than one expert report or an advice from a specialist solicitor or counsel—

(a) the defendant at the end of Stage 2 may refuse to pay; or

(b) the court at Stage 3 may refuse to allow,

the costs of any report or advice not reasonably required.

(2) Therefore, where the claimant obtains more than one expert report or obtains an advice from a specialist solicitor or counsel—

(a) the claimant should explain in the Stage 2 Settlement Pack why they obtained a further report or such advice; and

(b) if relevant, the defendant should in the Stage 2 Settlement Pack identify the report or reports or advice for which they will not pay and explain why they will not pay for that report or reports or advice.

Submitting the Stage 2 Settlement Pack to the defendant

7.32 The Stage 2 Settlement Pack must comprise—

(1) the Stage 2 Settlement Pack Form;

(2) a medical report or reports;

(3) evidence of pecuniary losses;

(4) evidence of disbursements (for example the cost of any medical report);

(4A) in a soft tissue injury claim, the invoice for the cost of obtaining the fixed cost medical report and any invoice for the cost of obtaining medical records;

(5) any non-medical expert report;

(6) any medical records/photographs served with medical reports; and

(7) any witness statements.

7.32A In a soft tissue injury claim, the Stage 2 Settlement Pack is of no effect unless the medical report is a fixed cost medical report. Where the claimant includes more than one medical report, the first report obtained must be a fixed cost medical report from an accredited medical expert selected via the MedCo Portal and any further report from an expert in any of the disciplines listed in paragraph 7.8B(3)(a) to (d) must also be a fixed cost medical report.

7.33 The claimant should send the Stage 2 Settlement Pack to the defendant within 15 days of the claimant approving —

(1) the final medical report and agreeing to rely on the prognosis in that report; or

(2) any non-medical expert report,

whichever is later.

7.34 Where the defendant alleges contributory negligence because of the claimant's failure to wear a seat belt, the Stage 2 Settlement Pack Form must also suggest a percentage reduction (which may be 0 per cent) in the amount of damages.

Consideration of claim

7.35 There is a 35 day period for consideration of the Stage 2 Settlement Pack by the defendant ("the total consideration period"). This comprises a period of up to 15 days for the defendant to consider the Stage 2 Settlement Pack ("the initial consideration period") and make an offer. The remainder of the total consideration period ("the negotiation period") is for any further negotiation between the parties.

7.36 The total consideration period can be extended by the parties agreeing to extend either the initial consideration period or the negotiation period or both.

7.37 Where a party makes an offer 5 days or less before the end of the total consideration period (including any extension to this period under paragraph 7.36), there will be a further period of 5 days after the end of the total consideration period for the relevant party to consider that offer. During this period ("the further consideration period") no further offers can be made by either party.

Defendant accepts offer or makes counter-offer

7.38 Within the initial consideration period (or any extension agreed under paragraph 7.36) the defendant must either accept the offer made by the claimant on the Stage 2 Settlement Pack Form or make a counter-offer using that form.

7.39 The claim will no longer continue under this Protocol where the defendant gives notice to the claimant within the initial consideration period (or any extension agreed under paragraph 7.36) that the defendant—

(a) considers that, if proceedings were started, the small claims track would be the normal track for that claim; or

(b) withdraws the admission of causation as defined in paragraph

1.1(1)(c).

7.40 Where the defendant does not respond within the initial consideration period (or any extension agreed under paragraph 7.36), the claim will no longer continue under this Protocol and the claimant may start proceedings under Part 7 of the CPR.

7.41 When making a counter-offer the defendant must propose an amount for each head of damage and may, in addition, make an offer that is higher than the total of the amounts proposed for all heads of damage. The defendant must also explain in the counter-offer why a particular head of damage has been reduced. The explanation will assist the claimant when negotiating a settlement and will allow both parties to focus on those areas of the claim that remain in dispute.

7.42 Where the defendant has obtained a certificate of recoverable benefits from the CRU the counter-offer must state the name and amount of any deductible amount.

7.43 On receipt of a counter-offer from the defendant the claimant has until the end of the total consideration period or the further consideration period to accept or decline the counter offer.

7.44 Any offer to settle made at any stage by either party will automatically include, and cannot exclude—

(1) the Stage 1 and Stage 2 fixed costs in rule 45.18;

(2) an agreement in principle to pay a sum equal to the Type C fixed costs of an additional advice on quantum of damages where such advice is justified under paragraph 7.10;

(3) an agreement in principle to pay relevant disbursements allowed in accordance with rule 45.19;

(3A) in a soft tissue injury claim, the cost of obtaining a medical report in rule 45.19(2A)(a); or

(4) where applicable, any success fee in accordance with rule 45.31(1) (as it was in force immediately before 1 April 2013).

7.44A In a soft tissue injury claim, an offer to settle made by either party before a fixed cost medical report has been obtained and disclosed will have no adverse costs consequences until after the report has been disclosed.

7.45 Where there is a dispute about whether an additional advice on quantum of damages is justified or about the amount or validity of any disbursement, the parties may use the procedure set out in rule 45.29.

(Rule 45.29 provides that where the parties to a dispute have a written agreement on all issues but have failed to agree the amount of the costs, they may start proceedings under that rule so that the court can determine the amount of those costs.)

Withdrawal of offer after the consideration period

7.46 Where a party withdraws an offer made in the Stage 2 Settlement Pack Form after the total consideration period or further consideration period, the claim will no longer continue under this Protocol and the claimant may start proceedings under Part 7 of the CPR.

Settlement

7.47 Except where the claimant is a child or paragraphs 7.49 and 7.50 apply, the defendant must pay—

(1) the agreed damages less any—

(a) deductible amount which is payable to the CRU; and

(b) previous interim payment;

(2) any unpaid Stage 1 fixed costs in rule 45.18;

(3) the Stage 2 fixed costs in rule 45.18;

(4) where an additional advice on quantum of damages is justified under paragraph 7.10, a sum equal to the Type C fixed costs to cover the cost of that advice;

(5) the relevant disbursements allowed in accordance with rule 45.19 including any disbursements fixed under rule 45.19(2A); and

(6) where applicable, any success fee in accordance with rule 45.31(1) (as it was in force immediately before 1 April 2013),

within 10 days of the parties agreeing a settlement.

(Rule 21.10 provides that the approval of the court is required where, before proceedings are started, a claim is made by a child and a settlement is reached. The provisions in paragraph 6.1 of Practice Direction 8B set out what must be filed with the court when an application is made to approve a settlement.)

7.48 Except where paragraph 7.51 applies, where the parties agree a settlement for a greater sum than the defendant had offered during the total consideration period or further consideration period and after the Court Proceedings Pack has been sent to the defendant but before proceedings are issued under Stage 3—

(1) paragraph 7.47 applies; and

(2) the defendant must also pay the fixed late settlement costs in rule 45.23A.

Application for certificate of recoverable benefits

7.49 Paragraph 7.50 applies where, at the date of the acceptance of an offer in the Stage 2 Settlement Pack, the defendant does not have a certificate of recoverable benefits that will remain in force for at least 10 days.

7.50 The defendant should apply for a fresh certificate of recoverable benefits as soon as possible, notify the claimant that it has done so and must pay the amounts set out in paragraph 7.47 within 30 days of the end of the relevant period in paragraphs 7.35 to 7.37.

Vehicle related damages - additional damages

7.51 Paragraph 7.52 applies where at the end of the relevant period in paragraphs 7.35 to 7.37 the claim ("the original damages") has not settled and there remain vehicle related damages ("the additional damages") being dealt with by a third party separate from the claim. The original damages include all elements of the claim in the existing Stage 2 Settlement Pack.

7.52 Where paragraph 7.51 applies the claimant must, in relation to the additional damages—

(1) notify the defendant that this separate claim is being considered;

(2) obtain all relevant information from the third party; and

(3) make a separate offer by amending the Stage 2 Settlement Pack Form.

7.53 Within 15 days of the claimant sending the offer under paragraph 7.52(3), the defendant must either agree the offer made by the claimant or make a counter-offer.

7.54 The counter offer must explain why a particular head of damage has been reduced to assist the claimant when negotiating a settlement and to allow both parties to focus on those areas of the claim that remain in dispute.

Original damages and additional damages are agreed

7.55 Where the original damages and additional damages are agreed within the period in paragraph 7.53 the defendant must pay the claimant in accordance with paragraph 7.62.

7.56 Where the parties agree a settlement for a greater sum than the Defendant had offered during the period in paragraph 7.53 but after the Court Proceedings Pack has been sent to the Defendant and before proceedings are issued under Stage 3,

(1) paragraph 7.55 applies; and

(2) the defendant must also pay the fixed late settlement costs in rule 45.23A.

Original damages are not agreed, additional damages are agreed

7.57 Paragraph 7.58 applies where—

(1) the original damages are not agreed; but

(2) the additional damages are agreed.

7.58 Where paragraph 7.57 applies—

(1) the defendant must pay the agreed amount of the additional damages within 10 days of agreeing those damages, and

(2) the claimant must continue with the provisions in paragraphs 7.64 to 7.75 of this Protocol.

Original damages are agreed, additional damages are not agreed

7.59 Paragraph 7.60 applies where—

(1) the original damages are agreed; but

(2) the additional damages are not agreed.

7.60 Where paragraph 7.59 applies—

(1) the defendant must, in relation to the original damages, pay the claimant in accordance with paragraph 7.62; and

(2) the claimant may start proceedings under Part 7 of the CPR in relation to the additional damages.

Original damages and additional damages are not agreed

7.61 Paragraphs 7.70 to 7.75 apply where the original and additional damages are not agreed.

Settlement after claim for additional damages

7.62 Except where the claimant is a child or paragraph 7.64 applies, the defendant must pay—

(1) the agreed damages less any—

(a) deductible amount which is payable to the CRU; and

(b) previous interim payment;

(2) any unpaid Stage 1 fixed costs in rule 45.18;

(3) the Stage 2 fixed costs in rule 45.18;

(4) where an additional advice on quantum of damages is justified under paragraph 7.10, a sum equal to the Type C fixed costs to cover the costs of that advice;

(5) the relevant disbursements allowed in accordance with rule 45.19 including any disbursements fixed under rule 45.19(2A); and

(6) where applicable, any success fee in accordance with rule 45.31 (as it was in force immediately before 1 April 2013) for Stage 1 and Stage 2 fixed costs, within 10 days of agreeing to pay the damages.

(Rule 21.10 provides that the approval of the court is required where, before proceedings are started, a claim is made by a child and a settlement is reached. The provisions in paragraph 6.1 of Practice Direction 8B set out what must be filed with the court when an application is made to approve a settlement.)

Application for certificate of recoverable benefits

7.63 Where at the date on which damages are agreed the defendant does not have a certificate of recoverable benefits that remains in force for at least 10 days the defendant should apply for a fresh certificate as soon as possible, notify the claimant that it has done so and must pay the amounts set out in paragraph 7.62 within 30 days of the date on which damages are agreed.

Failure to reach agreement - general

7.64 Where the parties do not reach an agreement on

(1) the original damages within the periods specified in paragraphs 7.35 to 7.37; or

(2) the original damages and, where relevant, the additional damages under paragraph 7.51,

the claimant must send to the defendant the Court Proceedings Pack (Part A and Part B) Form which must contain—

(a) in Part A, the final schedule of the claimant's losses and the defendant's responses comprising only the figures specified in subparagraphs (1) and (2) above, together with supporting comments and evidence from both parties on any disputed heads of damage; and

(b) in Part B, the final offer and counter offer from the Stage 2 Settlement Pack Form and, where relevant, the offer and any final counter offer made under paragraph 7.53.

7.65 The deductible amount should only be deducted from the personal injury damages.

7.66 Comments in the Court Proceedings Pack (Part A) Form must not raise anything that has not been raised in the Stage 2 Settlement Pack Form.

7.67 The defendant should then check that the Court Proceedings Pack (Part A and Part B) Form complies with paragraphs 7.64 to 7.66. If the defendant considers that the Court Proceedings Pack (Part A and Part B) Form does not comply it must be returned to the claimant within 5 days with an explanation as to why it does not comply.

7.68 Where the defendant intends to nominate a legal representative to accept service the name and address of the legal representative should be provided in the Court Proceedings Pack (Part A) Form.

7.69 Where the defendant fails to return the Court Proceedings Pack (Part A and Part B) Form within the period in paragraph 7.67, the claimant should assume that the defendant has no further comment to make.

Non-settlement payment by the defendant at the end of Stage 2

7.70 Except where the claimant is a child the defendant must pay to the claimant—

(1) the final offer of damages made by the defendant in the Court Proceedings Pack (Part A and Part B) Form less any—

(a) deductible amount which is payable to the CRU; and

(b) previous interim payment;

(2) any unpaid Stage 1 fixed costs in rule 45.18;

(3) the Stage 2 fixed costs in rule 45.18; and

(4) the disbursements in rule 45.19(2) that have been agreed including any disbursements fixed under rule 45.19(2A).

7.71 Where the amount of a disbursement is not agreed the defendant must pay such amount for the disbursement as the defendant considers reasonable.

7.72 Subject to paragraphs 7.73 and 7.74 the defendant must pay the amounts in paragraph 7.70 and 7.71 within 15 days of receiving the Court Proceedings Pack (Part A and Part B) Form from the claimant.

7.73 Paragraph 7.74 applies where the defendant is required to make the payments in paragraph 7.70 but does not have a certificate of recoverable benefits that remains in force for at least 10 days.

7.74 The defendant should apply for a fresh certificate of recoverable benefits as soon as possible, notify the claimant that it has done so and must pay the amounts set out in paragraph 7.70 within 30 days of receiving the Court Proceedings Pack (Part A and Part B) Form from the claimant.

7.75 Where the defendant does not comply with paragraphs 7.72 or 7.74 the claimant may give written notice that the claim will no longer continue under this Protocol and start proceedings under Part 7 of the CPR.

General provisions

7.76 Where the claimant gives notice to the defendant that the claim is unsuitable for this Protocol (for example, because there are complex issues of fact or law) then the claim will no longer continue under this Protocol. However, where the court considers that the claimant acted unreasonably in giving such notice it will award no more than the fixed costs in rule 45.18.

Stage 3

Stage 3 Procedure

8.1 The Stage 3 Procedure is set out in Practice Direction 8B.

Chapter 34

The Employers' Liability/ Public Liability Portal: the text

THE EMPLOYER'S LIABILITY & PUBLIC LIABILITY PORTAL – THE TEXT

This chapter contains Public Sector information licensed under the Open Government Licence V3.0.

Pre-Action Protocol for Low Value Personal Injury (Employers' Liability and Public Liability) Claims

Contents

SECTION III – THE STAGES OF THE PROCESS

SECTION I - INTRODUCTION

Definitions

1.1 In this Protocol—

(1) 'admission of liability' means the defendant admits that—

(a) the breach of duty occurred;

(b) the defendant thereby caused some loss to the claimant, the nature and extent of which is not admitted; and

(c) the defendant has no accrued defence to the claim under the Limitation Act 1980;

(2) 'bank holiday' means a bank holiday under the Banking and Financial Dealings Act 1971;

(3) 'business day' means any day except Saturday, Sunday, a bank holiday, Good Friday or Christmas Day;

(4) 'certificate of recoverable benefits' has the same meaning as in rule 36.22(1)(e)(i) of the Civil Procedure Rules 1998.

(5) 'child' means a person under 18;

(6) 'claim' means a claim, prior to the start of proceedings, for payment of damages under the process set out in this Protocol;

(7) 'claimant' means a person starting a claim under this Protocol ; unless the context indicated that it means the claimant's legal representative;

(8) 'clinical negligence' has the same meaning as in section 58C of the Courts and Legal Services Act 1990;

(9) 'CNF' means a Claim Notification Form;

(10) 'deductible amount' has the same meaning as in rule 36.22(1)(d) of the Civil Procedure Rules 1998;

(11) 'defendant' includes, where the context indicates, the defendant's insurer or legal representative;

(12) 'disease claim' means a claim within sub-paragraph (14)(b);

(13) 'employee' has the meaning given to it by section 2(1) of the Employers' Liability (Compulsory Insurance) Act 1969;

(14) 'employers' liability claim' means a claim by an employee against their employer for damages arising from—

(a) a bodily injury sustained by the employee in the course of employment; or

(b) a disease that the claimant is alleged to have contracted as a consequence of the employer's breach of statutory or common law duties of care in the course of the employee's employment, other than a physical or psychological injury caused by an accident or other single event;

(15) 'legal representative' has the same meaning as in rule 2.3(1) of the Civil Procedure Rules 1998;

(16) 'medical expert' means a person who is—

(a) registered with the General Medical Council;

(b) registered with the General Dental Council; or

(c) a Psychologist or Physiotherapist registered with the Health Professions Council;

(17) 'pecuniary losses' means past and future expenses and losses; and

(18) 'public liability claim'—

(a) means a claim for damages for personal injuries arising out of a breach of a statutory or common law duty of care made against—

(i) a person other than the claimant's employer; or

(ii) the claimant's employer in respect of matters arising other than in the course the claimant's employment; but

(b) does not include a claim for damages arising from a disease that the claimant is alleged to have contracted as a consequence of breach of statutory or common law duties of care, other than a physical or psychological injury caused by an accident or other single event;

(19) 'Type C fixed costs' has the same meaning as in rule 45.18(2) of the Civil Procedure Rules 1998; and

(20) 'vulnerable adult' has the same meaning as in paragraph 3(5) of Schedule 1 to the Legal Aid, Sentencing and Punishment of Offenders Act 2012

1.2 A reference to a rule or practice direction, unless otherwise defined, is a reference to a rule in the Civil Procedure Rules 1998 ('CPR') or a practice direction supplementing them.

1.3 Subject to paragraph 1.4 the standard forms used in the process set out in this Protocol are available from Her Majesty's Courts and Tribunals Service ('HMCTS') website at www.justice.gov.uk/forms/hmcts—

(1) Claim Notification Form ('Form EL1', 'Form ELD1' and 'Form PL1'– which are referred to in this Protocol as 'the CNF');

(2) Defendant Only Claim Notification Form ('Form EL2', 'Form ELD2' and 'Form PL2');

(3) Medical Report Form ('Form EPL3');

(4) Interim Settlement Pack Form ('Form EPL4');

(5) Stage 2 Settlement Pack Form ('Form EPL5');

(6) Court Proceedings Pack (Part A) Form ('Form EPL6'); and

(7) Court Proceedings Pack (Part B) Form ('Form EPL7').

1.4 The information required in Form EPL3 may be provided in a different format to that set out in that Form.

Preamble

2.1 This Protocol describes the behaviour the court expects of the parties prior to the start of proceedings where a claimant claims damages valued at no more than £25,000 in an employers' liability claim or in a public liability claim. The Civil Procedure Rules 1998 enable the court to impose costs sanctions where this Protocol is not followed.

Aims

3.1 The aim of this Protocol is to ensure that—

(1) the defendant pays damages and costs using the process set out in the Protocol without the need for the claimant to start proceedings;

(2) damages are paid within a reasonable time; and

(3) the claimant's legal representative receives the fixed costs at each appropriate stage.

Scope

4.1 This Protocol applies where—

(1) either—

(a) the claim arises from an accident occurring on or after 31 July 2013; or

(b) in a disease claim, no letter of claim has been sent to the defendant before 31 July 2013;

(2) the claim includes damages in respect of personal injury;

(3) the claimant values the claim at not more than £25,000 on a full liability basis including pecuniary losses but excluding interest ('the upper limit'); and

(4) if proceedings were started the small claims track would not be the normal track for that claim.

(Rule 26.6 provides that the small claims track is not the normal track where the value of any claim for damages for personal injuries (defined as compensation for pain, suffering and loss of amenity) is more than £1,000.)

4.2 This Protocol ceases to apply to a claim where, at any stage, the claimant notifies the defendant that the claim has now been revalued at more than the upper limit.

4.3 This Protocol does not apply to a claim—

(1) where the claimant or defendant acts as personal representative of a deceased person;

(2) where the claimant or defendant is a protected party as defined in rule 21.1(2);

(3) in the case of a public liability claim, where the defendant is an individual ('individual' does not include a defendant who is sued in their business capacity or in their capacity as an office holder);

(4) where the claimant is bankrupt;

(5) where the defendant is insolvent and there is no identifiable insurer;

(6) in the case of a disease claim, where there is more than one employer defendant;

(7) for personal injury arising from an accident or alleged breach of duty occurring outside England and Wales;

(8) for damages in relation to harm, abuse or neglect of or by children or vulnerable adults;

(9) which includes a claim for clinical negligence;

(10) for mesothelioma;

(11) for damages arising out of a road traffic accident (as defined in paragraph 1.1(16) of the Pre-Action Protocol for Low Value Personal Injury Claims in Road Traffic Accidents).

4.4 The fixed costs in rule 45.18 apply in relation to a claimant only where a claimant has a legal representative.

SECTION II – GENERAL PROVISIONS

Communication between the parties

5.1 Subject to paragraphs 6.1 and 6.2, where the Protocol requires information to be sent to a party it must be sent via www.claimsportal.org.uk (or any other Portal address that may be prescribed from time to time). The claimant will give an e-mail address for contact in the Claim Notification Form ("CNF"). All written communications not required by the Protocol must be sent by e-mail.

5.2 Where the claimant has sent the CNF to the wrong defendant, the claimant may, in this circumstance only, resend the relevant form to the correct defendant. The period in paragraph 6.12 starts from the date that the form was sent to the correct defendant.

Time periods

5.3 A reference to a fixed number of days is a reference to business days as defined in paragraph 1.1(3).

5.4 Where a party should respond within a fixed number of days, the period for response starts the first business day after the information was sent to that party.

5.5 All time periods, except those stated in—

(1) paragraph 6.11 (response);

(2) paragraph 7.34 (the further consideration period),

may be varied by agreement between the parties.

5.6 Where this Protocol requires the defendant to pay an amount within a fixed number of days the claimant must receive the cheque or the transfer of the amount from the defendant before the end of the period specified in the relevant provision.

Limitation period

5.7 Where compliance with this Protocol is not possible before the expiry of the limitation period the claimant may start proceedings and apply to the court for an order to stay (i.e. suspend) the proceedings while the parties take steps to follow this Protocol. Where proceedings are started in a case to which this paragraph applies the claimant should use the procedure set out under Part 8 in accordance with Practice Direction 8B ("the Stage 3 Procedure").

5.8 Where the parties are then unable to reach a settlement at the end of Stage 2 of this Protocol the claimant must, in order to proceed to Stage 3, apply to lift the stay and request directions in the existing proceedings.

Claimant's reasonable belief of the value of the claim

5.9 Where the claimant reasonably believes that the claim is valued at between £1,000 and £25,000 but it subsequently becomes apparent that the value of the claim is less than £1,000, the claimant is entitled to the Stage 1 and (where relevant) the Stage 2 fixed costs.

Claimants without a legal representative

5.10 Where the claimant does not have a legal representative, on receipt of the CNF the defendant must explain—

(1) the period within which a response is required; and

(2) that the claimant may obtain independent legal advice.

Discontinuing the Protocol process

5.11 Claims which no longer continue under this Protocol cannot subsequently re-enter the process.

SECTION III – THE STAGES OF THE PROCESS

Stage 1

Completion of the Claim Notification Form

6.1

(1) The claimant must complete and send—

(a) the CNF to the defendant's insurer, if known; and

(b) the Defendant Only Claim Notification Form ("Defendant Only CNF") to the defendant,

but the requirement to send the form to the defendant may be ignored in a disease claim where the CNF has been sent to the insurer and the defendant has been dissolved, is insolvent or has ceased to trade.

(2) If—

(a) the insurer's identity is not known; or

(b) the defendant is known not to hold insurance cover,
the CNF must be sent to the defendant's registered office or principal place of business and no Defendant Only CNF is required.

(3) Where the insurer's identity is not known, the claimant must make a reasonable attempt to identify the insurer and, in an employers' liability claim, the claimant must have carried out a database search through the Employers' Liability Tracing Office.

(4) In a disease claim, the CNF should be sent to the insurer identified as the insurer last on risk for the employer for the material period of employment.

6.2 If the CNF or Defendant Only CNF cannot be sent to the defendant via the prescribed Portal address, it must be sent via first class post; and this must be done, in a case where the CNF is sent to the insurer, at the same time or as soon as practicable after the CNF is sent.

6.3 All boxes in the CNF that are marked as mandatory must be completed before it is sent. The claimant must make a reasonable attempt to complete those boxes that are not marked as mandatory.

6.4 Where the claimant is a child, this must be noted in the relevant section of the CNF.

6.5 The statement of truth in the CNF must be signed either by the claimant or by the claimant's legal representative where the claimant has authorised the legal representative to do so and the legal representative can produce written evidence of that authorisation. Where the claimant is a child the statement of truth may be signed by the parent or guardian. On the electronically completed CNF the person may enter their name in the signature box to satisfy this requirement.

Rehabilitation

6.6 The claimant must set out details of rehabilitation in the CNF. The parties should at all stages consider the Rehabilitation Code which may be found at: http://www.iua.co.uk/IUA_Member/Publications

Failure to complete the Claim Notification Form

6.7 Where the defendant considers that inadequate mandatory information has been provided in the CNF that shall be a valid reason for the defendant to decide that the claim should no longer continue under this Protocol.

6.8 Rule 45.24(2) sets out the sanctions available to the court where it considers that the claimant provided inadequate information in the CNF.

Response

6.9 The defendant must send to the claimant an electronic acknowledgment the next day after receipt of the CNF.

6.10 If the claimant has sent the CNF to the defendant in accordance with paragraph 6.1(2)—

(a) the defendant must send to the claimant an electronic acknowledgment the next day after receipt of the CNF and send the CNF to the insurer at the same time and advise the claimant that they have done so;

(b) the insurer must send to the claimant an electronic acknowledgment the next day after its receipt by the insurer;

and

(c) the claimant must then submit the CNF to the insurer via the Portal as soon as possible and, in any event, within 30 days of the day upon which the claimant first sent it to the defendant.

6.11 The defendant must complete the 'Response' section of the CNF ("the CNF response") and send it to the claimant—

(a) in the case of an employers' liability claim, within 30 days of the step taken pursuant to paragraph 6.1; and

(b) in the case of a public liability claim, within 40 days of the step taken pursuant to paragraph 6.1.

Application for a certificate of recoverable benefits

6.12 The defendant must, before the end of Stage 1, apply to the Compensation Recovery Unit (CRU) for a certificate of recoverable benefits.

Contributory Negligence, liability not admitted or failure to respond

6.13 The claim will no longer continue under this Protocol where the defendant, within the relevant period in paragraph 6.11 —

(1) makes an admission of liability but alleges contributory negligence;

(2) does not complete and send the CNF response;

(3) does not admit liability; or

(4) notifies the claimant that the defendant considers that—

(a) there is inadequate mandatory information in the CNF; or

(b) if proceedings were issued, the small claims track would be the normal track for that claim.

6.14 Where the defendant does not admit liability the defendant must give brief reasons in the CNF response.

6.15 Where paragraph 6.13 applies the claim will proceed under the relevant Pre-Action Protocol and the CNF will serve as the letter of claim (except where the claim no longer continues under this Protocol because the CNF contained inadequate information). Time will be treated as running under the relevant Pre-Action Protocol from the date the form of acknowledgment is served under paragraph 6.9 or 6.10.

(For admissions made in the course of the process under this Protocol, see rule 14.1B.)

(Paragraph 2.10A of the Pre-Action Protocol on Personal Injury and paragraph 6.10A of the Pre-Action Protocol for Disease and Illness Claims provide that the CNF can be used as the letter of claim except where the claim no longer continues under this Protocol because the CNF contained inadequate information.)

Stage 1 fixed costs

6.16 Except where the claimant is a child, where liability is admitted the defendant must pay the Stage 1 fixed costs in rule 45.18 within 10 days after receiving the Stage 2 Settlement Pack.

6.17 Where the defendant fails to pay the Stage 1 fixed costs within the period specified in paragraph 6.16 the claimant may give written notice that the claim will no longer continue under this Protocol. Unless the claimant's notice is sent to the defendant within 10 days after the expiry of the period in paragraph 6.16 the claim will continue under this Protocol.

Stage 2

Medical reports

7.1 The claimant should obtain a medical report, if one has not already been obtained.

7.2 It is expected that most claimants will obtain a medical report from one expert but additional medical reports may be obtained from other experts where the injuries require reports from more than one medical discipline.

7.3 The claimant must check the factual accuracy of any medical report before it is sent to the defendant. There will be no further opportunity for the claimant to challenge the factual accuracy of a medical report after it has been sent to the defendant.

7.4

(1) The medical expert should identify within the report—

(a) the medical records that have been reviewed; and

(b) the medical records considered relevant to the claim.

(2) The claimant must disclose with any medical report sent to the defendant any medical records which the expert considers relevant.

7.5 Any relevant photograph(s) of the claimant's injuries upon which the claimant intends to rely should also be disclosed with the medical report.

Subsequent medical reports

7.6 A subsequent medical report from an expert who has already reported must be justified. A report may be justified where—

(1) the first medical report recommends that further time is required before a prognosis of the claimant's injuries can be determined; or

(2) the claimant is receiving continuing treatment; or

(3) the claimant has not recovered as expected in the original prognosis.

Non-medical reports

7.7

(1) In most cases, a report from a non-medical expert will not be required, but a report may be obtained where it is reasonably required to value the claim.

(2) Paragraph 7.2 applies to non-medical expert reports as it applies to expert medical reports.

Specialist legal advice

7.8 In most cases under this Protocol, it is expected that the claimant's legal representative will be able to value the claim. In some cases with a value of more than £10,000, an additional advice from a specialist solicitor or from counsel may be justified where it is reasonably required to value the claim.

Details of loss of earnings

7.9 In an employers' liability claim, the defendant must, within 20 days of the date of admission of liability, provide earnings details to verify the claimant's loss of earnings, if any.

Witness Statements

7.10 In most cases, witness statements, whether from the claimant or otherwise, will not be required. One or more statements may, however, be provided where reasonably required to value the claim.

Stay of process

7.11 Where the claimant needs to obtain a subsequent medical report or a report from a non-medical expert the parties should agree to stay the process in this Protocol for a suitable period. The claimant may then request an interim payment in accordance with paragraphs 7.12 to 7.20.

Request for an interim payment

7.12 Where the claimant requests an interim payment of £1,000, the defendant should make an interim payment to the claimant in accordance with paragraph 7.17.

7.13 The claimant must send to the defendant the Interim Settlement Pack and initial medical reports (including any recommendation that a subsequent medical report is justified) in order to request the interim payment.

7.14 The claimant must also send evidence of pecuniary losses and disbursements. This will assist the defendant in considering whether to make an offer to settle the claim.

7.15 Where an interim payment of more than £1,000 is requested the claimant must specify in the Interim Settlement Pack the amount requested, the heads of damage which are the subject of the request and the reasons for the request.

7.16 Unless the parties agree otherwise—

(a) the interim payment of £1,000 is only in relation to general damages; and

(b) where more than £1,000 is requested by the claimant, the amount in excess of £1,000 is only in relation to pecuniary losses.

Interim payment of £1,000

7.17

(1) Where paragraph 7.12 applies the defendant must pay £1,000 within 10 days of receiving the Interim Settlement Pack.

(2) Sub-paragraph (1) does not apply in a claim in respect of a disease to which the Pneumoconiosis etc. (Workers' Compensation) Act 1979 applies unless there is a valid CRU certificate showing no deduction for recoverable lump sum payments.

Interim payment of more than £1,000

7.18 Subject to paragraphs 7.19 and 7.21, where the claimant has requested an interim payment of more than £1,000 the defendant must pay—

(1) the full amount requested less any deductible amount which is payable to the CRU;

(2) the amount of £1,000; or

(3) some other amount of more than £1,000 but less than the amount requested by the claimant,

within 15 days of receiving the Interim Settlement Pack.

7.19 Where a payment is made under paragraphs 7.18(2) or (3) the defendant must briefly explain in the Interim Settlement Pack why the full amount requested by the claimant is not agreed.

7.20 Where the claim is valued at more than £10,000, the claimant may use the procedure at paragraphs 7.12 to 7.19 to request more than one interim payment.

7.21 Nothing in this Protocol is intended to affect the provisions contained in the Rehabilitation Code.

Application for a certificate of recoverable benefits

7.22 Paragraph 7.23 applies where the defendant agrees to make a payment in accordance with paragraph 7.18(1) or (3) but does not yet have a certificate of recoverable benefits or does not have one that will remain in force for at least 10 days from the date of receiving the Interim Settlement Pack.

7.23 The defendant should apply for a certificate of recoverable benefits as soon as possible, notify the claimant that it has done so and must make the interim payment under paragraph 7.18(1) or (3) no more than 30 days from the date of receiving the Interim Settlement Pack.

Request for an interim payment where the claimant is a child

7.24 The interim payment provisions in this Protocol do not apply where the claimant is a child. Where the claimant is a child and an interim payment is reasonably required proceedings must be started under Part 7 of the CPR and an application for an interim payment can be made within those proceedings.

(Rule 21.10 provides that no payment, which relates to a claim by a child, is valid without the approval of the court.)

7.25 Paragraph 7.24 does not prevent a defendant from making a payment direct to a treatment provider.

Interim payment – supplementary provisions

7.26 Where the defendant does not comply with paragraphs 7.17 or 7.18 the claimant may start proceedings under Part 7 of the CPR and apply to the court for an interim payment in those proceedings.

7.27 Where the defendant does comply with paragraph 7.18(2) or (3) but the claimant is not content with the amount paid, the claimant may still start proceedings. However, the court will order the defendant to pay no more than the Stage 2 fixed costs where the court awards an interim payment of no more than the amount offered by the defendant or the court makes no award.

7.28 Where paragraph 7.26 or 7.27 applies the claimant must give notice to the defendant that the claim will no longer continue under this Protocol. Unless the claimant's notice is sent to the defendant within 10 days after the expiry of the period in paragraphs 7.17, 7.18 or 7.23 as appropriate, the claim will continue under this Protocol.

Costs of expert medical and non-medical reports and specialist legal advice obtained

7.29

(1) Where the claimant obtains more than one expert report or an advice from a specialist solicitor or counsel—

(a) the defendant at the end of Stage 2 may refuse to pay; or

(b) the court at Stage 3 may refuse to allow,

the costs of any report or advice not reasonably required.

(2) Therefore, where the claimant obtains more than one expert report or obtains an advice from a specialist solicitor or counsel—

(a) the claimant should explain in the Stage 2 Settlement Pack why they obtained a further report or such advice; and

(b) if relevant, the defendant should in the Stage 2 Settlement Pack identify the report or reports or advice for which they will not pay and explain why they will not pay for that report or reports or advice.

Submitting the Stage 2 Settlement Pack to the defendant

7.30 The Stage 2 Settlement Pack must comprise—

(1) the Stage 2 Settlement Pack Form;

(2) a medical report or reports;

(3) evidence of pecuniary losses;

(4) evidence of disbursements (for example the cost of any medical report);

(5) any non-medical expert report;

(6) any medical records/photographs served with medical reports; and

(7) any witness statements.

7.31 The claimant should send the Stage 2 Settlement Pack to the defendant within 15 days of the claimant approving —

(1) the final medical report and agreeing to rely on the prognosis in that report; or

(2) any non-medical expert report,

whichever is later.

Consideration of claim

7.32 There is a 35 day period for consideration of the Stage 2 Settlement Pack by the defendant ("the total consideration period"). This comprises a period of up to 15 days for the defendant to consider the Stage 2 Settlement Pack ("the initial consideration period") and make an offer. The remainder of the total consideration period ("the negotiation period") is for any further negotiation between the parties.

7.33 The total consideration period can be extended by the parties agreeing to extend either the initial consideration period or the negotiation period or both.

7.34 Where a party makes an offer 5 days or less before the end of the total consideration period (including any extension to this period under paragraph 7.32), there will be a further period of 5 days after the end of the total consideration period for the relevant party to consider that offer. During this period ("the further consideration period") no further offers can be made by either party.

Defendant accepts offer or makes counter-offer

7.35 Within the initial consideration period (or any extension agreed under paragraph 7.33) the defendant must either accept the offer made by the claimant on the Stage 2 Settlement Pack Form or make a counter-offer using that form.

7.36 The claim will no longer continue under this Protocol where the defendant gives notice to the claimant within the initial consideration period (or any extension agreed under paragraph 7.33) that the defendant—

(a) considers that, if proceedings were started, the small claims track would be the normal track for that claim; or

(b) withdraws the admission of causation as defined in paragraph 1.1(1)(b).

7.37 Where the defendant does not respond within the initial consideration period (or any extension agreed under paragraph 7.33), the claim will no longer continue under this Protocol and the claimant may start proceedings under Part 7 of the CPR.

7.38 When making a counter-offer the defendant must propose an amount for each head of damage and may, in addition, make an offer that is higher than the total of the amounts proposed for all heads of damage. The defendant must also explain in the counter-offer why a particular head of damage has been reduced. The explanation will assist the claimant when negotiating a settlement and will allow both parties to focus on those areas of the claim that remain in dispute.

7.39 Where the defendant has obtained a certificate of recoverable benefits from the CRU the counter offer must state the name and amount of any deductible amount.

7.40 On receipt of a counter-offer from the defendant the claimant has until the end of the total consideration period or the further consideration period to accept or decline the counter offer.

7.41 Any offer to settle made at any stage by either party will automatically include, and cannot exclude—

(1) the Stage 1 and Stage 2 fixed costs in rule 45.18;

(2) an agreement in principle to pay a sum equal to the Type C fixed costs of an additional advice on quantum of damages where such advice is justified under paragraph 7.8;

(3) an agreement in principle to pay relevant disbursements allowed in accordance with rule 45.19; or

(4) where applicable, any success fee in accordance with rule 45.31(1) (as it was in force immediately before 1 April 2013).

7.42 Where there is a dispute about whether an additional advice on quantum of damages is justified or about the amount or validity of any disbursement, the parties may use the procedure set out in rule 46.14.

(Rule 46.14 provides that where the parties to a dispute have a written agreement on all issues but have failed to agree the amount of the costs, they may start proceedings under that rule so that the court can determine the amount of those costs.)

Withdrawal of offer after the consideration period

7.43 Where a party withdraws an offer made in the Stage 2 Settlement Pack Form after the total consideration period or further consideration period, the claim will no longer continue under this Protocol and the claimant may start proceedings under Part 7 of the CPR.

Settlement

7.44 Except where the claimant is a child or paragraphs 7.46 and 7.47 apply, the defendant must pay—

(1) the agreed damages less any—

(a) deductible amount which is payable to the CRU; and

(b) previous interim payment;

(2) any unpaid Stage 1 fixed costs in rule 45.18;

(3) the Stage 2 fixed costs in rule 45.18;

(4) where an additional advice on quantum of damages is justified under paragraph 7.8, a sum equal to the Type C fixed costs to cover the cost of that advice;

(5) the relevant disbursements allowed in accordance with rule 45.19; and

(6) where applicable, any success fee in accordance with rule 45.31(1) (as it was in force immediately before 1 April 2013),

within 10 days of the parties agreeing a settlement.

(Rule 21.10 provides that the approval of the court is required where, before proceedings are started, a claim is made by a child and a settlement is reached. The provisions in paragraph 6.1 of Practice Direction 8B set out what must be filed with the court when an application is made to approve a settlement.)

7.45 Where the parties agree a settlement for a greater sum than the defendant had offered during the total consideration period or further consideration period and after the Court Proceedings Pack has been sent to the defendant but before proceedings are issued under Stage 3,

(1) paragraph 7.44 applies; and

(2) the defendant must also pay the fixed late settlement costs in rule 45.23A.

Application for certificate of recoverable benefits

7.46 Paragraph 7.47 applies where, at the date of the acceptance of an offer in the Stage 2 Settlement Pack, the defendant does not have a certificate of recoverable benefits that will remain in force for at least 10 days.

7.47 The defendant should apply for a fresh certificate of recoverable benefits as soon as possible, notify the claimant that it has done so and must pay the amounts set out in paragraph 7.44 within 30 days of the end of the relevant period in paragraphs 7.32 to 7.34.

Failure to reach agreement - general

7.48 Where the parties do not reach an agreement on the damages to be paid within the periods specified in paragraphs 7.32 to 7.34, the claimant must send to the defendant the Court Proceedings Pack (Part A and Part B) Form which must contain—

(a) in Part A, the final schedule of the claimant's losses and the defendant's responses comprising only the figures specified during the periods in paragraphs 7.32 to 7.34, together with supporting comments and evidence from both parties on any disputed heads of damage; and

(b) in Part B, the final offer and counter offer from the Stage 2 Settlement Pack Form.

7.49 Comments in the Court Proceedings Pack (Part A) Form must not raise anything that has not been raised in the Stage 2 Settlement Pack Form.

7.50 The defendant should then check that the Court Proceedings Pack (Part A and Part B) Form complies with paragraphs 7.48 to 7.49. If the defendant considers that the Court Proceedings Pack (Part A and Part B) Form does not comply it must be returned to the claimant within 5 days with an explanation as to why it does not comply.

7.51 Where the defendant intends to nominate a legal representative to accept service the name and address of the legal representative should be provided in the Court Proceedings Pack (Part A) Form.

7.52 Where the defendant fails to return the Court Proceedings Pack (Part A and Part B) Form within the period in paragraph 7.50, the claimant should assume that the defendant has no further comment to make.

Non-settlement payment by the defendant at the end of Stage 2

7.53 Except where the claimant is a child the defendant must pay to the claimant—

(1) the final offer of damages made by the defendant in the Court Proceedings Pack (Part A and Part B) Form less any—

(a) deductible amount which is payable to the CRU; and

(b) previous interim payment(s);

(2) any unpaid Stage 1 fixed costs in rule 45.18;

(3) the Stage 2 fixed costs in rule 45.18; and

(4) the disbursements in rule 45.19(2) that have been agreed.

7.54 Where the amount of a disbursement is not agreed the defendant must pay such amount for the disbursement as the defendant considers reasonable.

7.55 Subject to paragraphs 7.56 and 7.57 the defendant must pay the amounts in paragraph 7.53 and 7.54 within 15 days of receiving the Court Proceedings Pack (Part A and Part B) Form from the claimant.

7.56 Paragraph 7.57 applies where the defendant is required to make the payments in paragraph 7.53 but does not have a certificate of recoverable benefits that remains in force for at least 10 days.

7.57 The defendant should apply for a fresh certificate of recoverable benefits as soon as possible, notify the claimant that it has done so and must pay the amounts set out in paragraph 7.53 within 30 days of receiving the Court Proceedings Pack (Part A and Part B) Form from the claimant.

7.58 Where the defendant does not comply with paragraphs 7.55 or 7.57 the claimant may give written notice that the claim will no longer continue under this Protocol and start proceedings under Part 7 of the CPR.

General provisions

7.59 Where the claimant gives notice to the defendant that the claim is unsuitable for this Protocol (for example, because there are complex issues of fact or law or where claimants contemplate applying for a Group Litigation Order) then the claim will no longer continue under this Protocol. However, where the court considers that the claimant acted unreasonably in giving such notice it will award no more than the fixed costs in rule 45.18.

Stage 3

Stage 3 Procedure

8.1 The Stage 3 Procedure is set out in Practice Direction 8B

Chapter 35

Practice Direction 8B re Stage 3: the text

PRACTICE DIRECTION 8B RE STAGE 3 – THE TEXT

This chapter contains Public Sector information licensed under the Open Government Licence V3.0.

PRACTICE DIRECTION 8B – PRE-ACTION PROTOCOL FOR LOW VALUE PERSONAL INJURY CLAIMS IN ROAD TRAFFIC ACCIDENTS AND LOW VALUE PERSONAL INJURY (EMPLOYERS' LIABILITY AND PUBLIC LIABILITY) CLAIMS – STAGE 3 PROCEDURE

This Practice Direction supplements rule 8.1(6)

Contents of this Practice Direction

General

1.1 This Practice Direction sets out the procedure ('the Stage 3 Procedure') for a claim where –

(1) the parties –

(a) have followed the Pre-Action Protocol for Low Value Personal Injury Claims in Road Traffic Accidents ('the RTA Protocol') or the Pre-Action Protocol for Low Value Personal Injury (Employers' Liability and Public Liability) Claims ("the EL/PL Protocol"); but

(b) are unable to agree the amount of damages payable at the end of Stage 2 of the relevant Protocol;

(2)

(a) the claimant is a child;

(b) a settlement has been agreed by the parties at the end of Stage 2 of the relevant Protocol; and

(c) the approval of the court is required in relation to the settlement in accordance with rule 21.10(2); or

(3) compliance with the relevant Protocol is not possible before the expiry of a limitation period and proceedings are started in accordance with paragraph 16 of this Practice Direction.

1.2 A claim under this Practice Direction must be started in a county court and will normally be heard by a district judge.

Modification of Part 8

2.1 The claim is made under the Part 8 procedure as modified by this Practice Direction and subject to paragraph 2.2.

2.2 The claim will be determined by the court on the contents of the Court Proceedings Pack. The following rules do not apply to a claim under this Practice Direction –

(1) rule 8.2A (issue of claim form without naming defendants);

(2) rule 8.3 (acknowledgment of service);

(3) rule 8.5 (filing and serving written evidence);

(4) rule 8.6 (evidence – general);

(5) rule 8.7 (part 20 claims);

(6) rule 8.8 (procedure where defendant objects to use of the Part 8 procedure); and

(7) rule 8.9(c).

Definitions

3.1 References to 'the Court Proceedings Pack (Part A) Form', 'the Court Proceedings Pack (Part B) Form' and 'the CNF Response Form' are references to the forms used in the Protocols.

3.2 'Protocol offer' has the meaning given by rule 36.17.

3.3 'Settlement hearing' means a hearing where the court considers a settlement agreed between the parties (whether before or after proceedings have started) and the claimant is a child.

3.4 'Stage 3 hearing' means a final hearing to determine the amount of damages that remain in dispute between the parties.

3.5 Accredited medical expert', 'fixed costs medical report', 'MedCo' and 'soft tissue injury claim' have the same meaning as in paragraph 1.1(A1), (10A), (12A), and (16A), respectively, of the RTA Protocol.

Types of claim in which this modified Part 8 procedure may be followed

4.1 The court may at any stage order a claim that has been started under Part 7 to continue under the Part 8 procedure as modified by this Practice Direction.

An application to the court to determine the amount of damages

5.1 An application to the court to determine the amount of damages must be started by a claim form.

5.2 The claim form must state –

(1) that the claimant has followed the procedure set out in the relevant Protocol;

(2) the date when the Court Proceedings Pack (Part A and Part B) Form was sent to the defendant. (This provision does not apply where the claimant is a child and the application is for a settlement hearing);

(3) whether the claimant wants the claim to be determined by the court on the papers (except where a party is a child) or at a Stage 3 hearing;

(4) where the claimant seeks a settlement hearing or a Stage 3 hearing, the dates which the claimant requests should be avoided; and

(5) the value of the claim.

Filing and serving written evidence

6.1 The claimant must file with the claim form –

(1) the Court Proceedings Pack (Part A) Form;

(2) the Court Proceedings Pack (Part B) Form (the claimant and defendant's final offers) in a sealed envelope. (This provision does not apply where the claimant is a child and the application is for a settlement hearing);

(3) copies of medical reports;

(4) evidence of special damages; and

(5) evidence of disbursements (for example the cost of any medical report) in accordance with rule 45.19(2).

6.1A

(1) In a soft tissue injury claim, the claimant may not proceed unless the medical report is a fixed cost medical report. Where the claimant includes more than one medical report, the first report obtained must be a fixed cost medical report from an accredited medical expert selected via the MedCo Portal (website at: www.medco.org.uk) and any further report from an expert in any of the following disciplines must also be a fixed cost medical report—

(a) Consultant Orthopaedic Surgeon;

(b) Consultant in Accident and Emergency Medicine;

(c) General Practitioner registered with the General Medical Council;

(d) Physiotherapist registered with the Health and Care Professions Council.

(2) The cost of obtaining a further report from an expert not listed in paragraph (1)(a) to (d) is not subject to rule 45.19(2A)(b), but the use of that expert and the cost must be justified.

6.2 The filing of the claim form and documents set out in paragraph 6.1 represent the start of Stage 3 for the purposes of fixed costs.

6.3 Subject to paragraph 6.5 the claimant must only file those documents in paragraph 6.1 where they have already been sent to the defendant under the relevant Protocol.

6.4 The claimant's evidence as set out in paragraph 6.1 must be served on the defendant with the claim form.

6.5 Where the claimant is a child the claimant must also provide to the court the following in relation to a settlement made before or after the start of proceedings –

(1) the draft consent order;

(2) the advice by counsel, solicitor or other legal representative on the amount of damages; and

(3) a statement verified by a statement of truth signed by the litigation friend which confirms whether the child has recovered in accordance with the prognosis and whether there are any continuing symptoms. This statement will enable the court to decide whether to order the child to attend the settlement hearing.

6.6 Where the defendant is uninsured and the Motor Insurers' Bureau ('MIB') or its agents have consented in the CNF Response Form to the MIB being joined as a defendant, the claimant must name the MIB as the second defendant and must also provide to the court a copy of the CNF Response Form completed by or on behalf of the MIB.

6.7 Where this Practice Direction requires a step to be taken by the defendant, it will be sufficient for this step to be taken by the MIB.

Evidence – general

7.1 The parties may not rely upon evidence unless –

(1) it has been served in accordance with paragraph 6.4;

(2) it has been filed in accordance with paragraph 8.2 and 11.3: or

(3) (where the court considers that it cannot properly determine the claim without it), the court orders otherwise and gives directions.

7.2 Where the court considers that –

(1) further evidence must be provided by any party; and

(2) the claim is not suitable to continue under the Stage 3 Procedure,

the court will order that the claim will continue under Part 7, allocate the claim to a track and give directions.

7.3 Where paragraph 7.2 applies the court will not allow the Stage 3 fixed costs.

Acknowledgment of Service

8.1 The defendant must file and serve an acknowledgment of service in Form N210B not more than 14 days after service of the claim form.

8.2 The defendant must file and serve with the acknowledgment of service, or as soon as possible thereafter, a certificate that is in force.

('Certificate' is defined in rule 36.15(1)(e)(i).)

8.3 The acknowledgment of service must state whether the defendant –

(1)

(a) contests the amount of damages claimed;

(b) contests the making of an order for damages;

(c) disputes the court's jurisdiction; or

(d) objects to the use of the Stage 3 Procedure;

(2) wants the claim to be determined by the court on the papers or at a Stage 3 hearing.

8.4 Where the defendant objects to the use of the Stage 3 Procedure reasons must be given in the acknowledgment of service.

8.5 The acknowledgment of service may be signed and filed by the defendant's insurer who may give their address as the address for service.

Dismissal of the claim

9.1 Where the defendant opposes the claim because the claimant has –

(1) not followed the procedure set out in the relevant Protocol; or

(2) filed and served additional or new evidence with the claim form that had not been provided under the relevant Protocol,

the court will dismiss the claim and the claimant may start proceedings under Part 7.

(Rule 45.24 sets out the costs consequences of failing to comply with the relevant Protocol.)

Withdrawal of the Protocol offer

10.1 A party may only withdraw a Protocol offer after proceedings have started with the court's permission. Where the court gives permission the claim will no longer continue under the Stage 3 Procedure and the court will give directions. The court will only give permission where there is good reason for the claim not to continue under the Stage 3 Procedure.

Consideration of the claim

11.1 The court will order that damages are to be assessed –

(1) on the papers; or

(2) at a Stage 3 hearing where –

(a) the claimant so requests on the claim form;

(b) the defendant so requests in the acknowledgment of service (Form N210B); or

(c) the court so orders,

and on a date determined by the court.

11.2 The court will give the parties at least 21 days notice of the date of the determination on the papers or the date of the Stage 3 hearing.

11.3 Where further deductible amounts have accrued since the final offer was made by both parties in the Court Proceedings Pack (Part B) Form, the defendant must file an up to date certificate at least 5 days before the date of a determination on the papers.

11.4 Where the claim is determined on the papers the court will give reasons for its decision in the judgment.

('Deductible amount' is defined in rule 36.15(1)(d).)

Settlement at Stage 2 where the claimant is a child

12.1 Paragraphs 12.2 to 12.5 apply where –

(1) the claimant is a child;

(2) there is a settlement at Stage 2 of the Protocol; and

(3) an application is made to the court to approve the settlement.

12.2 Where the settlement is approved at the settlement hearing the court will order the costs to be paid in accordance with rule 45.21(2).

12.3 Where the settlement is not approved at the first settlement hearing and the court orders a second settlement hearing at which the settlement is approved, the court will order the costs to be paid in accordance with rule 45.21(4) to (6).

12.4 Where the settlement is not approved at the first settlement hearing and the court orders that the claim is not suitable to be determined under the Stage 3 Procedure, the court will order costs to be paid in accordance with rule 45.23 and will give directions.

12.5 Where the settlement is not approved at the second settlement hearing the claim will no longer continue under the Stage 3 Procedure and the court will give directions.

Settlement at Stage 3 where the claimant is a child

13.1 Paragraphs 13.2 and 13.3 apply where –

(1) the claimant is a child;

(2) there is a settlement after proceedings have started under the Stage 3 Procedure; and

(3) an application is made to the court to approve the settlement.

13.2 Where the settlement is approved at the settlement hearing the court will order the costs to be paid in accordance with rule 45.22(2).

13.3 Where the settlement is not approved at the settlement hearing the court will order the claim to proceed to a Stage 3 hearing.

Adjournment

14.1 Where the court adjourns a settlement hearing or a Stage 3 hearing it may, in its discretion, order the costs to be paid in accordance with rule 45.27.

Appeals – determination on the papers

15.1 The court will not consider an application to set aside a judgment made after a determination on the papers. The judgment will state the appeal court to which an appeal lies.

Limitation

16.1 Where compliance with the relevant Protocol is not possible before the expiry of a limitation period the claimant may start proceedings in accordance with paragraph 16.2.

16.2 The claimant must –

(1) start proceedings under this Practice Direction; and

(2) state on the claim form that –

(a) the claim is for damages; and

(b) a stay of proceedings is sought in order to comply with the relevant Protocol.

16.3 The claimant must send to the defendant the claim form together with the order imposing the stay.

16.4 Where a claim is made under paragraph 16.1 the provisions in this Practice Direction, except paragraphs 1.2, 2.1, 2.2 and 16.1 to 16.6, are disapplied.

16.5 Where –

(1) a stay is granted by the court;

(2) the parties have complied with the relevant Protocol; and

(3) the claimant wishes to start the Stage 3 Procedure,

the claimant must make an application to the court to lift the stay and request directions.

16.6 Where the court orders that the stay be lifted –

(1) the provisions of this Practice Direction will apply; and

(2) the claimant must –

(a) amend the claim form in accordance with paragraph 5.2; and

(b) file the documents in paragraph 6.1.

16.7 Where, during Stage 1 or Stage 2 of the relevant Protocol –

(1) the claim no longer continues under that Protocol; and

(2) the claimant wishes to start proceedings under Part 7,

the claimant must make an application to the court to lift the stay and request directions.

Modification to the general rules

17.1 The claim will not be allocated to a track. Parts 26 to 29 do not apply.

Chapter 36

Pre-Action Protocol for Personal Injury Claims: the text

PRE-ACTION PROTOCOL FOR PERSONAL INJURY CLAIMS

This chapter contains Public Sector information licensed under the Open Government Licence V3.0.

Pre-Action Protocol for Personal Injury Claims

Contents

1. Introduction

1.1

1.1.1 This Protocol is primarily designed for personal injury claims which are likely to be allocated to the fast track and to the entirety of those claims: not only to the personal injury element of a claim which also includes, for instance, property damage. It is not intended to apply to claims which proceed under—

(a) the Pre-Action Protocol for Low Value Personal Injury Claims in Road Traffic Accidents from 31 July 2013;

(b) the Pre-Action Protocol for Low Value Personal Injury (Employers' Liability and Public Liability) Claims;

(c) the Pre-Action Protocol for the Resolution of Clinical Disputes; and

(d) the Pre-Action Protocol for Disease and Illness Claims.

1.1.2 If at any stage the claimant values the claim at more than the upper limit of the fast track, the claimant should notify the defendant as soon as possible. However, the "cards on the table" approach advocated by this Protocol is equally appropriate to higher value claims. The spirit, if not the letter of the Protocol, should still be followed for claims which could potentially be allocated multi-track.

1.2 Claims which exit either of the low value pre-action protocols listed at paragraph 1.1.1(a) and (b) ("the low value protocols") prior to Stage 2 will proceed under this Protocol from the point specified in those protocols, and as set out in paragraph 1.3.

1.3

1.3.1 Where a claim exits a low value protocol because the defendant considers that there is inadequate mandatory information in the Claim Notification Form ("CNF"), the claim will proceed under this Protocol from paragraph 5.1.

1.3.2 Where a defendant—

(a) alleges contributory negligence;

(b) does not complete and send the CNF Response; or

(c) does not admit liability,

the claim will proceed under this Protocol from paragraph 5.5.

1.4

1.4.1 This Protocol sets out conduct that the court would normally expect prospective parties to follow prior to the commencement of proceedings. It establishes a reasonable process and timetable for the exchange of information relevant to a dispute, sets standards for the content and quality of letters of claim, and in particular, the conduct of pre-action negotiations. In particular, the parts of this Protocol that are concerned with rehabilitation are likely to be of application in all claims.

1.4.2 The timetable and the arrangements for disclosing documents and obtaining expert evidence may need to be varied to suit the circumstances of the case. Where one or both parties consider the detail of the Protocol is not appropriate to the case, and proceedings are subsequently issued, the court will expect an explanation as to why the Protocol has not been followed, or has been varied.

1.5 Where either party fails to comply with this Protocol, the court may impose sanctions. When deciding whether to do so, the court will look at whether the parties have complied in substance with the relevant principles and requirements. It will also consider the effect any non-compliance has had on another party. It is not likely to be concerned with minor or technical shortcomings (see paragraphs 13 to 15 of the Practice Direction on Pre-Action Conduct and Protocols).

Early Issue

1.6 The Protocol recommends that a defendant be given three months to investigate and respond to a claim before proceedings are issued. This may not always be possible, particularly where a claimant only consults a legal representative close to the end of any relevant limitation period. In these circumstances, the claimant's solicitor should give as much notice of the intention to issue proceedings as is practicable and the parties should consider whether the court might be invited to extend time for service of the claimant's supporting documents and for service of any defence, or alternatively, to stay the proceedings while the recommended steps in the Protocol are followed.

Litigants in Person

1.7 If a party to the claim does not have a legal representative they should still, in so far as reasonably possible, fully comply with this Protocol. Any reference to a claimant in this Protocol will also mean the claimant's legal representative.

2. Overview of Protocol – General Aim

2.1 The Protocol's objectives are to—

(a) encourage the exchange of early and full information about the dispute;

(b) encourage better and earlier pre-action investigation by all parties;

(c) enable the parties to avoid litigation by agreeing a settlement of the dispute before proceedings are commenced;

(d) support the just, proportionate and efficient management of proceedings where litigation cannot be avoided; and

(e) promote the provision of medical or rehabilitation treatment (not just in high value cases) to address the needs of the Claimant at the earliest possible opportunity.

3. The Protocol

An illustrative flow chart is attached at Annexe A which shows each of the steps that the parties are expected to take before the commencement of proceedings.

Letter of Notification

3.1 The claimant or his legal representative may wish to notify a defendant and/or the insurer as soon as they know a claim is likely to be made, but before they are able to send a detailed Letter of Claim, particularly, for instance, when the defendant has no or limited knowledge of the incident giving rise to the claim, or where the claimant is incurring significant expenditure as a result of the accident which he hopes the defendant might pay for, in whole or in part.

3.2 The Letter of Notification should advise the defendant and/or the insurer of any relevant information that is available to assist with determining issues of liability/suitability of the claim for an interim payment and/or early rehabilitation.

3.3 If the claimant or his legal representative gives notification before sending a Letter of Claim, it will not start the timetable for the Letter of Response. However the Letter of Notification should be acknowledged within 14 days of receipt.

4. Rehabilitation

4.1 The parties should consider as early as possible whether the claimant has reasonable needs that could be met by medical treatment or other rehabilitative
measures. They should discuss how these needs might be addressed.

4.2 The Rehabilitation Code (which can be found at: http://www.iua.co.uk/IUA_Member/Publications) is likely to be helpful in considering how to identify the claimant's needs and how to address the cost of providing for those needs.

4.3 The time limit set out in paragraph 6.3 of this Protocol shall not be shortened, except by consent to allow these issues to be addressed.

4.4 Any immediate needs assessment report or documents associated with it that are obtained for the purposes of rehabilitation shall not be used in the litigation except by consent and shall in any event be exempt from the provisions of paragraphs 7.2 to 7.11 of this Protocol. Similarly, persons conducting the immediate needs assessment shall not be a compellable witness at court.

4.5 Consideration of rehabilitation options, by all parties, should be an ongoing process throughout the entire Protocol period.

5. Letter of Claim

5.1 Subject to paragraph 5.3 the claimant should send to the proposed defendant two copies of the Letter of Claim. One copy of the letter is for the defendant, the second for passing on to the insurers, as soon as possible, and, in any event, within 7 days of the day upon which the defendant received it.

5.2 The Letter of Claim should include the information described on the template at Annexe B1. The level of detail will need to be varied to suit the particular circumstances. In all cases there should be sufficient information for the defendant to assess liability and to enable the defendant to estimate the likely size and heads of the claim without necessarily addressing quantum in detail.

5.3 The letter should contain a clear summary of the facts on which the claim is based together with an indication of the nature of any injuries suffered, and the way in which these impact on the claimant's day to day functioning and prognosis. Any financial loss incurred by the claimant should be outlined with an indication of the heads of damage to be claimed and the amount of that loss, unless this is
impracticable.

5.4 Details of the claimant's National Insurance number and date of birth should be supplied to the defendant's insurer once the defendant has responded to the Letter of Claim and confirmed the identity of the insurer. This information should not be supplied in the Letter of Claim.

5.5 Where a claim no longer continues under either low value protocol, the CNF
completed by the claimant under those protocols can be used as the Letter of Claim
under this Protocol unless the defendant has notified the claimant that there is inadequate information in the CNF.

5.6 Once the claimant has sent the Letter of Claim no further investigation on liability should normally be carried out within the Protocol period until a response is received from the defendant indicating whether liability is disputed.

Status of Letters of Claim and Response

5.7 Letters of Claim and Response are not intended to have the same formal status as a statement of case in proceedings. It would not be consistent with the spirit of the Protocol for a party to 'take a point' on this in the proceedings, provided that there was no obvious intention by the party who changed their position to mislead the other party.

6. The Response

6.1 Attached at Annexe B2 is a template for the suggested contents of the Letter of Response: the level of detail will need to be varied to suit the particular circumstances.

6.2 The defendant must reply within 21 calendar days of the date of posting of the letter identifying the insurer (if any). If the insurer is aware of any significant omissions from the letter of claim they should identify them specifically. Similarly, if they are aware that another defendant has also been identified whom they believe would not be a correct defendant in any proceedings, they should notify the claimant without delay, with reasons, and in any event by the end of the Response period. Where there has been no reply by the defendant or insurer within 21 days, the claimant will be entitled to issue proceedings. Compliance with this paragraph will be taken into account on the question of any assessment of the defendant's costs.

6.3 The defendant (insurer) will have a maximum of three months from the date of acknowledgment of the Letter of Claim (or of the CNF where the claim commenced in a portal) to investigate. No later than the end of that period, The defendant (insurer) should reply by no later than the end of that period, stating if liability is admitted by admitting that the accident occurred, that the accident was caused by the defendant's breach of duty, and the claimant suffered loss and there is no defence under the Limitation Act 1980.

6.4 Where the accident occurred outside England and Wales and/or where the defendant is outside the jurisdiction, the time periods of 21 days and three months should normally be extended up to 42 days and six months.

6.5 If a defendant denies liability and/or causation, their version of events should be supplied. The defendant should also enclose with the response, documents in their possession which are material to the issues between the parties, and which would be likely to be ordered to be disclosed by the court, either on an application for pre-action disclosure, or on disclosure during proceedings. No charge will be made for providing copy documents under the Protocol.

6.6 An admission made by any party under this Protocol may well be binding on that party in the litigation. Further information about admissions made under this Protocol is to be found in Civil Procedure Rules ("CPR") rule 14.1A.

6.7 Following receipt of the Letter of Response, if the claimant is aware that there may be a delay of six months or more before the claimant decides if, when and how to proceed, the claimant should keep the defendant generally informed.

7. Disclosure

7.1 Documents

7.1.1 The aim of early disclosure of documents by the defendant is not to encourage 'fishing expeditions' by the claimant, but to promote an early exchange of relevant information to help in clarifying or resolving issues in dispute. The claimant's solicitor can assist by identifying in the Letter of Claim or in a subsequent letter the particular categories of documents which they consider are relevant and why, with a brief explanation of their purported relevance if necessary.

7.1.2 Attached at Annexe C are specimen, but non-exhaustive, lists of documents likely to be material in different types of claim.

7.1.3 Pre-action disclosure will generally be limited to the documents required to be enclosed with the Letter of Claim and the Response. In cases where liability is admitted in full, disclosure will be limited to the documents relevant to quantum, the parties can agree that further disclosure may be given. If either or both of the parties consider that further disclosure should be given but there is disagreement about some aspect of that process, they may be able to make an application to the court for pre-action disclosure under Part 31 of the CPR. Parties should assist each other and avoid the necessity for such an application.

7.1.4 The protocol should also contain a requirement that the defendant is under a duty to preserve the disclosure documents and other evidence (CCTV for example). If the documents are destroyed, this could be an abuse of the court process.

Experts

7.2 Save for cases likely to be allocated to the multi-track, the Protocol encourages joint selection of, and access to, quantum experts, and, on occasion liability experts e.g. engineers. The expert report produced is not a joint report for the purposes of CPR Part 35. The Protocol promotes the practice of the claimant obtaining a medical report, disclosing it to the defendant who then asks questions and/or agrees it and does not obtain their own report. The Protocol provides for nomination of the expert by the claimant in personal injury claims.

7.3 Before any party instructs an expert, they should give the other party a list of the name(s) of one or more experts in the relevant speciality whom they consider are suitable to instruct.

7.4 Some solicitors choose to obtain medical reports through medical agencies, rather than directly from a specific doctor or hospital. The defendant's prior consent to this should be sought and, if the defendant so requests, the agency should be asked to provide in advance the names of the doctor(s) whom they are considering instructing.

7.5 Where a medical expert is to be instructed, the claimant's solicitor will organise access to relevant medical records – see specimen letter of instruction at Annexe D.

7.6 Within 14 days of providing a list of experts the other party may indicate an objection to one or more of the named experts. The first party should then instruct a mutually acceptable expert assuming there is one (this is not the same as a joint expert). It must be emphasised that when the claimant nominates an expert in the original Letter of Claim, the defendant has a further 14 days to object to one or more of the named experts after expiration of the 21 day period within which they have to reply to the Letter of Claim, as set out in paragraph 6.2.

7.7 If the defendant objects to all the listed experts, the parties may then instruct experts of their own choice. It will be for the court to decide, subsequently and if proceedings are issued, whether either party had acted unreasonably.

7.8 If the defendant does not object to an expert nominated by the claimant, they shall not be entitled to rely on their own expert evidence within that expert's area of expertise unless—

(a) the claimant agrees;

(b) the court so directs; or

(c) the claimant's expert report has been amended and the claimant is not prepared to disclose the original report.

7.9 Any party may send to an agreed expert written questions on the report, via the first party's solicitors. Such questions must be put within 28 days of service of the expert's report and must only be for the purpose of clarification of the report. The expert should send answers to the questions simultaneously to each party.

7.10 The cost of a report from an agreed expert will usually be paid by the instructing first party: the costs of the expert replying to questions will usually be borne by the party which asks the questions.

7.11 If necessary, after proceedings have commenced and with the permission of the court, the parties may obtain further expert reports. It would be for the court to decide whether the costs of more than one expert's report should be recoverable.

8. Negotiations following an admission

8.1

8.1.1 Where a defendant admits liability which has caused some damage, before proceedings are issued, the claimant should send to that defendant—

(a) any medical reports obtained under this Protocol on which the claimant relies; and

(b) a schedule of any past and future expenses and losses which are claimed, even if the schedule is necessarily provisional. The schedule should contain as much detail as reasonably practicable and should identify those losses that are ongoing. If the schedule is likely to be updated before the case is concluded, it should say so.

8.1.2 The claimant should delay issuing proceedings for 21 days from disclosure of (a) and (b) above (unless such delay would cause his claim to become time-barred), to enable the parties to consider whether the claim is capable of settlement.

8.2 CPR Part 36 permits claimants and defendants to make offers to settle pre-proceedings. Parties should always consider if it is appropriate to make a Part 36 Offer before issuing. If such an offer is made, the party making the offer must always try to supply sufficient evidence and/or information to enable the offer to be properly considered.

The level of detail will depend on the value of the claim. Medical reports may not be necessary where there is no significant continuing injury and a detailed schedule may not be necessary in a low value case.

9. Alternative Dispute Resolution

9.1

9.1.1 Litigation should be a last resort. As part of this Protocol, the parties should consider whether negotiation or some other form of Alternative Dispute Resolution ("ADR") might enable them to resolve their dispute without commencing proceedings.

9.1.2 Some of the options for resolving disputes without commencing proceedings are—

(a) discussions and negotiation (which may or may not include making Part 36 Offers or providing an explanation and/or apology);

(b) mediation, a third party facilitating a resolution;

(c) arbitration, a third party deciding the dispute; and

(d) early neutral evaluation, a third party giving an informed opinion on the dispute.

9.1.3 If proceedings are issued, the parties may be required by the court to provide evidence that ADR has been considered. It is expressly recognised that no party can or should be forced to mediate or enter into any form of ADR but unreasonable refusal to consider ADR will be taken into account by the court when deciding who bears the costs of the proceedings.

9.2 Information on mediation and other forms of ADR is available in the Jackson ADR Handbook (available from Oxford University Press) or at—

- http://www.civilmediation.justice.gov.uk/
- http://www.adviceguide.org.uk/england/law_e/law_legal_system_e/law_taking_legal_action_e/alternatives_to_court.htm

10. Quantification of Loss - Special damages

10.1 In all cases, if the defendant admits liability, the claimant will send to the defendant as soon as reasonably practicable a schedule of any past and future expenses and losses which he claims, even if the schedule is necessarily provisional. The schedule should contain as much detail as reasonably practicable and should identify those losses that are ongoing. If the schedule is likely to be updated before the case is concluded, it should say so. The claimant should keep the defendant informed as to the rate at which his financial loss is progressing throughout the entire Protocol period.

11. Stocktake

11.1 Where the procedure set out in this Protocol has not resolved the dispute between the parties, each party should undertake a review of its own positions and the strengths and weaknesses of its case. The parties should then together consider the evidence and the arguments in order to see whether litigation can be avoided or, if that is not possible, for the issues between the parties to be narrowed before proceedings are issued. Where the defendant is insured and the pre-action steps have been taken by the insurer, the insurer would normally be expected to nominate solicitors to act in the proceedings and to accept service of the claim form and other documents on behalf of the defendant. The claimant or their solicitor is recommended to invite the insurer to nominate the insurer to nominate solicitors to act in the proceedings and do so 7 to 14 days before the intended issue date.

Annex A: Illustrative flow chart

- Annex A: Illustrative flow chart

Annex B: Templates for letters of claim and response

B1 Letter of Claim

To

Defendant

Dear Sirs

Re:

Claimant's full name

Claimant's full address

Claimant's Clock or Works Number

Claimant's Employer (name and address)

We are instructed by the above named to claim damages in connection with an **accident at work/road traffic accident/tripping accident** on day of **(year)** at **(place of accident which must be sufficiently detailed to establish location)**

Please confirm the identity of your insurers. Please note that the insurers will need to see this letter as soon as possible and it may affect your insurance cover and/or the conduct of any subsequent legal proceedings if you do not send this letter to them.

Clear summary of the facts

The circumstances of the accident are:

(brief outline)

Liability

The reason why we are alleging fault is:

(simple explanation e.g. defective machine, broken ground)

We are obtaining a police report and will let you have a copy of the same upon your undertaking to meet half the fee.

Injuries

A description of our clients' injuries is as follows:

(brief outline) The description should include a non-exhaustive list of the main functional effects on daily living, so that the defendant can begin to assess value / rehabilitation needs.

(In cases of road traffic accidents)

Our client (state hospital reference number) received treatment for the injuries at name and address of hospital).

Our client is still suffering from the effects of his/her injury. We invite you to participate with us in addressing his/her immediate needs by use of rehabilitation.

Loss of Earnings

He/She is employed as **(occupation)** and has had the following time off work
(dates of absence). His/Her approximate weekly income is (insert if known).

If you are our client's employers, please provide us with the usual earnings details which will enable us to calculate his financial loss.

Other Financial Losses

We are also aware of the following (likely) financial losses:

Details of the insurer

We have also sent a letter of claim to **(name and address)** and a copy of that letter is attached. We understand their insurers are **(name, address and claims number if known)**.

At this stage of our enquiries we would expect the documents contained in parts **(insert appropriate parts of standard disclosure list)** to be relevant to this action.

A copy of this letter is attached for you to send to your insurers. Finally we expect an acknowledgment of this letter within 21 days by yourselves or your insurers.

Yours faithfully

B2 Letter of response

To Claimant's legal representative

Dear Sirs

Letter of Response

[Claimant's name] v [Defendant's name]

Parties

We have been instructed to act on behalf of [defendant] in relation to your client's accident on [ ]. We note that you have also written to [defendant] in connection with this claim. We [do/do not] believe they are a relevant party because [ ]. [In addition we believe your claim should be directed against [defendant] for the following reasons:

Liability

In respect of our client's liability for this accident we

admit the accident occurred and that our client is liable for loss and damage to the
claimant the extent of which will require quantification.

Or

admit the accident occurred but deny that our client is responsible for any loss or
damage alleged to have been caused for the following reasons:-

Or

do not admit the accident occurred either in the manner described in your letter of
claim [or at all] because:

Limitation

[We do not intend to raise any limitation defence]

Documents

We attach copies of the following documents in support of our client's position:
You have requested copies of the following documents which we are not enclosing
as we do not believe they are relevant for the following reasons:

[It would assist our investigations if you could supply us with copies of the following documents]

Next Steps

In admitted cases

Please advise us which medical experts you are proposing to instruct.

Please also supply us with your client's schedule of past and future expenses [if any] which are claimed, even if this can only be supplied on a provisional basis at present to assist us with making an appropriate reserve.

If you have identified that the claimant has any immediate need for additional medical treatment or other early rehabilitation intervention so that we can take instructions pursuant to the Rehabilitation Code.

In non-admitted cases

Please confirm we may now close our file. Alternatively, if you intend to proceed
please advise which experts you are proposing to instruct.

Alternative Dispute Resolution

Include details of any options that may be considered whether on a without prejudice basis or otherwise.

Yours faithfully

Annex C: Pre-Action Personal Injury Protocol Standard Disclosure Lists

RTA CASES

SECTION A

In all cases where liability is at issue–

(i) documents identifying nature, extent and location of damage to defendant's vehicle where there is any dispute about point of impact;

(ii) MOT certificate where relevant;

(iii) maintenance records where vehicle defect is alleged or it is alleged by defendant that there was an unforeseen defect which caused or contributed to the accident.

SECTION B

Accident involving commercial vehicle as defendant–

(i) tachograph charts or entry from individual control book;

(ii) maintenance and repair records required for operators' licence where vehicle
defect is alleged or it is alleged by defendant that there was an unforeseen defect which caused or contributed to the accident.

SECTION C

Cases against local authorities where highway design defect is alleged—

(i) documents produced to comply with Section 39 of the Road Traffic Act 1988 in
respect of the duty designed to promote road safety to include studies into road
accidents in the relevant area and documents relating to measures recommended to prevent accidents in the relevant area;

(ii) any Rule 43 reports produced at the request of a coroner pursuant to Schedule 5 of the Coroners & Justice Act 2009, for accidents occurring in the same locus as one covered by an earlier report.

HIGHWAY TRIPPING CLAIMS

Documents from Highway Authority for a period of 12 months prior to the accident–

(i) records of inspection for the relevant stretch of highway;

(ii) maintenance records including records of independent contractors working in
relevant area;

(iii) records of the minutes of Highway Authority meetings where maintenance or
repair policy has been discussed or decided;

(iv) records of complaints about the state of highways;

(v) records of other accidents which have occurred on the relevant stretch of highway.

WORKPLACE CLAIMS

GENERAL DOCUMENTS

(i) accident book entry;

(ii) other entries in the book or other accident books, relating to accidents or injuries similar to those suffered by our client (and if it is contended there are no such entries please confirm we may have facilities to inspect all accident books);

(iii) first aider report;

(iv) surgery record;

(v) foreman/supervisor accident report;

(vi) safety representative's accident report;

(vii) RIDDOR (Reporting of Injuries, Diseases and Dangerous Occurrences Regulations) reported to HSE or relevant investigatory agency;

(viii) back to work interview notes and report;

(ix) all personnel/occupational health records relating to our client;

(x) other communications between defendants and HSE or other relevant investigatory agency;

(xi) minutes of Health and Safety Committee meeting(s) where accident/matter
considered;

(xii) copies of all relevant CCTV footage and any other relevant photographs, videos and/or DVDs;

(xiii) copies of all electronic communications/documentation relating to the accident;

(xiv) earnings information where defendant is employer;

(xv) reports to DWP;

(xvi) manufacturer's or dealers instructions or recommendations concerning use of
the work equipment;

(xvii) service or maintenance records of the work equipment;

(xviii) all documents recording arrangements for detecting, removing or cleaning up any articles or substances on the floor of the premises likely to cause a trip or slip;

(xix) work sheets and all other documents completed by or on behalf of those responsible for implementing the cleaning policy and recording work done;

(xx) all invoices, receipts and other documents relating to the purchase of relevant
safety equipment to prevent a repetition of the accident;

(xxi) all correspondence, memoranda or other documentation received or brought
into being concerning the condition or repair of the work equipment/the premises;

(xxii) all correspondence, instructions, estimates, invoices and other documentation submitted or received concerning repairs, remedial works or other works to the work equipment/the premises since the date of that accident;

(xxiii) work sheets and all other documents recording work done completed by those responsible for maintaining the work equipment/premises;

(xxiv) all relevant risk assessments;

(xxv) all reports, conclusions or recommendations following any enquiry or investigation into the accident;

(xxvi) the record kept of complaints made by employees together with all other documents recording in any way such complaints or actions taken thereon;

(xxvii) all other correspondence sent, or received, relating to our client's injury prior to receipt of this letter of claim;

(xxviii) documents listed above relating to any previous/similar accident/matter
identified by the claimant and relied upon as proof of negligence including accident
book entries;

WORKPLACE CLAIMS – DISCLOSURE WHERE SPECIFIC REGULATIONS APPLY

SECTION A - Management of Health and Safety at Work Regulations 1999

Documents including—

(i) Pre-accident Risk Assessment required by Regulation 3(1);

(ii) Post-accident Re-Assessment required by Regulation 3(2);

(iii) Accident Investigation Report prepared in implementing the requirements of
Regulations 4, and 5;

(iv) Health Surveillance Records in appropriate cases required by Regulation 6;

(v) documents relating to the appointment of competent persons to assist required by Regulation 7;

(vi) documents relating to the employees health and safety training required by Regulation 8;

(vii) documents relating to necessary contacts with external services required by
Regulation 9;

(viii) information provided to employees under Regulation 10.

SECTION B– Workplace (Health Safety and Welfare) Regulations 1992

Documents including—

(i) repair and maintenance records required by Regulation 5;

(ii) housekeeping records to comply with the requirements of Regulation 9;

(iii) hazard warning signs or notices to comply with Regulation 17 (Traffic Routes).

SECTION C – Provision and Use of Work Equipment Regulations 1998

Documents including—

(i) manufacturers' specifications and instructions in respect of relevant work equipment establishing its suitability to comply with Regulation 4;

(ii) maintenance log/maintenance records required to comply with Regulation 5;

(iii) documents providing information and instructions to employees to comply with
Regulation 8;

(iv) documents provided to the employee in respect of training for use to comply with Regulation 9;

(v) risk assessments/documents required to comply with Regulation 12;

(vi) any notice, sign or document relied upon as a defence to alleged breaches of
Regulations 14 to 18 dealing with controls and control systems;

(vii) instruction/training documents issued to comply with the requirements of
Regulation 22 insofar as it deals with maintenance operations where the machinery
is not shut down;

(viii) copies of markings required to comply with Regulation 23;

(ix) copies of warnings required to comply with Regulation 24.

SECTION D – Personal Protective Equipment at Work Regulations 1992

Documents including—

(i) documents relating to the assessment of the Personal Protective Equipment to
comply with Regulation 6;

(ii) documents relating to the maintenance and replacement of Personal Protective
Equipment to comply with Regulation 7;

(iii) record of maintenance procedures for Personal Protective Equipment to comply
with Regulation 7;

(iv) records of tests and examinations of Personal Protective Equipment to comply
with Regulation 7;

(v) documents providing information, instruction and training in relation to the
Personal Protective Equipment to comply with Regulation 9;

(vi) instructions for use of Personal Protective Equipment to include the manufacturers' instructions to comply with Regulation 10.

SECTION E – Manual Handling Operations Regulations 1992

Documents including—

(i) Manual Handling Risk Assessment carried out to comply with the requirements of Regulation 4(1)(b)(i);

(ii) re-assessment carried out post-accident to comply with requirements of Regulation 4(1)(b)(i);

(iii) documents showing the information provided to the employee to give general
indications related to the load and precise indications on the weight of the load and
the heaviest side of the load if the centre of gravity was not positioned centrally to
comply with Regulation 4(1)(b)(iii);

(iv) documents relating to training in respect of manual handling operations and
training records.

SECTION F – Health and Safety (Display Screen Equipment) Regulations 1992

Documents including—

(i) analysis of work stations to assess and reduce risks carried out to comply with the requirements of Regulation 2;

(ii) re-assessment of analysis of work stations to assess and reduce risks following
development of symptoms by the claimant;

(iii) documents detailing the provision of training including training records to comply with the requirements of Regulation 6;

(iv) documents providing information to employees to comply with the requirements of Regulation 7.

SECTION G – Control of Substances Hazardous to Health Regulations 2002

Documents including—

(i) risk assessment carried out to comply with the requirements of Regulation 6;

(ii) reviewed risk assessment carried out to comply with the requirements of Regulation 6;

(iii) documents recording any changes to the risk assessment required to comply with Regulation 6 and steps taken to meet the requirements of Regulation 7;

(iv) copy labels from containers used for storage handling and disposal of carcinogenics to comply with the requirements of Regulation 7(2A)(h);

(v) warning signs identifying designation of areas and installations which may be
contaminated by carcinogenics to comply with the requirements of Regulation 7(2A)(h);

(vi) documents relating to the assessment of the Personal Protective Equipment to
comply with Regulation 7(3A);

(vii) documents relating to the maintenance and replacement of Personal Protective
Equipment to comply with Regulation 7(3A);

(viii) record of maintenance procedures for Personal Protective Equipment to comply with Regulation 7(3A);

(ix) records of tests and examinations of Personal Protective Equipment to comply
with Regulation 7(3A);

(x) documents providing information, instruction and training in relation to the
Personal Protective Equipment to comply with Regulation 7(3A);

(xi) instructions for use of Personal Protective Equipment to include the manufacturers' instructions to comply with Regulation 7(3A);

(xii) air monitoring records for substances assigned a maximum exposure limit or
occupational exposure standard to comply with the requirements of Regulation 7;

(xiii) maintenance examination and test of control measures records to comply with
Regulation 9;

(xiv) monitoring records to comply with the requirements of Regulation 10;

(xv) health surveillance records to comply with the requirements of Regulation 11;

(xvi) documents detailing information, instruction and training including training
records for employees to comply with the requirements of Regulation 12;

(xvii) all documents relating to arrangements and procedures to deal with accidents, incidents and emergencies required to comply with Regulation 13;

(xvii) labels and Health and Safety data sheets supplied to the employers to comply with the CHIP Regulations.

SECTION H – Construction (Design and Management) Regulations 2007

Documents including—

(i) notification of a project form (HSE F10) to comply with the requirements of
Regulation 7;

(ii) Health and Safety Plan to comply with requirements of Regulation 15;

(iii) Health and Safety file to comply with the requirements of Regulations 12 and 14;

(iv) information and training records provided to comply with the requirements of
Regulation 17;

(v) records of advice from and views of persons at work to comply with the requirements of Regulation 18;

(vi) reports of inspections made in accordance with Regulation 33;

(vii) records of checks for the purposes of Regulation 34;

(viii) emergency procedures for the purposes of Regulation 39.

SECTION I – Construction (Health, Safety & Welfare) Regulations 1996

Documents including—

(i) documents produced to comply with requirements of the Regulations.

SECTION J – Work at Height Regulations 2005

Documents including—

(i) documents relating to planning, supervision and safety carried out for
Regulation 4;

(ii) documents relating to training for the purposes of Regulation 5;

(iii) documents relating to the risk assessment carried out for Regulation 6;

(iv) documents relating to the selection of work equipment for the purposes
of
Regulation 7;

(v) notices or other means in writing warning of fragile surfaces for the
purposes of
Regulation 9;

(vi) documents relating to any inspection carried out for Regulation 12;

(vii) documents relating to any inspection carried out for Regulation 13;

(viii) reports made for the purposes of Regulation 14;

(ix) any certificate issued for the purposes of Regulation 15.

SECTION K – Pressure Systems and Transportable Gas Containers Regulations 1989

(i) information and specimen markings provided to comply with the
requirements of Regulation 5;

(ii) written statements specifying the safe operating limits of a system to
comply with the requirements of Regulation 7;

(iii) copy of the written scheme of examination required to comply with the
requirements of Regulation 8;

(iv) examination records required to comply with the requirements of Regulation 9;

(v) instructions provided for the use of operator to comply with Regulation 11;

(vi) records kept to comply with the requirements of Regulation 13;

(vii) records kept to comply with the requirements of Regulation 22.

SECTION L – Lifting Operations and Lifting Equipment Regulations 1998

Documents including—

(i) records kept to comply with the requirements of the Regulations including the
records kept to comply with Regulation 6.

SECTION M – The Noise at Work Regulations 1989

Documents including—

(i) any risk assessment records required to comply with the requirements of Regulations 4 and 5;

(ii) manufacturers' literature in respect of all ear protection made available to claimant to comply with the requirements of Regulation 8;

(iii) all documents provided to the employee for the provision of information to comply with Regulation 11.

SECTION N – Control of Noise at Work Regulations 1989

Documents including—

(i) documents relating to the assessment of the level of noise to which employees are exposed to comply with Regulation 5;

(ii) documents relating to health surveillance of employees to comply with Regulation 9;

(ii) instruction and training records provided to employees to comply with Regulation 10.

SECTION O – Construction (Head Protection) Regulations 1989

Documents including—

(i) pre-accident assessment of head protection required to comply with Regulation 3(4);

(ii) post-accident re-assessment required to comply with Regulation 3(5).

SECTION P – The Construction (General Provisions) Regulations 1961

Documents including—

(i) report prepared following inspections and examinations of excavations etc. to comply with the requirements of Regulation 9.

SECTION Q – Gas Containers Regulations 1989

Documents including—

(i) information and specimen markings provided to comply with the requirements of Regulation 5;

(ii) written statements specifying the safe operating limits of a system to comply with the requirements of Regulation 7;

(iii) copy of the written scheme of examination required to comply with the requirements of Regulation 8;

(iv) examination records required to comply with the requirements of Regulation 9;

(v) instructions provided for the use of operator to comply with Regulation 11.

SECTION R – Control of Noise at Work Regulations 2005

Documents including—

(i) risk assessment records required to comply with the requirements of Regulations 4 and 5;

(ii) all documents relating to steps taken to comply with regulation 6;

(iii) all documents relating to and/or arising out of actions taken to comply including providing consideration of alternative work that the claimant could have engaged to comply with Regulation 7.

SECTION S – Mine and Quarries Act 1954

Documents including—

(i) documents produced to comply with requirements of the Act.

SECTION T – Control of Vibrations at Work Regulations 2005

Documents including—

(i) risk assessments and documents produced to comply with requirements of Regulations 6 and 8;

(ii) occupational health surveillance records produced to comply with Regulation 7.

ANNEX D: Letter of instruction to medical expert

Dear Sir,

Re: **(Name and Address)**

D.O.B.–

Telephone No.–

Date of Accident –

We are acting for the above named in connection with injuries received in an accident which occurred on the above date. A summary of the main facts of the accident circumstances is provided below. The main injuries appear to have been **(describe main injuries and functional impact on day to day living as in Letter of Claim)**.

In order to assist with the preparation of your report we have enclosed the following documents:

Enclosures

1. Hospital Records
2. GP records
3. Statement of Events

We have not obtained [ ] records yet but will use our best endeavours to obtain these without delay if you request them.

We should be obliged if you would examine our Client and let us have a full and detailed report dealing with any relevant pre-accident medical history, the injuries sustained, treatment received and present condition, dealing in particular with the capacity for work and giving a prognosis.

It is central to our assessment of the extent of our Client's injuries to establish the extent and duration of any continuing disability. Accordingly, in the prognosis section we would ask you to specifically comment on any areas of continuing complaint or disability or impact on daily living. If there is such continuing disability you should comment upon the level of suffering or inconvenience caused and, if you are able, give your view as to when or if the complaint or disability is likely to resolve.

If our client requires further treatment, please can you advise of the cost on a private patient basis.

Please send our Client an appointment direct for this purpose. Should you be able to offer a cancellation appointment please contact our Client direct. We confirm we will be responsible for your reasonable fees.

We are obtaining the notes and records from our Client's GP and Hospitals attended and will forward them to you when they are to hand/or please request the GP and Hospital records direct and advise that any invoice for the provision of these records should be forwarded to us.

In order to comply with Court Rules we would be grateful if you would insert above your signature, the following statement: "I confirm that I have made clear which facts and matters referred to in this report are within my own knowledge and which are not. Those that are within my own knowledge I confirm to be true. The opinions I have expressed represent my true and complete professional opinions on the matters to which they refer".

In order to avoid further correspondence we can confirm that on the evidence we have there is no reason to suspect we may be pursuing a claim against the hospital
or its staff.

We look forward to receiving your report within _______ weeks. If you will not be able to prepare your report within this period please telephone us upon receipt of these instructions.

When acknowledging these instructions it would assist if you could give an estimate as to the likely time scale for the provision of your report and also an indication as to your fee.

Yours faithfully,

PART VII

THE OLD "PREDICTIVE" COSTS REGIME

Chapter 37

The Old "Predictive" Costs Regime

THE OLD "PREDICTIVE" COSTS REGIME

Predictive Costs Regime

Road traffic accident after 6 October 2003 - Up to £10,000 and settled pre-issue

When the accident occurred prior to 30 April 2010, it will fall to be dealt with under this scheme.

In relation to accidents occurring on or after 30 April 2010 they will have gone into the RTA Portal. If resolved in the portal then portal costs are payable.

Any such matter not resolved within the portal, but settled pre-issue is dealt with by this scheme as Fixed Recoverable Costs outside the portal did not come in until 31 July 2013.

Any accident occurring on or after 31 July 2013 will be subject to Fixed Recoverable Costs on exiting the portal, even if proceedings are not issued as Fixed Recoverable Costs cover matters settled pre-issue and post-issue, as well as matters which go to trial.

The only general exception to the rule that anything exiting a portal goes to Fixed Recoverable Costs is industrial disease claims, but, not being road traffic matters, they cannot come within the Predictive Costs regime as that only covers road traffic matters.

Any matter allocated to the multi-track is excluded from the Fixed Recoverable Costs scheme.

However there are some cases which are excluded from the portal process completely and where the old predictive costs regime still applies.

The Predictable, or Predictive Costs Regime is set out in Part II of CPR 45 and CPR 45.9(2) defines that part as applying where:-

> "(a) the dispute arises from a road traffic accident occurring on or after 6 October 2003;
>
> (b) the agreed damages include damages in respect of personal injury, damage to property, or both;
>
> (c) the total value of the agreed damages does not exceed £10,000; and

(d) if a claim had been issued for the amount of the agreed damages, the small claims track would not have been the normal track for that claim."

Note that in contrast to the portal scheme vehicle related damages are taken in to account in determining what the value of the claim is.

So a £12,000.00 settlement, including a £4,000 vehicle related damages claim, is valued at £12,000, not £8,000. In the portal it would be £8,000.

Also in contrast to the portal system, it is the amount actually settled for and if contributory negligence is involved that does not matter.

Thus a claim for £30,000 settles for £10,000 on the basis of 66.66% contributory negligence. That is within the scheme as it is considered to have a value of £10,000.

It would not be in the portal as the full liability value of the claim exceeds £25,000.

CPR 45.11 sets out the amount of those fixed costs as follows:-

"45.11

(4) Subject to paragraphs (2) and (3), the amount of fixed recoverable costs is the total of –

(a) £800;

(b) 20% of the damages agreed up to £5,000; and

(c) 15% of the damages agreed between £5,000 and £10,000.

(5) Where the claimant –

(a) lives or works in an area set out in Practice Direction 45; and

(b) instructs a legal representative who practices in that area, the fixed recoverable costs will include, in addition to the costs specified in paragraph (1), an amount equal to 12.5% of the costs allowable under that paragraph.

(6) Where appropriate, VAT may be recovered in addition to the amount of fixed recoverable costs and any reference in this Section to fixed recoverable costs is a reference to those costs net of any such VAT."

This original predictable costs regime continues to be relevant for claims not covered by the RTA Portal, but like the portal the scheme excludes small claims and unlike the portals it also excludes litigants in person.

For example this system continues to apply:-

- in relation to claims against persons other than road users;
- where one of the parties is a protected party, other than a child;
- the claimant is bankrupt;
- the defendant's vehicle is registered outside the United Kingdom.

This is not an exhaustive list and in any road traffic accident matter worth £10,000.00 or less, which does not go into the portal, you should check to see whether the reason it is excluded from the portal also excludes it from this scheme.

The predictive costs regime never has any application if the matter is issued.

Examples of cases covered by predictive costs but not the portals

Any accident which occurred before 30 April 2010 can never be entered on to a portal as the portals exclude accidents before that date. It is the date of the accident, not the Claim Notification Form, which is relevant.

Consequently there will be matters involving children who had accidents before 30 April 2010 where the matter will not go on to the portal, but if settled prior to the issue of proceedings for £10,000.00 or less, will be dealt with by the Old Predictive Costs Regime.

As we have seen earlier claims which on a full liability basis exceed £25,000 do not go into the RTA Portal, but if they settle for £10,000 or less then they are within this older scheme.

Does the ruling in *Nizami v Butt [2006] EWHC 159 (QB)* apply to the Old Predictive Costs Regime? In other words is the indemnity principle waived just as it is in the portal and Fixed Recoverable Costs scheme?

There is no direct authority on the point but it seems to me that by analogy, yes it does.

Success Fees

The usual rule applies, that is that if the conditional fee agreement was signed on or before 31 March 2013, then the success fee is recoverable.

Otherwise it is not.

Post Script

The figures in the Old Predictive Costs Regime were agreed between representatives of claimant solicitors' groups and insurers at a meeting of the Civil Justice Council in 2002.

After two days of heated discussions between the claimant and defendant camps no one was prepared actually to specify any figures, leading to an increasingly frustrated Master of the Rolls, Lord Phillips, to ask someone to put forward some figures to get matters going.

My business partner Robert Males came up with the figures and after a short discussion they were agreed.

History is often written on the proverbial back of a fag pack.

PART VIII

FROM PORTALS TO FIXED RECOVERABLE COSTS

Chapter 38

Overview

OVERVIEW

This part looks at some issues where a matter has exited the portal, for whatever reason, but where substantive Part 7 proceedings have not been issued.

Claimants should avoid being caught in this no man's land, as the costs barely rise above those in the portal, and if care is not taken a considerable amount of work will be done before the issue of proceedings and for almost no extra costs.

Once a matter drops out of either of the portals, which are themselves technically Pre-Action Protocols, they automatically go into the Pre-Action Protocol for Personal Injury Claims, the text of which is set out in chapter 36.

Time to elapse before issuing proceedings in an ex-portal matter

In an RTA matter the defendant has 21 calendar days from the date of the posting of the Letter of Claim, and a CNF lodged on the portal is deemed to be the Letter of Claim, to identify the insurer and identify specifically any significant omissions from the Letter of Claim.

The insurer then has a further three months from the date of that acknowledgment to investigate.

Hence the three months and 21 days maximum from the date of lodging the CNF to issuing Part 7 proceedings unless liability is positively admitted or positively denied earlier.

For an accident outside England and Wales the periods are 42 days and six months respectively.

Where the insurer is not identified, or where the MIB is involved the period is 42 days.

For a matter in the EL portal the period is 42 days and the PL portal 56 days.

Note that a matter that exits the RTA portal, or was never suitable for the RTA portal, but which settles pre-issue for £10,000.00 or less, is potentially within the old predictive costs regime, which is dealt with in chapter 37.

In this part I also deal with interim applications, including applications for pre-action disclosure, as these can occur when a matter has never been in the portal, or is in the portal, or has exited the portal.

CPR 45 now governs the costs position in relation to claims in the portal, claims which have exited the portal but not been issued, and issued ex-portal claims.

Thus CPR 45 covers everything, including the link between portal claims and issued ex-portal claims, and so I include the text in this part.

As the portal process spreads to all civil litigation it would make sense in my view to have a short limitation period once a matter has exited the portal.

Thus, in personal injury cases, allowing for the potential time to investigate by the defendant, there should be a provision that once a matter has exited the portal process for any reason then Part 7 proceedings must be issued within three months of that exit, failing which the claimant shall be debarred from bringing a claim.

It makes sense to have a seamless process for all civil litigation of all kinds and all values running from the moment the CNF is submitted to the end of a Supreme Court appeal hearing.

I deal with some of these issues in a little more detail in Part X – Extending Fixed Recoverable Costs, and they will be looked at extensively in my new book where I set out a scheme for fixed costs for everything without any upper value limit.

Chapter 39

Children

CHILDREN

No civil matter involving a child can ever be settled without the approval of the court and any such purported settlement is invalid, leaving the child free to issue proceedings once she or he attains majority, that is 18 years of age.

Limitation then begins to run, so in a personal injury case the time limit is three years from the child's 18th birthday.

So-called parental indemnities are worthless and unlawful and if facilitated by a solicitor involve serious professional misconduct.

CPR 21.10 could not be clearer.

"**21.10**

(1) Where a claim is made –

(a) by or on behalf of a child or protected party; or

(b) against a child or protected party,

no settlement, compromise or payment (including any voluntary interim payment) and no acceptance of money paid into court shall be valid, so far as it relates to the claim by, on behalf of or against the child or protected party, without the approval of the court.

(2) Where –

(a) before proceedings in which a claim is made by or on behalf of, or against, a child or protected party (whether alone or with any other person) are begun, an agreement is reached for the settlement of the claim; and

(b) the sole purpose of proceedings is to obtain the approval of the court to a settlement or compromise of the claim,

the claim must –

(i) be made using the procedure set out in Part 8 (alternative procedure for claims); and

(ii) include a request to the court for approval of the settlement or compromise.

(3) In proceedings to which Section II or Section III of Part 45 applies, the court will not make an order for detailed assessment of the costs payable to the child or protected party but will assess the costs in the manner set out in that Section.

(Rule 46.4 contains provisions about costs where money is payable to a child or protected party.)"

Here I do not deal with the general law in relation to children and infant approval settlements, but rather the procedure within the portals for obtaining the approval of the court and the costs consequences.

Generally I deal with Part 36 in chapter 22 but in this chapter I do look at the special provisions relating to Part 36 and children within the portal process.

I also look at the lacuna whereby the fixed costs in a case involving a child *drop* if the case exits the portal and settles before substantive Part 7 proceedings are issued.

Claims made by children are not thereby excluded from the portal process, but the process is modified as follows:-

- the CNF must state that the claimant is a child;

- the Statement of Truth may be signed by the child's parent or guardian as an alternative to the claimant or claimant's legal representative;

- the interim payment provisions do not apply and proceedings must be started in order to obtain the court's approval to a payment other than those made directly to treatment providers;

- court approval is necessary in relation to any proposed settlement and this is by way of a settlement hearing.

Once a case has exited the portal the usual rules and procedures apply in relation to obtaining the approval of the court and issuing an application for an infant approval hearing but there are special rules as to costs, which I deal with below.

The usual issues involving children apply to personal injury claims subject to the portal and Fixed Recoverable Costs regime, that is in relation to a Litigation Friend, conflict of interest, Part 36 etc.

Within the portal the child settlement process is governed by Practice Direction 8B. Paragraph 6.5 provides that where the claimant is a child and settlement has been agreed between the parties the following must be filed at court:-

- a draft Consent Order;
- an advice on quantum by counsel, solicitor or other legal representative;
- a statement verified by a Statement of Truth signed by the Litigation Friend which confirms whether the child has recovered in line with the prognosis, and whether there are any continuing symptoms.

There must be an oral hearing. The stage 3 paper hearing process cannot be used in a case involving a child.

Child Settlement Hearings and costs within the portal

Settlement within stage 2

First settlement hearing – settlement approved

The costs payable are:-

- Stage 1 and stage 2 fixed costs;
- Stage 3, type A, B and C fixed costs; and
- disbursements as per CPR 45.19.

First settlement hearing – settlement not approved

Stage 1 and stage 2 fixed costs only are payable.

Second settlement hearing – settlement approved

One set of stage 3, type A, B and C fixed costs are payable.

Note: stage 1 and stage 2 fixed costs will have been ordered at the first settlement hearing.

Thus where a matter is approved at a second settlement hearing the starting point is that the claimant gets no extra costs, but does not lose costs for failure to get the right figure at the first settlement hearing.

However the court has a discretion to order:-

- the defendant to pay an extra set of type A and/or type B fixed costs; or
- the claimant to pay type A and/or type B fixed costs.

Type A costs are preparation for the hearing and type B costs are for the advocacy.

Type C costs are costs of the advice. Thus only one set of advice costs is ever recoverable, even if there has been an additional advice. The court has no discretion to award more than one advice fee.

Qualified One-Way Costs Shifting

It is questionable whether CPR 42.21(6), which gives the court the power to order the client to pay type A and type B costs, survives the more recent CPR 44.13 – 17, dealing with Qualified One-Way Costs Shifting.

This situation is not one of the exceptions listed in the QOCS provisions and so yet again we have two Civil Procedure Rules, apparently of equal weight, contradicting one another.

No doubt time, or the Court of the Appeal, will tell.

This issue will become of greater importance as the portal and fixed costs scheme extends to much higher value claims as proposed by Lord Justice Jackson, who will report by 31 July 2017 in relation to Fixed Recoverable Costs.

Case unsuitable for stage 3

Where the court has not approved the settlement and orders that the claim is not suitable to be determined under the normal, effectively contested, stage 3 procedure the costs payable are:-

- stage 1 and stage 2 fixed costs; and
- stage 3, type A, B and C fixed costs.

The claim then exits the portal process.

Settlement within stage 3

First settlement hearing

Costs payable are:-

- stage 1 and stage 2 fixed costs;
- stage 3, type A, B and C fixed costs; and
- disbursements in accordance with CPR 45.19.

If the settlement is not approved, then the claim moves to the conventional stage 3 hearing and stage 1 and stage 2 fixed costs are payable, together with type A costs only

Stage 3 hearing

The position, including the court's discretionary powers and the issue of Qualified One-Way Costs Shifting, are as per settlement within stage 2 – second settlement hearing above.

FIXED COSTS

Fixed Costs under CPR 45 refer to the issuing of a claim under Part 7. Proceedings issued for an infant settlement hearing are Part 8 proceedings. CPR 21.10 reads:-

"(2) Where –

> (a) before proceedings in which a claim is made by or on behalf of, or against, a child or protected party (whether alone or with any other person) are begun, an agreement is reached for the settlement of the claim; and
>
> (b) the sole purpose of proceedings is to obtain the approval of the court to a settlement or compromise of the claim,

the claim must –

> (i) be made using the procedure set out in Part 8 (alternative procedure for claims); and
>
> (ii) include a request to the court for approval of the settlement or compromise."

CPR 45.21(2) provides that where the court approves the settlement at a settlement hearing the defendant shall pay Type C costs (£150 plus VAT) as well as other costs and disbursements.

A settlement hearing is essential in all cases involving children, whatever the value and whatever the procedure.

From the reports that I am getting judges are refusing to allow deductions from children's damages to fund the success fee/solicitor and own client costs.

This raises the issue of whether anyone will act for children in portal/Fixed Recoverable Costs cases where the recoverable fees in the portals are unprofitable, without an additional charge to the client.

This problem will be greatly exacerbated when the personal injury small claims limit goes up on 1 October 2018. For claims of that value or less, there will be no recovery from the other side beyond the £100.00 or so fixed small claims track costs.

If judges refuse to allow a charge to be made to the child, then almost no one will act for children in road traffic cases worth £5,000.00 or less. That covers about 90% of cases.

In *Dockerill and Healey v Tullett and Macefield v Bakos and Tubridy v Sarwar [2012] EWCA Civ 184*

the court recognized that this may well lead to solicitors not acting for children.

Note also that while the portal and the Fixed Recoverable Costs Scheme allow for an additional fee in relation to a matter involving a child there appears to be no provision for such an additional fee if the matter is settled after exiting the portal but before proceedings are issued.

There appears to be nothing to stop a claimant issuing proceedings while the matter is still in one of the portals, provided that the appropriate time has expired since lodging the Claim Notification Form, which stands as the Letter of Claim.

Claimants may wish to do this in children cases to avoid the lacuna whereby no additional fee is payable in a child case where the matter has exited the portal but not yet been issued.

EXAMPLE

If a child's claim settled for damages of £1,000.00 the following costs would be applicable at each stage:-

- **Settles within the portal**

  CPR 45.22 applies to cases where settlement at Stage 3 where the claimant is a child:-

  Stage 1 fee - £ 200.00

  Stage 2 fee - £ 300.00

  Stage 3 fee –

  - Type A costs £ 250.00

    Type A fixed costs' means the legal representative's costs

  - Type B costs £ 250.00

    Type B fixed costs' means the advocate's costs

  - Type C costs £ 150.00

    Type C fixed costs' means the costs for the advice on the amount of damages where the claimant is a child

  TOTAL **£1,150.00**

- **Settles outside the Portal but pre-issue**

CPR 45.29C Table B deals with the amount of Fixed costs in claims that no longer continue in the portal

"TABLE 6B

Fixed costs where a claim no longer continues under the RTA Protocol
A. If Parties reach a settlement prior to the claimant issuing proceedings under Part 7

Agreed damages	At least £1,000, but not more than £5,000
Fixed costs	The greater of— (a) £550; or (b) the total of— (i) £100; and (ii) 20% of the damages"

TOTAL **£ 550.00**

- **Settles post issue**

CPR 45.29C Table B deals with the amount of Fixed costs in claims that no longer continue in the portal

"TABLE 6B

B. If proceedings are issued under Part 7, but the case settles before trial

Stage at which case is settled	On or after the date of issue, but prior to the date of allocation under Part 26
Fixed costs	The total of— (a) £1,160; and (b) 20% of the damages"

Thus this will be:-

£1,160.00
£ 200.00

TOTAL **£1,360.00**

Children & Disbursements

CPR 45.12(2)(b) provides that the court may allow court fees payable on an application to the court and fees payable for instructing counsel where they are necessarily incurred by reason of one or more of the claimants being a child or protected party as defined in Part 21.

Thus counsel's fees are recoverable as a disbursement under that rule, but there is no additional fee if the solicitor prepares the advice herself or himself.

This reflects how badly the rules are written. In fact if you look at CPR 45.12(2)(b) what it actually says is that the court can allow fees payable for instructing counsel or court fees payable on an application to the court. Clearly the word "or" should be "and" and on a literal reading of that rule you either get counsel's fees or the court fees, but you cannot get both.

There are other similar confusions.

RTA Portal 7.10 reads:-

"7.10 In most cases under this Protocol, it is expected that the claimant's legal representative will be able to value the claim. In some cases with a value of more than £10,000 (excluding vehicle related damages), an additional advice from a specialist solicitor or from counsel may be justified where it is reasonably required to value the claim."

EL/PL 7.8 is in similar terms.

Thus it is unclear as to whether you can instruct a specialist solicitor in your own firm and get the extra fee in those circumstances.

That paragraph specifically states that it is expected that the claimant's legal representative, rather than counsel, will be able to value the claim and yet CPR 45.12 allows for the recovery of counsel's fees, but allows no extra cost for the solicitor, even though it is expected that the solicitor will be able to value the claim!

Thus the position in relation to children, in precisely the same case is:-

Settled in the portal: £150.00 extra fee payable to counsel or specialist solicitor;

Settled out of the portal pre-issue: no extra fee payable;

Settled after proceedings issued: £150.00 fee for counsel but no fee if the solicitor does the work.

After-the-Event insurance

CPR 21.12(2)(a) specifically allows for an After-the-Event insurance premium to be deducted from a child's damages upon application to the court.

Although an application has to be made, the Litigation Friend is entitled to recover the amount paid out if it has been reasonably incurred and is reasonable in amount (CPR 21.12(1)).

Infant approval hearing

Could an Infant Approval Hearing come within the definition of "trial" as set out in this Court of Appeal decision?

Is it in fact a disposal hearing within the meaning of Practice Direction 26.12.4?

On the face of it the answer to both questions is yes, in which case the third stage costs are payable.

This will be logical given that in a case involving a child the matter should be prepared fully in exactly the same way as for a disposal hearing, so that the court has all of the necessary information to enable it to decide whether or not the proposed settlement should be approved.

Can proceedings be issued while a matter is still in the portal?

To avoid falling into the out of portal but pre-issue lacuna of lower costs there appears to be nothing to stop substantive Part 7 proceedings being issued while the matter is still in the portal process and then immediately exiting that process.

This avoids any time when the matter is out of the portal without proceedings having been issued.

Success fees

CPR 21.12(1A)(b) gives the court power to order deduction of a success fee agreed by a Litigation Friend on behalf of a child and the wording of the rule is that the Litigation Friend is entitled to recover such success fee from damages if it has been reasonably incurred and is reasonable in amount, and provided that damages do not exceed £25,000.00.

The general rule is that there must be a detailed assessment of costs where there is any proposed charge to a child over and above any costs recovered from the other side (CPR 46.4).

However, if the only proposed charge is the success fee then the court can summarily assess the costs, that is the success fee (CPR 46.4(5)(B)).

If there is no charge to the child then there need not be any assessment and this allows the Litigation Friend, often the parent, to pay the success fee.

Practice Direction 46, paragraph 2.1(b) provides:-

"2.1 The circumstances in which the court need not order the detailed assessment of costs under rule 46.4(2) are as follows –

(a) …

(b) where another party has agreed to pay a specified sum in respect of the costs of the child or protected party and the legal representative acting for the child or protected party has waived the right to claim further costs;"

As court approval is only required to deduct money from the child's damages, it is perfectly lawful and proper to have an arrangement with the Litigation Friend, who after all is the person who enters into the agreement, that that person will pay a sum capped to 25% of damages in return for the solicitor agreeing to act for the child.

The Litigation Friend should be told that they must not take any part of the damages. That is not normally an immediate problem as the damages are invested by the court.

Making a charge to the parent and not the child may appear to involve an element of robbing Peter to pay Paul.

Historically courts would allow solicitors to recover costs in infant matters, even though the matter was a small claim and indeed insurers would normally pay up without argument.

That has all changed.

If the child attains majority during the case, then it is permissible to charge a success fee, or indeed any other agreed costs.

Thus if a case is settled when the claimant is 17 years and 11 months old the solicitor cannot charge anything, but if it is settled a month later then the full charge and success fee can be made.

Part 36

The whole issue of Part 36, a rule of the utmost complexity, is beyond the scope of this book but in chapter 22 I deal with Part 36 insofar as there are separate provisions in relation to portals and the fixed costs regime.

Here I look at the interplay between Part 36 and claims involving minors. I look at the basic rule and the discretion of the court within that rule.

I do not consider the case law that has developed around Part 36 offers in relation to children when the child's prognosis is not clear.

Where a child matches or beats its own offer then the normal benefits apply.

Where a minor beats a defendant's Part 36 offer then there are no consequences and the usual law applies.

The variation comes into play when a minor claimant fails to beat a defendant's Part 36 offer.

Then CPR 36.29(2) comes into play and the court must order the claimant to pay the fixed costs in CPR 45.26 and interest on those costs.

CPR 45.26 provides for the claimant to pay stage 3 type A fixed costs if it is a paper hearing and stage 3 type A and B fixed costs if it is an oral hearing, which a case involving a minor always will be.

CPR 45.26 provides for the claimant to pay any stage 3 disbursements allowed in accordance with CPR 45.19 and that specifically provides that CPR 45.19(2)(d) for court fees in respect of the stage 3 procedure to be paid.

However CPR 45.22 deals with settlement at stage 3 where the claimant is a child and reads:-

"Settlement at Stage 3 where the claimant is a child

45.22

(1) This rule applies where –

(a) the claimant is a child;

(b) there is a settlement after proceedings are started under the Stage 3 Procedure;

(c) the settlement is more than the defendant's relevant Protocol offer; and

(d) an application is made to the court to approve the settlement.

(2) Where the court approves the settlement at the settlement hearing it will order the defendant to pay –

(a) the Stage 1 and 2 fixed costs;

(b) the Stage 3 Type A, B and C fixed costs; and

(c) disbursements allowed in accordance with rule 45.19.

(3) Where the court does not approve the settlement at the settlement hearing it will order the defendant to pay the Stage 1 and 2 fixed costs.

(4) Paragraphs (5) and (6) apply where the court does not approve the settlement at the first settlement hearing but does approve the settlement at the Stage 3 hearing.

(5) At the Stage 3 hearing the court will order the defendant to pay –

(a) the Stage 3 Type A and C fixed costs for the settlement hearing;

(b) disbursements allowed in accordance with rule 45.19; and

(c) the Stage 3 Type B fixed costs for one of the hearings.

(6) The court in its discretion may also order –

(a) the defendant to pay an additional amount of either or both the Stage 3 –

(i) Type A fixed costs;

(ii) Type B fixed costs; or

(b) the claimant to pay an amount equivalent to either or both of the Stage 3 –

(i) Type A fixed costs;

(ii) Type B fixed costs.

(7) Where the settlement is not approved at the Stage 3 hearing the court will order the defendant to pay the Stage 3 Type A fixed costs."

It will be seen at "CPR 45.22(6)(b)" where the claimant is a child, a discretion to order the claimant to pay an amount equivalent to either or both of the stage 3 type A fixed costs and/or type B fixed costs.

The rule is not at all clear but I presume that that is intended to apply in the situation where a minor claimant fails to beat a defendant's Part 36 offer.

However, note that CPR 45.22 only applies where there is a settlement after proceedings have started under the stage 3 procedure and the settlement is more than the defendant's relevant protocol offer and an application is made to the court to approve the settlement.

Thus it does not deal with the situation where the matter goes to a stage 3 hearing on quantum, rather than simply to approve the settlement.

Given that limitation I am not sure in what circumstances the court would be able to exercise its discretion to order the claimant to pay costs.

The rules are immensely complex and my view is that a minor who at a stage 3 hearing fails to beat a defendant's Part 36 offer, is indeed liable for a stage 3 court fee as well as stage 3 costs.

It is true that a fee would have been payable anyway for an infant approval hearing, but that is a very different type of hearing and of course if the judge decides damages then there is no approval hearing as obviously the judge him or herself has approved the figure by determining it himself or herself.

Chapter 40

Interim application, including pre-action disclosure

INTERIM APPLICATIONS INCLUDING FOR PRE-ACTION DISCLOSURE

Interim Applications

Interim applications are dealt with by CPR 45.29H which states:-

"(1) Where the court makes an order for costs of an interim application to be paid by one party in a case to which this Section applies, the order shall be for a sum equivalent to one half of the applicable Type A and Type B costs in Table 6 or 6A.

(2) Where the party in whose favour the order for costs is made—

(a) lives, works or carries on business in an area set out in Practice Direction 45; and

(b) instructs a legal representative who practises in that area, the costs will include, in addition to the costs allowable under paragraph (1), an amount equal to 12.5% of those costs.

(3) If an order for costs is made pursuant to this rule, the party in whose favour the order is made is entitled to disbursements in accordance with rule 45.29I.

(4) Where appropriate, VAT may be recovered in addition to the amount of any costs allowable under this rule."

Thus CPR 45.29H(2) deals with the London uplift and CPR 45.29H(3) allows for any of the disbursements mentioned in CPR 45.29I, which will include the application fee, and CPR 45.29H(4) deals with VAT.

Table 6A is contained within CPR 45.18.

Table A costs are the preparation costs and Table B costs are the advocacy costs.

Type A fixed costs are always £250.00 as are Type B fixed costs.

Thus the potential sum is £125.00 (half of Type A costs) or £250.00 (half of Type A and Type B costs). Obviously it is not possible to have Type B costs alone as there cannot be advocacy without preparation, although there are plenty of judges and clients who might disagree!

There is no doubt that fixed costs apply to interim applications.

On such applications the court has the power to award an amount of costs exceeding fixed recoverable costs and that power is contained in CPR 45.29J which reads:-

"(1) If it considers that there are exceptional circumstances making it appropriate to do so, the court will consider a claim for an amount of costs (excluding disbursements) which is greater than the fixed recoverable costs referred to in rules 45.29B to 45.29H.

(2) If the court considers such a claim to be appropriate, it may—

(a) summarily assess the costs; or

(b) make an order for the costs to be subject to detailed assessment.

(3) If the court does not consider the claim to be appropriate, it will make an order—

(a) if the claim is made by the claimant, for the fixed recoverable costs; or

(b) if the claim is made by the defendant, for a sum which has regard to, but which does not exceed the fixed recoverable costs,

and any permitted disbursements only."

Note that CPR 45.29J specifically refers to rules CPR 45.29B to 45.29H, and that 45.29H deals only with interim applications.

Thus it is beyond doubt that the court has the power on an interim application to make an order exceeding fixed recoverable costs.

Pre-action disclosure applications

CPR 23 deals with applications for court orders and covers what are generally known as interim applications and CPR 23.2(4A) clearly envisages pre-action applications coming within that rule and being interim applications as it states:-

"(4A) An application made in the County Court before a claim has been started may be made at any County Court hearing centre, unless any enactment, rule or practice direction provides otherwise."

Practice Direction 23A, dealing with applications states:-

"5. All applications made before a claim is commenced should be made under Part 23 of the Civil Procedure Rules. Attention is drawn in particular to rule 23.2(4) and (4A)."

Thus an application for pre-action disclosure is treated in exactly the same way as any post-issue application.

I appreciate that a Pre-Action Disclosure Application is governed by CPR 31.16, but clearly other Civil Procedure Rules need to apply as that rule does not deal with matters such as service and so on and the fact that that rule imposes additional requirements does not change the general principle.

Costs in Pre-Action Disclosure are dealt with by CPR 46, and CPR 46.1 specifically refers to applications under Section 33 of the Senior Courts Act 1981 and Section 52 of the County Courts Act 1984 which are the statutory provisions concerning Pre-Action Disclosure.

The general rule is that the applicant will be ordered to pay the costs in any event.

This is by virtue of CPR 46.1(2) which provides:-

"(2) The general rule is that the court will award the person against whom the order is sought that person's costs –

(a) of the application; and

(b) of complying with any order made on the application."

CPR 46.1(3) goes on to provide:-

"(3) The court may however make a different order, having regard to all the circumstances, including –

(a) the extent to which it was reasonable for the person against whom the order was sought to oppose the application; and

(b) whether the parties to the application have complied with any relevant pre-action protocol."

That position is confirmed by the exception contained in CPR 44.13(1) in relation to Qualified One-Way Costs Shifting, that is that a Pre-Action Disclosure Application under either Section 33 or Section 52 is not protected by QOCS.

Obviously that reflects the fact that generally any applicant for Pre-Action Disclosure would, on the face of it, be protected by QOCS and it would be pointless ordering the claimant to pay but then giving them the protection of QOCS.

The dictionary definition of "interim" does not help. One of the definitions is:-

"A thing done in an interval; an interlude."

which does suggest that for there to be an interim application there must have been proceedings underway.

However as an adjective the definition is:-

"Done, made, provided, etc. in or for the meantime; provisional, temporary."

Is a Pre-Action Disclosure Application in a claim that has exited the portal an interim application that falls within the fixed costs of CPR 45.29H?

Pre-Action Disclosure is dealt with in CPR 31.16 and in accordance with CPR 31.16(1)

"This rule applies where an application is made to the court under any Act for disclosure before proceedings have started."

Such applications, before proceedings have started, are permitted in the High Court under section 33 of the Senior Courts Act 1981 and in the County Court under section 52 of the County Courts Act 1984.

An interim application is an application made in accordance with CPR 23 and CPR 23.2 gives details as to where an interim application should be made as follows:-

"**Where to make an application**

23.2

(1) …
(2) …
(3) …
(4) Subject to paragraph (4A), if an application is made before a claim has been started, it must be made to the court where it is likely that the claim to which the application relates will be started unless there is good reason to make the application to a different court.

(4A) An application made in the County Court before a claim has been started may be made at

any County Court hearing centre, unless any enactment, rule or practice direction provides

otherwise.

(5) ..."

CPR 23.2(4) allows for interim applications to be made where proceedings have not yet been started and thus an application for Pre-Action Disclosure is an interim application.

Rule 45.29(H) overs the costs of interim applications which as we have seen above can include an application for Pre-Action Disclosure.

Rule 45.29(H)(1) provides that where the court makes an order for costs of an interim application to be paid by one party in a case *to which this section applies* (my italics) the order shall be for a sum......

Rule 45.27 deals with the scope and interpretation of the section involving the Pre-Action protocol for low value personal injury claims in Road Traffic Accidents and set out in 45.27(1):

"This section applies to claims that have been or should have been started under Part 8 in accordance with Practice Direction 8B ("the Stage 3 Procedure")."

So a claim that has been started in the portal or should have been started in the portal even if it has subsequently left the portal still comes within the definition set out in Rule 45.27(1) and therefore on an interim application the fixed costs set out at Rule 45.29(H) apply to such an application.

If the application is an interim application then costs will be awarded in accordance with CPR 45.29H, the text of which is set out above.

The Court of Appeal agreed with this reasoning in *Sharp v Leeds City Council*, 1 February 2017, [2017] EWCA Civ 33, where it held that applications for Pre-Action Disclosure are covered by the fixed costs scheme for interim hearings.

PRE-ACTION DISCLOSURE APPLICATIONS ARE COVERED BY FIXED COSTS

In *Sharp v Leeds City Council [2017] EWCA Civ 33 (01 February 2017)* the Court of Appeal held that applications for Pre-Action Disclosure are covered by the Fixed Recoverable Costs Scheme for interim hearings in fixed costs matters.

This case involved a claim which started, but no longer continued, under the EL/PL portal, but the same principle applies to RTA matters.

Equally if the matter had never been in a portal, but should have been, then again the court would no doubt limit the costs to fixed costs for interim hearings.

Some courts had taken this view, that is that CPR 45 fixed costs applied, whereas had taken the view that CPR 46 applied and had thus allowed costs on the standard basis.

Applications for Pre-Action Disclosure may be made in the County Court under section 52(2) of the County Courts Act 1984 and in the High Court under section 33 of the Senior Courts Act 1981.

The jurisdiction is not confined to personal injury matters.

CPR 46 makes specific provision for the costs of such applications, both in the County Court and the High Court, and the general rule is that the applicant pays the costs, win or lose, but the court is free to make a different order.

In practice in ex-portal cases, an application nearly always arises due to the failure of the defendant to follow the Pre-Action Protocol and therefore the court virtually always does make a different order, that is orders the defendant to pay the applicant's costs.

CPR 44.13(1) dis-applies Qualified One-Way Costs Shifting in relation to Pre-Action Disclosure applications, so a defendant in a personal injury action can enforce any costs order.

No reference to this dis-application of QOCS is made in CPR 45, which governs fixed costs.

CPR 45.29H deals with interim applications in fixed costs matters.

CPR 45.29J deals with costs in excess of fixed costs if "there are exceptional circumstances".

The Court of Appeal, rightly in my view, held that:

"…the fixed costs regime plainly applies to the costs of a PAD application made by a claimant who is pursuing a claim for damages for personal injuries which began with the issue of a CNF in the Portal pursuant to the EL/PL Protocol but which, at the time of the PAD application, is no longer continuing under that Protocol. My reasons follow.

31. The starting point is that the plain object and intent of the fixed costs regime in relation to claims of this kind is that, from the moment of entry into the Portal pursuant to the EL/PL Protocol (and, for that matter, the RTA Protocol as well) recovery of the costs of pursuing or defending that claim at all subsequent stages is intended to be limited to the fixed rates of recoverable costs, subject only to a very small category of clearly stated exceptions. To recognise implied exceptions in relation to such claim-related activity and expenditure would be destructive of the clear purpose of the fixed costs regime, which is to pursue the elusive objective of proportionality in the conduct of the small or relatively modest types of claim to which that regime currently applies.

32. That conclusion is, in my view, expressly prescribed by the clear words of Part 45.29A(1) and 45.29D. In particular, paragraph D provides that the fixed costs and disbursements prescribed by the regime (in paragraphs 29E and I respectively) are "the only costs allowed". Although this is subject to paragraphs F, H and J, they are each part of the fixed costs regime, even though they permit different or enlarged recovery in certain precisely defined circumstances.

33. That this is what Section IIIA of Part 45 is clearly designed to achieve is powerfully reinforced by its context, namely those other provisions in Part 45 (already described) which ensure that a case which starts under the EL/PL Protocol and continues within it to settlement or Stage 3 determination is also subject to the fixed costs regime throughout, as I have described. Furthermore, the fixed costs regime plainly applies to cases which no longer continue under the EL/PL Protocol but which never reach the stage when court proceedings are issued. This is what is provided by Part 45.29E and Part A of Table 6C in particular. The same applies to RTA Protocol cases: see Part 45.29C, and Part A of Table 6B."

The Court of Appeal recognised that its decision might mean that a recalcitrant defendant may not be incentivised to comply with the protocol in this regard.

It had this to say generally:

"39. But in my judgment the answer to this submission lies not in subjecting the fixed costs regime to an implied exception for PAD applications which exposed recalcitrant defendants to an altogether higher but variable level of recoverable costs liability, to be determined by assessment. Rather, the answer lies in the availability of an application under Part 45.29J, if exceptional circumstances can be shown or, for the future, in a recognition by the Rule Committee that the fixed costs regime needs to be kept under review, and defects in it remedied by adjustment of the fixed allowances where that can be shown to be justified.

40. It may well be that the frequency with which defendants fail to comply with their Protocol disclosure obligations may make it difficult to pass the exceptional circumstances hurdle in Part 45.29J, although I would not regard deliberate disregard of those obligations as unexceptional merely because it was frequently encountered. It may be that the very limited recovery of expenditure on a PAD application under the fixed costs regime means that such applications are not as effective as a means of sanctioning breach of Protocol disclosure obligations as they should be. If that is made good by appropriate evidence, then it seems to me that some consideration by way of review to the establishment of a more generous, but still fixed, recovery of costs of such applications would be justified.

41. By contrast, to throw open PAD applications generally to the recovery of assessed costs would in my view be to risk giving rise to an undesirable form of satellite litigation in which there would be likely to be incentives for the incurring of disproportionate expense, which is precisely what the fixed costs regime, viewed as a whole, is designed to avoid. The fixed costs regime inevitably contains swings and roundabouts, and lawyers who assist claimants by participating in it are accustomed to taking the rough with the smooth, in pursuing legal business which is profitable overall."

This is in marked contrast to the Court of Appeal's own decision in *Qader & Others v Esure Ltd & Khan v McGee [2016] EWCA Civ 1109, 16 November 2016*, just 77 days earlier.

Sharp is right and Qader is wrong, in my view.

However, in spite of the way that the Court of Appeal sought to distinguish Qader in Sharp, there are now two different lines of authority, one saying that the Court of Appeal can change the CPR and one saying that it cannot, one saying the escape provision is the appropriate remedy, one saying that it is not.

This leaves open the issue of a claim which has exited the portal but might be allocated to the multi-track. Following the decision of the Court of Appeal in *Qader & Others v Esure Ltd & Khan v McGee [2016] EWCA Civ 1109, 16 November 2016* a matter which is allocated to the multi-track is not subject to Fixed Recoverable Costs, even if it was previously in one of the portals.

Clearly if an interim application is made after it has been allocated to the multi-track then Fixed Recoverable Costs do not apply.

It is unclear what the position is in relation to a pre-action disclosure application, when obviously the matter has not been allocated. Supposing both parties agree at that application that the matter is suitable for the multi-track – does that give the court the power to order other than Fixed Recoverable Costs?

The court is free to do so by exercising the escape provision set out above.

Any doubts about the Qader decision have been ended by Rule 8.1 of The Civil Procedure (Amendment) Rules 2017, effective 6 April 2017, which provides that fixed recoverable costs only apply " for as long as the case is not allocated to the multi-track."

Rule 8 amends the tables in CPR 29 to omit the words "but not more than £25,000" to make it clear that ex-portal claims which are not allocated to the multi-track are subject to Fixed Recoverable Costs, whatever their value.

Case law

In *Annable v Fields, Bains v Jenkins and Harvey v Gizem Ltd, Preston County Court, 6 December 2016, Claim numbers C00PR338/PR14/2016*

the claimants had sought standard, rather than fixed, costs in relation to pre-action disclosure applications.

Bizarrely the District Judge awarded no costs at all on the basis that costs were fixed by CPR 45.29 and the claimants should have produced a schedule seeking those fixed costs.

HH Judge Butler allowed the appeals in all three cases, holding that a minimum of fixed costs is mandatory and therefore there is nothing wrong in seeking full costs and then later conceding fixed costs.

It is not a case of all or nothing.

Is an allocation hearing an interim hearing?

I do not know and so I asked the good people of Twitterland:-

Any thoughts on whether an allocation hearing is an interim hearing for CPR 45.29H costs purposes? Mention in the book for answerer. ☺

Here are the responses:-

Sarah Robson @portal_queen:-

"I've had judges say anything that isn't a final hearing is an interim hearing. But you were going to mention me anyway ;)"

Alec Hancock @AJhancokCILEX:-

"due to argue that in a schedule of costs post settlement. One hearing was a result of an app, other was allocation hearing"

Anna Symington @adrsymington

"I say (with no authority) no as it refers to "interim application" not interim hearing"

Alec Hancock @AJhancokCILEX:-

"would submit that absence of ref of cmc or allocation/ listing hearing suggests that interim hearing was meant to cover all"

Gerard McDermott @McDermottQC

"I'm with Anna ... do I get a mention too? (#vainsilk)"

Sarah Robson @portal_queen:-

"but if that was the case, there'd be no costs for an interim hearing not from an application"

Anna Symington @adrsymington

"presumably because they did not envisage any interim hearings absent apps (rightly or wrongly)"

So no one knows. I am glad of that as I would have felt disconcerted if I had had a flood of replies saying that it was obvious and I should look at CPR XX or whatever.

It also shows the enormous value of Twitter.

Once anyone does find the answer, perhaps you could let me know. ☺

It may be that the Court of Appeal has provided the answer in *Sharp v Leeds City Council*, 1 February 2017, [2017] EWCA Civ 33, that is that any hearing that is not a trial, that is a final contested hearing, in an interim hearing for costs purposes.

Chapter 41

Exiting the portal

EXITING THE PORTAL

Any matter exiting the portal process becomes subject to the Pre-Action Protocol for Personal Injury Claims, the text of which is at chapter 36.

The stage at which a claim exits the portal determines where it is picked up in that protocol.

The protocol treats the Claim Notification Form as the Letter of Claim, providing that it gives sufficient information.

The claim will no longer continue under either protocol where the defendant within the relevant period:-

(1) makes an admission of liability but alleges contributory negligence, other than in relation to a claimant's admitted failure to wear a seat belt in an RTA matter; (6.15(1) RTA, 6.13(1) Employers' Liability and Public Liability)

(2) does not complete and send the CNF response (6.15(2) RTA, 6.13(2) Employers' Liability and Public Liability)

(3) does not admit liability (6.15(3) RTA, 6.13(3) Employers' Liability and Public Liability)

(4) notifies the claimant that the defendant considers that –

   (a) there is inadequate information in the CNF; or

   (b) if proceedings were issued, the small claims track would be the normal track for that claim. (6.45(4) RTA, 6.13(4) Employers' Liability and Public Liability).

Statistics

Full statistics are set out in Chapter 28.

RTA

In the RTA Portal 1,579,217 out of 5,073,532, that is 31.13% of claims lodged between 30 April 2010 and 31 August 2016, exited the portal by the end of Stage 1.

Of those 1,579,217 the reason for exit was

i.	Liability Decision Timeout	1,067,103
ii.	Liability not admitted or admitted with contributory negligence other than failure to wear a seatbelt.	512,114
	Total	1,579,217

Thus exit for Liability Decision Timeout was the reason in 67.57% of cases exiting the portal at Stage 1 and 21.03% of all cases submitted on the portal.

Exit because liability was not admitted, or was admitted with an allegation of contributory negligence other than failure to wear a seatbelt, accounted for 32.43% of matters exiting the portal at Stage 1, and 10.09% of all cases submitted on the portal.

3,494,315, that is 68.87% of the total, proceeded to Stage 2.

Employers Liability

In the EL Portal 65,219 out of 142,984, that is 45.61% of claims lodged between 31 July 2013 and 31 August 2016, exited the portal by the end of Stage 1.

Of those 65,219 the reason for exit was

i.	Liability Decision Timeout	33,349
ii.	Liability not admitted or admitted with contributory negligence alleged	31,870
	Total	65,219

Thus exit for Liability Decision Timeout was the reason in 51.13% of cases exiting the portal at Stage 1, and 23.32% of all cases submitted on the portal.

Exit because liability was not admitted, or was admitted with an allegation of contributory negligence, accounted for 48.87% of matters exiting the portal at Stage 1, and 22.29% of all cases submitted on the portal.

77,765, that is 54.39% of the total, proceeded to Stage 2.

Public Liability

In the PL Portal 116,719 out of 203,383, that is 57.39% of claims lodged between 31 July 2013 and 31 August 2016, exited the portal by the end of Stage 1.

Of those 116,719 the reason for exit was

i.	Liability Decision Timeout	42,389
ii.	Liability not admitted or admitted with contributory negligence alleged	74,330
	Total	116,719

Thus exit for Liability Decision Timeout was the reason in 36.32% of cases exiting the portal at Stage 1, and 20.84% of all cases submitted on the portal.

Exit because liability was not admitted, or was admitted with an allegation of contributory negligence, accounted for 63.68% of matters exiting the portal at Stage 1, and 36.55% of all cases submitted on the portal.

86,664 that is 42.61% of the total, proceeded to Stage 2.

Where a party withdraws a Stage 2 offer the matter exits the portal (7.46 RTA, 7.43 Employers' Liability and Public Liability).

Where the defendant fails to make a counter-offer within the specified period the matter exits the portal (7.40 RTA, 7.37 Employers' Liability and Public Liability).

There are a number of instances where it is unclear what the sanction is for failure to comply with the protocol requirements, notably:-

- failure by defendant to acknowledge the CNF the next day, that is electronic acknowledgement of the CNF and sending the claim to the insurer within one working day where the CNF is received directly by the insured;

- failure by an insurer in an Employers' Liability case to provide wages information within 20 days where liability has been admitted;

- failure to pay settlement monies, including Stage 2 costs, within 10 days of settlement;

- failure to resubmit CNF to the insurer within 30 days where first CNF issued to the defendant (Employers' Liability and Public Liability only).

- defendant's failure to comply with obligation where an interim payment is requested and ISP submitted.

Failure to pay the settlement monies on time is a serious and frequent problem. One answer would be to impose an immediate 10% uplift on damages if payment is late with a further 1% uplift for each additional day's lateness. That would soon stop the problem.

Unreasonably causing matter to exit the portal

Paragraph 7.76 of RTA portal and 7.59 EL and PL portal provides that where a court considers that the claimant acted unreasonably in serving notice that the claim was unsuitable for the portal it will award no more that CPR 45.18 fixed costs.

Note that the provision in the old portal whereby a case exited the portal if a defendant failed to acknowledge the CNF within one day of receipt has gone.

Although 6.10 of the road traffic portal requires the defendant to send to the claimant an electronic acknowledgement the next day after receipt of the CNF, failure to do so no longer carries with it the penalty of the claim exiting the portal.

6.11 requires the defendant to complete the Insurer Response section of the CNF, the CNF Response, and send it to the claimant within 15 days and failure to do so does cause the matter to exit the portal (6.15(2)).

In the Employers' Liability and Public Liability portal the electronic acknowledgement requirement is at 6.10(a) and the CNF Response requirement is at 6.11 and again the matter does not exit the portal on the defendant's failure to acknowledge, but does exit on failure to send the CNF Response (3.13(2)).

My view is that it would be unreasonable for a claimant to exit the portal merely because a defendant had failed to send the acknowledgement and that that would result in the claimant recovering only portal fees, even though the defendant is in breach of a requirement.

If the matter exits due to the defendant's failure to complete and send the CNF Response, then the claimant gets Fixed Recoverable Costs.

There are at least three other areas where there is no sanction for breach of the rules:-

- failure by the claimant to re-submit CNF within 30 days of first issue to insurer in Employers' Liability and Public Liability claims;

- failure by the claimant to provide details of earnings claim within 20 days of the defendant making an admission of liability in an Employers' Liability claim;

- failure by the defendant to pay the settlement monies within 10 days of the agreed settlement, including Stage 2 fixed costs.

Unnecessary Part 7 proceedings

In *Uppal v Daudia* LTLPI 9 July 2012

the defendant successfully argued that the claimant had unreasonably removed the case from the portal.

This resulted in the claimant failing to recover over £20,000 in costs claimed and being ordered to pay the defendant's costs on the indemnity basis.

The claimant had argued that it was entitled to remove the claim from the portal because the defendant had not made an offer in response to the claimant's counter-offer within the total consideration period.

The Judge held that there was no such requirement and that the defendant was only required to respond to the claimant's first offer within the initial consideration period.

The defendant was awarded indemnity costs for having to defend unnecessarily Part 7 proceedings and the claimant was denied its claimed costs of over £20,000.00.

Technical non-compliance is not a ground to remove claim from portal

In *Jaykishan Patel v Fortis Insurance Ltd* LTL 11 January 2012 (2011) the defendant successfully argued that technical non-compliance with the portal was not a ground for a claimant to remove a case from the portal and recover Part 7 costs.

Here the defendant had used the A2A system to access the portal, which was unable to send acknowledgements of Claim Notification Forms, contrary to paragraph 6.10 of the portal protocol.

However within 48 hours the defendant had responded with the Full Insurer Response, accepting the claim and admitting responsibility. On the same day the claimant removed the matter from the portal.

The court held that this was not a ground for removal and that the claimant's conduct was unreasonable. Parties should not lightly remove claims from the portal and should never do it on technical grounds.

Once a party had communicated its decision not to continue with the portal process, then that process was at an end and the parties were not at liberty to resume it, even if Part 7 proceedings had not been commenced and even if the case was still physically in the portal.

Here the claimant was restricted to CPR 45.36 portal costs, compared with a Part 7 costs schedule claiming over £16,000. The defendant was awarded some of its costs of defending the claim, reflecting costs that would not have been incurred had the matter remained in the portal.

In *Ilahi v Usman, Manchester County Court 29 November 2012*

the court held that the claimant had behaved unreasonably in withdrawing its stage 2 portal offer and thus causing the matter to exit the portal and consequently should only get portal costs.

Although this is only a County Court decision by a Circuit Judge leave to appeal to the Court of Appeal was refused by Lord Justice Jackson who gave brief reasons as follows:-

"I agree with the analysis of the provisions of the Pre-action Protocol for Low Value PI Claims in RTAs made by Judge Platts. I also agree with the judge's application of those provision to the facts of this case."

This is not a Court of Appeal decision binding on other courts, but it is a decision with which Lord Justice Jackson has specifically agreed.

Throughout I refer to the wording of the portal at the relevant time.

Paragraph 7.55 of the portal at the time provided that if agreement was not reached during stage 2 then the claimant "must" send to the defendant a Court Proceedings Pack thus initiating the stage 3 procedure and under paragraph 7.61 the defendant must pay to the claimant its final offer of damages (in this case £2,400.00).

Instead the claimant withdrew its offer without explanation thus causing the matter to exit the portal under 7.39. At the time that paragraph read:-

"7.39 Where a party withdraws an offer made in the Stage 2 Settlement Pack Form after the total consideration period or further consideration period, the claim will no longer continue under this Protocol and the claimant may start proceedings under Part 7 of the CPR."

The matter went to a disposal hearing.

The District Judge awarded the claimant costs on the standard, open basis.

The District Judge failed to consider CPR 45.36 which provided:-

"(1) This rule applies where the claimant –

(a) does not comply with the process set out in the RTA Protocol; or

(b) elects not to continue with that process,

and starts proceedings under Part 7.

(2) Where a judgment is given in favour of the claimant but –

(a) the court determines that the defendant did not proceed with the process set out in the RTA Protocol because the claimant provided insufficient information on the Claim Notification Form;

(b) the court considers that the claimant acted unreasonably –

(i) by discontinuing the process set out in the RTA Protocol and starting proceedings under Part 7;

(ii) by valuing the claim at more than £10,000, so that the claimant did not need to comply with the RTA Protocol; or

(iii) except for paragraph (2)(a), in any other way caused the process in the RTA Protocol to be discontinued; or

(c) the claimant did not comply with the RTA Protocol at all despite the claim falling within the scope of the RTA Protocol;

the court may order the defendant to pay no more than the fixed costs in rule 45.29 together with the disbursements allowed in accordance with rule 45.30 and success fee in accordance with rule 45.31(3)."

On appeal the Judge held that by taking a step – withdrawing the offer – which would cause the matter automatically to exit the portal, the claimant was electing not to continue with the portal and therefore CPR 45.36 was engaged.

The Appeal Judge went on to hold that the claimant had acted unreasonably in withdrawing her offer and that her reason for doing so was to get much higher costs and that that was against "the spirit if not the letter of the Protocol".

In the alternative the same considerations should have applied if the court had exercised its discretion under CPR 44.3.

CPR 44.3 gives courts a very wide discretion in relation to costs and specifically provides that the court must have regard to all circumstances including the conduct of all the parties and that includes conduct before, as well as during, the proceedings and in particular the extent to which the parties followed the Practice Direction (Pre-Action Conduct) or any relevant Pre-Action Protocol.

The Appeal Judge held that the principles set out by the Court of Appeal in

Voice and Script International Ltd v Alghafar [2003] EWCA Civ 736

applied here. In that decision the Court of Appeal said that the court was free to impose small claims costs even if the matter had not been allocated and even if that approach was not expressly stated in the CPR "it follows from two essential principles, first, the discretionary nature of costs orders and second, the overriding requirement of proportionality in civil litigation generally".

Keeping it in the portal

In *Phillips v Willis [2016] EWCA Civ 401*

the Court of Appeal said that the starting point should be that any matter that has started in the portal should stay within it and not be transferred to the Small Claims Track, or any other track, unless absolutely necessary and the decision here to transfer the matter to the Small Claims Track was wrong in law and irrational.

"Once a case is within the RTA protocol, it does not automatically exit when the personal injury claim is settled. On the contrary, the RTA process is carefully designed to whittle down the disputes between the parties as the case passes through the various stages. It is to be expected that the sum in issue between the parties will be much smaller when the case reaches Stage 3 than it was back in Stage 1. The mere fact that the personal injury claim has been resolved is not specified as being a reason to exit from the RTA process."

Here the claimant was injured in a road traffic accident and liability was admitted and general damages for personal injury, together with other losses, were agreed and the only issue remaining in dispute related to car hire charges

The matter proceeded to Stage 3 of the portal by virtue of the claimant issuing a claim under Part 8 of the Civil Procedure Rules.

However when the parties attended the hearing the District Judge transferred the matter to the Small Claims Track and made directions and this was on the basis that the only issue remaining was car hire charges and that the matter should proceed under Part 7.

The claimant appealed to the Circuit Judge who upheld the decision of the District Judge.

However the Court of Appeal overturned the District Judge's decision. The Court of Appeal was critical of the District Judge saying that he had caused the parties to incur substantial extra costs as a result of the order which he made of his own motion in circumstances where both parties were happy to have the matter dealt with within Stage 3 of the portal.

The Court of Appeal said:-

"29. The costs which the district judge caused the parties to incur were totally disproportionate to the sum at stake. First, the parties would have to pay a further court fee of £335.00 as a result of the district judge's order. Secondly, the parties would incur the costs of complying with the district judge's elaborate directions."

The Court of Appeal then set out those extensive directions and pointed out that the remaining sum in dispute was just £462.00.

The Court of Appeal went on to say:-

"30. I dread to think what doing all that would have cost, but that was not the end of the matter. Both parties would need to instruct representatives to attend the further hearing. They would also have to write off the costs of the 9 April hearing [the Stage 3 Portal Hearing]. At the end of all that, the winning party would recover virtually no costs, because the case was now proceeding on the small claims track.

In my view, the district judge's decision taken on 9 April 2014 that further evidence was necessary to resolve the outstanding dispute between the parties was irrational. The district judge was not entitled to reach that conclusion."

The Court of Appeal recognized that the issue in the appeal is how courts should deal with low value road traffic accident claims where the personal injury element has been resolved and only a modest dispute about car hire charges remains.

Although this case involved the pre-31 July 2013 portal, the principle applies to the current portals.

The Court of Appeal gives a helpful summary of the Stage 1 and Stage 2 portal procedure and says that if the matter is not settled by the end of Stage 2, the "case then proceeds to Stage 3, which is litigation."

The Court of Appeal then went on to say:-

"9. At this point, Practice Direction 8B takes centre stage. PD 8B requires the claimant to issue proceedings in the County Court under CPR Part 8. The practice direction substantially modifies the Part 8 procedure so as to make it suitable for low value RTA claims where only quantum is in dispute. This modified procedure is designed to minimise the expenditure of further costs and in the process to deliver fairly rough justice. This is justified because the sums in issue are usually small, and it is not appropriate to hold a full blown trial. The evidence which the parties can rely upon at Stage 3 is limited to that which is contained in the court proceedings pack. A court assesses the items of damages which remain in dispute, either on paper or at a single "Stage 3 hearing"."

The Court of Appeal stated that the provision which was of key importance to the present case is paragraph 7 of Practice Direction 8B, relating to the Stage 3 process, which reads:-

"7.1. The parties may not rely upon evidence unless —

(1) it has been served in accordance with paragraph 6.4;

(2) it has been filed in accordance with paragraph 8.2 and 11.3; or

(3) (where the court considers that it cannot properly determine the claim without it), the court orders otherwise and gives directions.

7.2. Where the court considers that —

(1) further evidence must be provided by any party; and

(2) the claim is not suitable to continue under the Stage 3 procedure,

the court will order that the claim will continue under Part 7, allocate the claim to a track and give directions.

7.3. Where paragraph 7.2 applies the court will not allow stage 3 fixed costs."

The Court of Appeal dismissed as irrelevant the fact that the personal injury element of the claim had been settled and that that personal injury element was the gateway to the portal.

The court held that the District Judge had no power under paragraph 7.2 of Practice Direction 8B to direct that the case should proceed under Part 7, rather than Part 8.

As to when that paragraph could ever apply the Court of Appeal suggested that there might be cases involving complex issue of law or fact which are not suitable for resolution at a Stage 3 hearing.

The Court of Appeal also considered CPR 8.1(3) which provides:-

"The court may at any stage order the claim to continue as if the claimant had not used the Part 8 procedure and, if it does so, the court may give any directions it considers appropriate."

The Court of Appeal accepted that the language of that rule is wider than that in paragraph 7.2 of the Practice Direction but said that "CPR 8.1(3) cannot be used to subvert the protocol process".

The Court of Appeal said that in any event the District Judge here was relying upon paragraph 7.2 of the Practice Direction, and not CPR 8.1(3) but if they were wrong in that view then it would have been an impermissible exercise of the power under CPR 8.1(3) to transfer this particular case out of Part 8 and into Part 7 of the CPR.

I am grateful to Steven Turner, Counsel for the Respondent, for background information in relation to this matter.

Zero counter-offer with no explanation

Paragraph 7.41 of the RTA portal states:

"The defendant must also explain in the counter-offer why a particular head of damage has been reduced. The explanation will assist the claimant when negotiating a settlement and will allow both parties to focus on those areas of the claim that remain in dispute."

Thus making an offer of zero is not a breach of the protocol, rather it is the defendant's failure to provide an explanation for reducing that head of damages which is the breach.

In *Dickinson v Langford, Birkenhead County Court, 14 February 2013*

the defendant counter-offered zero for care and assistance, but there the judge held that that did not justify exiting the portal as that head of damage could have been dealt with by a witness statement and a Schedule of Loss.

This followed another unreported decision, Lamb v Gregory in 2011.

Consequently the claimant was restricted to portal costs and the defendant was awarded all of its post portal costs.

Clearly there is a difference between where an offer of zero is made and an explanation given, as compared with the situation where an offer of zero is made and no explanation is given.

In practice, to avoid the costs risks, a claimant should put the defendant on notice that it is in breach of the protocol and ask for information as to why a zero offer has been made to be given, so as to enable the claimant to negotiate a settlement and for both parties to focus on those areas of the claim that remain in dispute, as per paragraph 7.41.

What if the zero counter-offer is in relation to vehicle related damages?

There is potentially a different procedure for dealing with vehicle related damages. However, if the claimant has brought such a claim within the portal, as it is entitled to do, then the same situation applies.

The claimant is free **not** to bring such claim within the portal.

Paragraph 6.4 reads:

"6.4. A claim for vehicle related damages will ordinarily be dealt with outside the provisions of this Protocol under industry agreements between relevant organisations and insurers. Where there is a claim for vehicle related damages the claimant must:

(1) state in the CNF that the claim is being dealt with by a third party; or

(2)

(a) explain in the CNF that the legal representative is dealing with the recovery of these additional costs; and

(b) attach any relevant invoices and receipts to the CNF or explain when they are likely to be sent to the defendant."

There is a lot of misunderstanding about the situation of vehicle related damages in the portal.

Fresh evidence in Part 7 proceedings

It is clear from both *Phillips v Willis [2016] EWCA Civ 401 Mulholland v Hughes and Conjoined Appeals, No. AP20/15, Newcastle-upon-Tyne County Court, 18*

September 2015 that neither the claimant nor defendant can raise matters at stage 3 that have not been raised at stage 2.

It is not clear whether a court in dealing with the matter in Part 7 proceedings should allow in evidence not raised in stage 2, which would therefore not have been allowed in at stage 3 of the portal process.

The Civil Procedure Rules are silent on the point and on the face of it the court has discretion to allow such evidence in and arguably it must do so.

There is no authority on this issue, that is can or should a court dealing with an ex-portal matter under Part 7 allow in evidence which would not have been admissible at stage 3.

If the court does admit such evidence then it is a way of bypassing the portal process and avoiding the restriction on getting evidence in at stage 3 that had not been disclosed at stage 2.

Thus a party which has failed to disclose evidence at stage 2 simply exits the portal and issues Part 7 proceedings to get that evidence in.

That does not seem right and nor is it consistent with the message in *Phillips v Willis* that the starting point is that any matter that has started in the portal should stay in it wherever possible.

Transfer from Part 8 to Part 7 generally

At paragraph 11 of *Phillips v Willis* the Court of Appeal said:-

"It is important to note that the RTA process has an inexorable character. If a case falls within the parameters of the RTA process, the parties must take the designated steps or accept the consequences. The rules specify what those consequences are. The rules also specify when a case must remain in the RTA process, when it must drop out of the process, and when it may drop out of the process."

It is clear that, in an appropriate case, the court can order a Part 8 claim to continue under Part 7, allocate the claim to a track and give directions.

This is governed by Practice Direction 8B, paragraph 7.2:-

"**7.2** Where the court considers that –

(1) further evidence must be provided by any party; and

(2) the claim is not suitable to continue under the Stage 3 Procedure,

the court will order that the claim will continue under Part 7, allocate the claim to a track and give directions."

Note the word "and". The mere fact that further evidence may be desirable does not allow either the admission of that evidence, nor transfer to Part 7, a point made by the Court of Appeal in Phillips.

In paragraph 36 of the judgment the Court of Appeal considered the circumstances in which paragraph 7.2 might ever apply and referred to cases possibly involving complex areas of law or fact which are not suitable for resolution at a stage 3 hearing.

CPR 8.1(3) provides:-

"8.1(3) (3) The court may at any stage order the claim to continue as if the claimant had not used the Part 8 procedure and, if it does so, the court may give any directions it considers appropriate."

The Court of Appeal accepted that the language of that rule is wider than that in paragraph 7.2 of the Practice Direction but said that "CPR 8.1(3) cannot be used to subvert the protocol process".

The reality is that a claimant can at any time cause any matter to exit the portal and can then issue Part 7 proceedings.

Clearly such a party can be punished in costs for unreasonably exiting the portal and I discuss that elsewhere.

Although the power appears not yet to have been exercised, it seems that the court could strike out as an abuse of process a claim which has been unreasonably exited from the portal process and made subject to Part 7 proceedings.

Evidence that arises post-portal exit

It is not clear whether fresh evidence that only became available post-portal exit should be admitted in Part 7 proceedings, for example a flare-up of symptoms.

One argument is that no prejudice is caused and no harm done and that justice demands such evidence be admitted.

The counterargument is that finality is of key importance and that such evidence should only be allowed in if, post-trial and judgment in any other case, it would be sufficient to give grounds for an appeal and re-trial.

Can a matter be transferred from Part 7 to Part 8?

There is no authority on this point, which is not the same as the Court of Appeal holding that the initial transfer from Part 8 to Part 7 was invalid and must be quashed.

In practice the circumstances where a court might consider transferring the matter from Part 7 to Part 8 probably mean that the case could be dealt with by a disposal hearing, by the same judge in the same list as a stage 3 hearing.

Exiting the portal because the claim is over the upper limit

Supposing a claim is placed on the portal through a Claim Notification Form and subsequently it becomes apparent that the damages on a full liability basis would exceed £25,000.00, but that contributory negligence is almost bound to reduce it below that sum.

Thus let us say that it becomes apparent that the claim is worth £48,000.00 on a full liability basis but there is likely to be 50% contributory negligence.

By paragraph 1.2 (1) (a) of the RTA Portal, £25,000.00 is the "Protocol Upper Limit" if the accident occurred on or after 31 July 2013 and that is on a full liability basis, including pecuniary loss but excluding interest.

In the EL/PL Portal the relevant provision is paragraph 4.1(3).

By paragraph 4.3 of the RTA Portal "This Protocol ceases to apply where, at any stage, the claimant notifies the defendant that the claim has now been revalued at more than the Protocol Upper Limit."

Paragraph 4.2 of the EL/PL Portal is in identical terms.

Thus if the solicitor notifies the defendant accordingly the matter exits the portal. This must be done via the portal and not by post – see paragraph 5.1 of the RTA portal and paragraph 5.1 of the EL/PL portal.

Under paragraph 6.15(1) of the RTA Portal the claim will no longer continue in the portal if the defendant makes an admission of liability but alleges contributory negligence (other than in relation to the claimant's admitted failure to wear a seatbelt).

Under paragraph 6.13 (1) of the EL/PL Portal the claim will no longer continue in the portal if the defendant makes an admission of liability but alleges contributory negligence.

Assuming the matter exits the portal the issue is which cost regime applies, Fixed Recoverable Costs or open costs?

The figures in the Tables under the CPR refer to the amount that the case settles for, not the amount claimed, so on the face of it a claim exiting the portal and settling for £24,000.00 does indeed result in fixed costs under the Table.

However if a claim for £48,000.00 never enters the portal, as indeed it should not, and settles for £24,000.00, it is not within the Fixed Recoverable Costs Scheme.

At CPR 45.29E (4)(b) in relation to table 6C - which is the relevant one for EL/PL Fixed Recoverable Costs – states that "unless stated otherwise, a reference to "damages" means agreed damages", that is £24,000.00 in the example given here.

There is no doubt that for the purposes of assessing value for the portals the relevant figure is that on a full liability basis and thus, for example, a claim worth £48,000.00 on a full liability basis which is settled on a 50/50 basis resulting in payment of £24,000.00, should never have been on the portal and is subject to open, standard costs and not Fixed Recoverable Costs.

The relevant part of the protocol is paragraph 1.2 which reads:-

"1.2

(1) The 'Protocol upper limit' is—

(a) £25,000 where the accident occurred on or after 31 July 2013; or

(b) £10,000 where the accident occurred on or after 30 April 2010 and before 31 July 2013, on a full liability basis including pecuniary losses but excluding interest."

In relation to the Pre-Action Protocol for Low Value Personal Injury (Employers' Liability and Public Liability) claims, the relevant provision is paragraph 4.1 which provides:-

"Scope

4.1. This Protocol applies where—

(1) either –

(a) the claim arises from an accident occurring on or after 31 July 2013; or

(b) in a disease claim, no Letter of Claim has been sent to the defendant before 31 July 2013;

(2) the claim includes damages in respect of personal injury;

(3) the claimant values the claim at not more than £25,000.00 on a full liability basis including pecuniary losses but excluding interest ("the upper limit"); and

(4) if proceedings were started the small claims track would not be the normal track for that claim.

(Rule 26.6 provides that the small claims track is not the normal track where the value of any claim for damages for personal injuries (defined as compensation for pain, suffering and loss of amenity) is more than £1,000.)"

Thus there should be no problem. The law is clear.

Having said that, matters are not quite that simple.

If in fact the matter was put on either of the portals and then exits for whatever reason, including that the full liability value is above the upper limit, then fixed recoverable costs do indeed apply, except if the matter is allocated to the multi –track - see the Court of Appeal decision in Qader.

Note that under fixed recoverable costs the calculation of costs is based on the amount actually ordered by the court, or settled for, and not the amount on a full liability basis.

Let us take a claim which, at full liability, is worth £20,000.00 and which correctly goes on the portal but then exits because contributory negligence is alleged and then settles for £10,000.00. The basis for assessing fixed recoverable costs is £10,000.00 and not £20,000.00.

However if the case, on a full liability basis, is valued at above the protocol upper limit and is never put on the portal, then it never becomes subject to fixed recoverable costs.

Thus a claim is genuinely worth £30,000.00 on a full liability basis and so does not go on the portal. It settles for £15,000.00, which is within the portal and fixed recoverable costs limit. However it is not subject to fixed recoverable costs as it quite rightly never went on the portal.

Another problem can arise concerning why the matter settles for a lower sum. In the example that I have just given there is no problem if it is genuinely agreed that the matter was worth £30,000.00 on a full liability basis but settles for half due to a 50/50 split on liability.

However let us say that the matter settles for £15,000.00 but without any stated split on liability and the defendant then argues that the matter was never worth more than £25,000.00, even on a full liability basis.

If the defendant is successful then the claimant is likely to be restricted to portal costs only, whether or not the matter ever went on the portal. See for example *Ilahi v Usman, Manchester County Court, 29 November 2012* which involved unreasonably exiting the portal.

Although this is only a County Court decision by a Circuit Judge, leave to appeal to the Court of Appeal was refused by Lord Justice Jackson and thus it is not a Court of Appeal decision but it is one with which Lord Justice Jackson has specifically agreed.

Lisbie v SKS Scaffolding Ltd [2011] EWHC 90203

concerns a different point. What the court did there is to look at the actual agreed damages and find that they were within the small claims limit. The portal process does not apply to small claims and therefore no costs would be awarded.

That throws up an interesting point. The upper limit for the portals is governed by the value of a claim on a *full liability* basis but the lower limit appears to be the actual value, and not the value on a full liability basis.

Thus a £30,000 clam with 50% contributory negligence is out with the portal process as it is worth £30,000 on a full liability basis, but a £2,000 claim with 50% contributory negligence is valued at £1,000 and thus is a small claim.

This will become of much greater importance once the small claims limit in personal injury claims goes up on 1 October 2018.

Lisbie cannot properly be used to argue that the claim genuinely for £40,000.00 on a full liability basis but which settles for say £20,000.00 on a 50/50 basis is therefore retrospectively captured by the portal/fixed recoverable costs scheme. The rules, as set out above, are clear in that regard.

If, as a matter of law, fixed costs do apply then in my view CPR 44.2(4) has no application as fixed costs are covered by CPR 45 and the wording of CPR 45 is mandatory, although I accept that CPR 44 does not specifically exclude fixed costs cases from its remit.

I am reinforced in that view by CPR 45.13 which lays down a specific regime for allowing a claim in excess of fixed recoverable costs, but only if there are "exceptional circumstances making it appropriate to do so".

I look at this case in a little more detail below.

Proportionality

Proportionality does not apply to fixed costs claims, for obvious reasons. However if the matter is not a fixed costs claim then it does apply and costs are proportionate if they bear a reasonable relationship to "the sums in issue in the proceedings".

That leaves open the issue of whether a claim for £40,000.00, settled for £20,000.00 on a 50/50 liability split involves a sum in issue of £40,000.00, or a sum in issue of £20,000.00.

That may depend upon the circumstances of the case. For example if it was agreed from the beginning what the liability split should be – and in a seatbelt case for example that may well be the case – then it is the lower sum which is truly in issue and will be the basis on which proportionality applies.

Each case will depend upon its merits and this whole area is one of extreme complexity.

Claim never on portal

Supposing that it is generally agreed by both parties that the claim is worth over £25,000.00 and thus it is not put on the portal, but for whatever reason it then settles for below £25,000.00.

On the face of it there is no entitlement to costs of any kind. The matter has not been issued and it is settled law that pre-issue there is no entitlement to costs in the absence of contractual agreement.

The portal and pre-issue Fixed Recoverable Costs scheme is an exception to that general rule.

However unless a matter has been on the portal it cannot be subject to Fixed Recoverable Costs.

Thus in such a case the claimant would need to get the normal contractual agreement of the defendant to pay costs, and that is likely to be on the basis of fixed portal costs or Fixed Recoverable Costs.

If the defendant unequivocally said that the claim was worth over £25,000.00, then there may be an argument of equitable estoppel.

Such a claim, if an RTA matter is settled for £10,000 or less, would be subject to the old, but still living, predictive costs.

Offer over portal limit in portal claim

What happens if a matter is in the portal but the defendant then makes a pre-settlement pack offer, or indeed any other offer, for a sum above the portal limit? Does the matter fall out of the portal? What costs are payable?

The matter should exit the portal as it must be apparent at that stage that it is valued over the portal limit and exiting the portal will cause pre-issue Fixed Recoverable Costs to come into play.

That leaves the matter in the undecided territory of a claim above the maximum limit, currently £25,000.00, which has not been allocated.

With effect from 6 April 2017 the upper Fixed Recoverable Costs limit is removed by Rule 8 of The Civil Procedure (Amendment) Rules 2017, but it is not clear if that is retrospective or whether it changes, rather than merely clarifies, the law.

Industrial disease: matter settles against one of two defendants

In an industrial disease claim against two defendants commencing December 2013. Therefore the claim does not enter the portal.

The claim settles against one defendant only for £6,000.00 on a unilateral basis pre-issue and then the claimant decides to no longer pursue the second defendant due to causation arguments and only a small proportion of exposure. The claim concludes against the second defendant on a drop hands basis.

The claimant prepares a Bill of Costs for the defendant to consider as standard basis costs apply.

The defendant against which the claimant succeeds argues fixed costs apply under CPR 45.24.

The claimant genuinely pursued two defendants whom he believed exposed him to noise and was a reasonable step to take, albeit he only succeeds against one. Is the court likely to agree with the defendant or, if the claimant can recover costs, do standard basis costs apply?

My view is that the starting point is indeed that standard basis costs apply as the matter did not go onto the portal and nor could it have gone onto the portal, as disease claims where there is more than one employer defendant, are excluded by paragraph 4.3(6) of the Employers' Liability and Public Liability Portal.

However I can see the logic of the paying party's argument and the court has a very wide discretion in relation to costs and one option open to the court would be to assess the bill on the standard basis but then make an award equivalent to the fixed costs sum applicable had the matter gone onto the portal.

The counterargument to the defendants' contention is that the solicitor has acted sensibly and in accordance with the overriding objective in choosing not to pursue the claim against the second defendant.

The alternative is absurd, that is that you issue proceedings against the second defendant and immediately discontinue, with the only expense being the client's court fee as Qualified One-Way Costs Shifting would apply to the claim and therefore there would be no liability for the second defendant's costs on discontinuance by the solicitor.

That would then rule out any possibility of the matter having gone on the portal and thus would undermine the defendant's argument in relation to fixed costs.

In *Lisbie v SKS Scaffolding Ltd [2011] EWHC 90203,*

the court specifically dealt with fixed costs.

That was an RTA claim for £1,475.00 at full value but with 50% contributory negligence meaning that the actual agreed damages were £737.50 and thus below the minimum cost bearing limit of £1,000.00.

At paragraph 27 the judge considered the term "agreed damages";

"The term "agreed damages", used in CPR 45.7(2)(d), is not defined in the rules. In the absence of particular definition, words should be given their usual meanings. It seems to me that the usual meaning of "agreed damages" is the amount of compensation which the parties have agreed should be paid. It is not the value of the claim before any deduction for contributory negligence. That would be an artificial meaning."

Consequently it was held that the claim fell outside the Fixed Recoverable Costs scheme, as the damages were under £1,000.00 and therefore it was not cost bearing at all.

Ex-portal claims

Any type of claim, that is a road traffic accident claim, an employer's liability claim or a public liability claim that has been in the portal, but exits the portal, then goes in principle to the Fixed Recoverable Costs Scheme rather than to standard costs.

However there are two significant exceptions and they are in relation to industrial disease claims and any claim issued and then allocated to the multi-track.

Although industrial disease claims go onto the EL/PL Protocol to start with they never go to Fixed Recoverable Costs if they exit the portal.

The authority for that statement is CPR 45.29A (2) which states:-

"(2) This section does not apply to a disease claim which is started under the EL/PL Protocol."

CPR 45.29A is itself headed "Scope and Interpretation" and is the first part of section IIIA claims which no longer continue under the RTA or EL/PL Pre-Action Protocols – Fixed Recoverable Costs.

In other words section IIIA deals with former portal claims and CPR 45.29A sets out the scope of the Fixed Recoverable Costs Scheme and CPR 45.29A (2) specifically excludes from the scope of Fixed Recoverable Costs a disease claim which had started under the EL/PL Protocol.

As far as I am aware that is the only *type* of ex-portal claim that is not subject to Fixed Recoverable Costs.

Below I deal with ex-portal claims which are of a type that can go to Fixed Recoverable Costs, but which may or may not for various reasons.

The fact that a claim has ever been in the portal has significant consequences for the rest of that claim's life.

The starting point is that any claim which has ever been in any portal remains subject forever to Fixed Recoverable Costs. This can have unexpected consequences.

Before any claim is placed on any portal a senior lawyer should review it. Here are some reasons why. Non personal injury lawyers need to

start getting to grips with portal and fixed costs concepts, which are not always straightforward.

Fixed Costs do not apply to an Ex-Portal Claim allocated to the Multi-Track

In *Qader & Others v Esure Ltd & Khan v McGee [2016] EWCA Civ 1109, 16 November 2016*

the Court of Appeal held that the Fixed Recoverable Costs Regime does not apply to a claim started in the RTA Portal, which subsequently exited the portal and was allocated to the multi-track after proceedings were issued under Part 7 of the Civil Procedure Rules.

The result may be just, but the Court of Appeal accepted that to achieve that result it needed to add in words to the Civil Procedure Rules, even though there was no irrationality in the wording and no irrationality or inherent unfairness in giving effect to that clear wording.

The lead, and only judgment, was given by Lord Justice Briggs, author of the extremely controversial report proposing to abolish court hearings for most claims under £25,000. Here, as a judge, he re-writes the law passed by Parliament, to reflect what he thinks was the minister's and the Government's – not Parliament's mind – intention.

Whatever view you take this decision has significant constitutional implications. The full contribution of Lords Justice Gross and Tomlinson sitting on this appeal were: "I agree".

Well, I disagree, but I am bothering to explain why.

The Court of Appeal recognized that it could re-write what is secondary legislation if it is in conflict with the Human Rights Act, as Parliament has given it that power in the Human Rights Act itself.

Clearly restricting a winning party to fixed costs where they have incurred significant costs is a potential breach of the European Convention on Human Rights, scheduled to the Human Rights Act as it could constitute breach of, among other things the right to a fair trial under Article 6.

To go down that legitimate route would have called in to question the whole issue of fixed costs, no costs, QOCS, small claims etc. – so they chose not to.

The Court of Appeal set out the problem in the first paragraph of the judgment:-

"The issue turns mainly on the interpretation of section IIIA of CPR Part 45, read together with the relevant provisions of the RTA Protocol, and against the background of the process of consultation which preceded the making of that section in 2013, by way of implementation of fixed costs proposals in the reports of Jackson LJ in his Review of Civil Litigation Costs. It requires the court not merely to interpret the relevant provisions, but to consider whether they suffer from an obvious drafting mistake which can be put right so as to bring them into compatibility with the intention of the relevant legislator, namely the Civil Procedure Rule Committee, pursuant to the court's exceptional jurisdiction to do so as explained by Lord Nicholls in *Inco Europe Limited v First Choice Distribution* [2000] 1 WLR 586, at 592."

At paragraph 8 of the judgment the Court of Appeal made it clear that although this judgment concerns cases started within the RTA Portal "it is likely that that outcome will affect the interpretation and application of the similar and indeed overlapping provisions in Part 45 about the EL/PL Protocol."

At paragraph 9 the court said:-

"Viewed as a whole, at first sight section IIIA appears to make comprehensive provision for the recovery only of fixed costs in all cases which start but no longer continue under either of the relevant Protocols, subject only to expressly stated exceptions."

The only stated exception is disease claims – see CPR 45.29A(2).

The court recognised that claims allocated to the multi-track would involve higher, and often much higher, expenditure of costs than claims resolved in the fast-track.

"Just as personal injury claims for less than £1,000 are inappropriate for the Protocols, so are claims for more than £25,000, so that there is an initial apparent symmetry between the scope of the Protocols and the fast track, in terms of the amount claimed." (Paragraph 15 of the judgment).

The Court of Appeal then looked at three situations where an ex-portal matter was likely to be allocated to the multi-track:-

- where it is revalued at a substantially higher level than the upper portal limit of £25,000.00;
- where vehicle-related damages, excluded for portal purposes from the calculation of the upper limit, means that the claim is a substantial one;
- as here where there is an allegation of fraud.

The second example is an interesting one as that envisages a claim worth say £75,000.00 being suitable for the portal process, but not the fast track, which is a curious conclusion.

The court recognised that the wording of the rules means that fixed costs apply to all ex-portal claims:-

"On the contrary, the language of Part 45.29A and B, taken together, appears unambiguously to apply the fixed costs regime to all cases which start within the relevant Protocols but no longer continue under them."

The Court of Appeal recognised the existence of the escape provision in CPR 45.29J.

Nevertheless the Court of Appeal held that fixed costs should be "**automatically dis-applied** in any case allocated to the multi-track, without the requirement for the claimant to have recourse to Part 45.29J." (Paragraph 35). (My emphasis).

The court made the point that to achieve the escape under CPR 45.29J the claimant has to show exceptional circumstances.

Thus the law now is that **any** case allocated to the multi-track for any reason takes the case out of Fixed Recoverable Costs.

The Court of Appeal here accepted that the clear wording of the rules, and indeed the judgments of the two lower courts, where not "irrational or, on its face, ones which could not possibly have been intended, so as to compel the court to some other conclusion, even though it would, subject to relief under Part 45.29J, lead potentially, albeit only until the end of the trial, to rough justice for some claimants." (Paragraph 35(c) of the judgment).

Thus the Court of Appeal here, following no canons of construction known to me, have, apparently for policy reasons, altered the wording of the Civil Procedure Rules which have been approved by Parliament by way of a Statutory Instrument.

Traditionally courts could never have recourse to anything discussed in Parliament, but had to look at the wording of legislation as passed by Parliament and without considering any background material. That rule was changed by the case of *Pepper v Hart [1992] UKHL 3* which held that in certain exceptional circumstances Hansard, the official record of the proceedings of Parliament, could be referred to in order to assist in the interpretation of Parliamentary legislation.

This decision extends that principle enormously with the Court of Appeal taking the view that it is able to consider the process of consultation which proceeded the Civil Procedure Rules which "demonstrate that it was not in fact the intention of those legislating for this regime in 2013 that it should ever apply to a case allocated to the multi-track." (Paragraph 35(d) of the judgment).

The Court of Appeal went on to say:-

"A conclusion that it should so apply is a result which can only have arisen from a drafting mistake, which the court has power to put right by way of interpretation even if, as here, it requires the addition of words, rather than giving the words actually used a meaning different from their natural and ordinary meaning. It should normally be possible to understand procedure rules just by reading them in their context, but this is a rare case where something has gone wrong, and where the court's interpretative powers must be used, as far as possible, to bring the language into accord with what it is confident was the underlying intention."

This is dangerous territory. If a court is free at any time to change the wording of laws to reflect "the intention of those legislating" then where does it stop?

Members of Parliament voting for a particular provision may have very different intentions. For example Michael Foot and Enoch Powell joined together to defeat the reform of the House of Lords because Enoch Powell wanted it to stay exactly as it was and Michael Foot wanted it scrapped altogether.

How would a court interpret those totally different intentions?

The key in any legislation is the wording as passed by Parliament. To start looking at "the intention of those legislating" gives the court virtually unfettered power to rewrite laws as it wants.

It should also be remembered that the Rules Committee did allow for an escape– that is what CPR 45.29J is all about and therefore there is an existing mechanism to avoid injustice to claimants.

The Court of Appeal went on to say at paragraph 43:-

"But for what I am about to describe about the background to the making section IIIA of Part 45, it could not be said that it would have been irrational for the Rule Committee to have gone down the more rigorous route of making fixed costs applicable to all cases coming out of the relevant Protocols, leaving the combination of Part 45.29J and Part 36 to make appropriate provision, where necessary, for cases allocated to the multi-track. Looking simply and objectively at the CPR, that would appear to have been what the Rules Committee intended."

To justify rewriting the clear wording of the Civil Procedure Rules, and the clear intention, the Court of Appeal then looked at what it called "the history of the making of this fixed costs scheme".

It had this to say:-

"44. It is however clear that this rigorous approach is not what the Rule Committee actually intended. The original impetus for what became the fixed costs scheme for RTA and EL/PL Protocol cases came from Jackson LJ's reports. At appendix 5 to his December 2009 Final Report is to be found a composite table ("table B") of fixed costs for RTA, EL and PL cases which, although the amounts recoverable are different, has a structure which was eventually adopted almost precisely in Tables 6B, 6C and 6D in section IIIA of Part 45. His appendix is entitled "Fixed costs matrix for fast track personal injury claims".

45. In March 2011 the Ministry of Justice published a consultation paper headed "Solving disputes in the County Courts: creating a simpler, quicker and more proportionate system". At paragraphs 57 to 59 it noted Jackson LJ's proposals for a regime of fixed recoverable costs for personal injury cases in the fast track. At paragraph 83 it noted that Jackson LJ's fast track proposals could be used for cases which

left the RTA Protocol process, for example where liability was not admitted. Paragraph 60 made express reference to the fixed costs table B in appendix 5 to Jackson LJ's final report.

46. In February 2012 the Ministry of Justice published the Government's response to that consultation. At paragraph 15 it announced its intention to increase the financial limit of the RTA Protocol to £25,000. At paragraph 20 it announced the Government's intention to extend the system of fixed recoverable costs, subject to further discussions with stakeholders, in a way similar to that proposed by Jackson LJ in his review.

47. In a consultation letter dated 19 November 2012 Helen Grant MP, the Parliamentary Under-Secretary of State for Justice, notified stakeholders of the Government's intention to introduce a matrix of fixed recoverable costs which would apply to RTA, EL and PL claims which "exit the Protocol process" based on Jackson LJ's table B (in appendix 5 to his Final Report), but amended to take account of inflation since the table was produced in 2009, and reduced throughout by an amount intended to reflect the forthcoming ban on referral fees. She attached as Annexe B to her letter a tabular form of her proposals, modelled on Jackson LJ's template and containing, for the most part, precisely the amounts now set out in Table 6B for RTA Protocol cases. She sought further views and evidence on (among other things):

"The interface between proposed FRC arrangements within and outside the Protocols, particularly with regard to incentives for either side to exit."

48. In a further response to consultation dated 27 February 2013 the Ministry of Justice stated, at paragraph 6, that it was the Government's intention to ask the Rule Committee to make rules which would fix recoverable costs in low-value personal injury cases at the level set in Annexe A. Annexe A continued to adopt the structure of Jackson LJ's table B, with amounts which in all respects, save for slightly different trial advocacy fees, were later included in Table 6B for RTA Protocol cases.

49. Paragraph 87 of that response stated as follows:
"Respondents were unclear as to whether the proposals are intended to apply to multi-track, as well as fast track, cases between £10,001 and £25,000. There was a clear view (whilst still arguing the proposed levels of FRCSs were too low in any event) that any proposals should only apply to fast track cases. It

has always been the Government's intention that these proposals apply only to cases in the fast track and if a case falling out of the protocols is judicially determined to be suitable for multi-track, normal multi-track costs rules will apply"."

So the Court of Appeal now thinks it acceptable to take into account consultations, results of those consultations, ministerial letters etc.

On that basis virtually any piece of legislation could be reworded in any way the court wants at any time.

The Court of Appeal justifies its decision by saying "there is no evidence that the government ordered its policy in relation to multi-track cases falling outside the fixed costs regime…"

Legislation is that which is passed by Parliament. It is not necessarily Government policy. Parliament is a check on the Government.

More worryingly the Court of Appeal said:-

"Furthermore it is plain that the fixed amounts recoverable were all based upon a table originally proposed by Jackson LJ and then amended after consultation, specifically chosen for fast track cases."

So the Judiciary commission a report from a senior Judge on and then amend the wording of the Civil Procedure Rules so that the law is as that senior Judge recommended, and not as passed by Parliament.

It may well be that here the outcome is sensible and just. That is not the point. Parliament makes the laws and the courts interpret them.

The Court of Appeal here unequivocally add words to the Civil Procedure Rules. At paragraph 56 the court says:-

"The best way to give effect to that intention seems to me to be to add this phrase to Part 45.29B, after the reference to 45.29J:

"…and for so long as the claim is not allocated to the multi-track…""'

That has now been done by Rule 8.1 of the Civil Procedure (Amendment) Rules 2017, effective 6 April 2017.

The £25,000.00 limit

The Court of Appeal discussed this at some length – that is the fact that Part A of Table B has a reference to an upper damages ceiling of £25,000.00 and thus it remains unclear as to whether a claim which is for over £25,000.00, and where it is determined by settlement or judgment, but which is in the fast-track is subject to Fixed Recoverable Costs or not.

The Court of Appeal had this to say:-

"I recognise also that my proposed insertion of words to Part 45.29B does nothing about the anomaly represented by the £25,000 apparent damages ceiling in part A of Table 6B. It is unnecessary in the context of these appeals to do so, both because neither of them reached settlement prior to the issuing of Part 7 proceedings, and because the damages claimed are well below £25,000. It is a continuing anomaly which, in my view, the Rule Committee should be invited to consider at the earliest available opportunity. It may also be minded to devise an amendment to section IIIA of Part 45 which fully reflects the concerns which underlie this judgment, not merely in relation to the RTA Protocol, but to the EL/PL Protocol as well."

The irony of this is that Lord Justice Jackson has himself proposed that fixed costs should apply to the lower reaches of the multi-track and so it is strongly arguable that the Rules Committee have drafted the rules in accordance with Lord Justice Jackson's intentions, as they now are, and with which I agree entirely.

All of the talk about more work in the multi-track etc. making it unsuitable for a fixed costs regime is going to look a bit weak next July if Lord Justice Jackson proposes an extension of fixed costs, to include a significant number of multi-track claims.

Rule 8 of the Civil Procedure (Amendment) Rules 2017 removes the £25,000 upper limit for Fixed Recoverable Costs.

Complexity

Paragraph 7.76 of the RTA Portal reads:-

"General provisions

7.76 Where the claimant gives notice to the defendant that the claim is unsuitable for this Protocol (for example, because there are complex issues of fact or law) then the claim will no longer continue under this Protocol. However, where the court considers that the claimant acted unreasonably in giving such notice it will award no more than the fixed costs in rule 45.18."

Paragraph 7.59 of the EL/PL Portal is in similar terms with an additional, stated potential ground for the claim being unsuitable, namely that the claimants are contemplating applying for a Group Litigation Order.

Thus the claimant is able to exit either portal at any time by giving notice but will only get portal fixed costs if the giving of the notice was unreasonable.

There appears to be no case law insofar as the issue of exiting due to complexity, that is what degree of complexity makes exiting reasonable, or rather what lack of complexity makes exiting unreasonable.

It will certainly require a very high degree of complexity, especially considering the additions to the new Portals in that they envisage witness statements, multiple medical reports, non-medical expert reports and advice from specialist solicitor or Counsel within them.

Care needs to be taken. A matter which becomes complex because of the claimant's behaviour, or more likely the solicitor's behaviour, may still involve an unreasonable exit from the portal.

The starting point is that all cases within the specified jurisdictions, road traffic, Employers' Liability and Public Liability, where the damages are under £25,000.00 and where there is no defence and no allegation of contributory negligence, are suitable for the portal as the only issues would be those of quantum and in low value claims this should not be particularly complex.

Even where there is an allegation of contributory negligence in relation to failure to wear a seatbelt the matter stays within the RTA portal if that allegation is admitted.

Supposing a claimant instructs a forensic accountant to report on lost earnings, or on pension loss.

That may make the matter complex but was it reasonable to engage a forensic accountant on a sub £25,000.00 claim?

Does proportionality come into play, that is that it is disproportionate to instruct a forensic account in a low value claim?

I have heard of at least two cases where an insurer has instructed a forensic accountant to negotiate low value lost earnings separately to other damages claimed in stage 2 proceedings, causing the claimant to exit the portal.

That seems a tactical mistake by the claimant in any event as in the portal process there is no entitlement to obtain a forensic accountant's report and thus the report would not have been admitted in the portal process and thus would not have influenced any award.

Outside the portal if the claim goes to the fast-track and is subject to Fixed Recoverable Costs then it is most unlikely that the court would admit such a request, although it would be free to allocate the matter to the multi-track, in which case fixed costs do not apply – see *Qader & Others v Esure Ltd & Khan v McGee [2016] EWCA Civ 1109, 16 November 2016.*

In such circumstances the court could award the claimant only portal costs, on the basis that it was unreasonable to exit the portal in response to the defendant's conduct, as the defendant could never have got such evidence before the court in the portal.

Given that it was the defendant who commissioned the forensic accountant's report the court is likely in such a case to exercise its discretion to find that the claimant did not unreasonably exit the portal.

Any other outcome would result in the defendant getting a windfall due to its own misconduct.

Exiting the portal on apparent complexity grounds needs careful thought.

Such a case would remain subject to fixed costs on exiting the portal. If the court takes the view that it is sufficiently complex to be allocated to the multi-track then fixed costs do not apply following the Court of Appeal's decision in Qader.

The decision in *Qader* must be treated with considerable caution, partly because it is fairly obviously wrong, but more significantly because just 77 days later the Court of Appeal, while claiming to distinguish it, effectively disagreed with it in *Sharp v Leeds City Council*, 1 February 2017, [2017] EWCA Civ 33.

The Court of Appeal had this to say at paragraph 39

"But in my judgment the answer to this submission lies not in subjecting the fixed costs regime to an implied exception for PAD applications which exposed recalcitrant defendants to an altogether higher but variable level of recoverable costs liability, to be determined by assessment. Rather, the answer lies in the availability of an application under Part 45.29J, if exceptional circumstances can be shown or, for the future, in a recognition by the Rule Committee that the fixed costs regime needs to be kept under review, and defects in it remedied by adjustment of the fixed allowances where that can be shown to be justified."

This is in marked contrast to its own decision in *Qader and Others v Esure Services Limited* [2016] EWCA Civ 1109, 16 November 2016, that is 77 days earlier.

Any doubts about the Qader decision have been ended by Rule 8.1 of The Civil Procedure (Amendment) Rules 2017, effective 6 April 2017, which provides that fixed recoverable costs only apply " for as long as the case is not allocated to the multi-track."

Complexity – the statistics

Those who argue that their particular type of work is so complex that it is not suitable for the portal process have nothing to fear as a claimant's solicitor has the unfettered right to exit the portal on grounds of complexity at any stage.

Complexity was raised by claimant personal injury lawyers dealing with employers' liability work and public liability work, where the portals were extended to cover that work on 31 July 2013.

Figures for the first 37 months of the EL and PL portal process, that is up to 31 August 2016, show that:

- in the EL portal out of 142, 984 portal claims just 243 exited the process as too complex, that is one in every 588 claims or 0.17%;
- for public liability claims out of 203,383 portal claims just 295 exited the portal as too complex, that is one in every 689 or 0.145%.
- for road traffic matters of 5,073,532 portal claims, 9 937 exited due to complexity, that is one in every 510 claims, or 0.19%.

The more complex the case the more there is to be gained by quick and cheap resolution in the portal, as demonstrated by these figures.

Over a vast number of claims there is no significant difference between the percentages exiting for complexity in what are considered to be very simple cases, that is RTA matters, and much more complex cases, that is Employer's Liability and Public Liability.

Indeed the very simple category – RTA- has the highest percentage of exits due to complexity!

The argument for the immediate introduction of a portal process for all civil litigation without limitation on type of work or value of claim is unanswerable.

Group litigation orders

The fact that the claimants are considering applying for a group litigation order is given as a specific potential reason for exiting the EL/PL portal (paragraph 7.59).

What Fixed Recoverable Costs?

Table 6 is not entirely clear. In relation to pre-issue work for both portals it has three value bands, £1,000.00 to £5,000.00, £5,001.00 to £10,000.00 and £10,001.00 to £25,000.00. That suggests that Fixed Recoverable Costs cannot apply to a pre-issue settlement of over £25,000.00.

Any doubt has now been removed by Rule 8 of the Civil Procedure (Amendment) Rules 2017, which remove that upper limit.

However there is no such limit in relation to the next three categories, that is:-

- issued – post-issue pre-allocation
- issued – post-allocation pre-listing
- issued – post-listing pre-trial

Neither is there any such limit in relation to the final column of Table 6, that is trial advocacy fees.

If a road traffic accident matter settles post-issue then the structure of Fixed Recoverable Costs is that there is a fixed fee that increases through the stages, that is it is £1,160.00 for the first stage rising to £1,880.00 for the second stage and £2,655.00 for the third stage.

In addition, whatever stage has been reached, there are additional recoverable costs of 20% of damages. Thus the Fixed Recoverable Costs on a £50,000.00 matter settled just after issue would be £11,160.00 plus VAT and court fees etc.

Might we have the irony of a claimant lawyer arguing that Fixed Recoverable Costs apply and a defendant lawyer seeking to invoke the escape clause?

Sub-Contractors

A claim is submitted in the Public Liability Portal but the defendant denies liability and blames its sub-contractors. What happens?

The possibility of more than one defendant does not of itself cause the matter to drop out of the portal; that only applies in industrial disease cases – see EL/PL 4.3 (6).

If there has been a denial of liability then the matter no longer continues in the portal- see EL/PL 6.13. (3) which provides that if the defendant does not admit liability within 40 days in a PL matter (6.11 (b)) then it no longer continues under the portal.

By virtue of EL/PL 5.11 claims which no longer continue under the Protocol cannot re-enter it.

Consequently the matter is out of the portal and cannot go back in and must proceed in the usual way with a letter of claim against the sub-contractors and proceedings issued if appropriate.

What costs regime then applies – Fixed Recoverable Costs or open costs? On balance my view is Fixed Recoverable Costs as the matter, albeit now with additional parties, is ex-portal.

However if the claimant decides not to proceed against the original defendant, but rather only against the sub-contractor, then that goes into the portal as that particular matter would never have gone into the portal, and obviously could never have dropped out.

Supposing the claimant issues against both and then discontinues, or even does not serve the original defendant. That is then a claim against the sub-contractors only which could not have been issued in the portal and is now not ex-portal in relation to the remaining parties. Do open costs apply?

On balance I think that Fixed Recoverable Costs apply. Supposing the court allocates the matter to the Multi-Track because of a multiplicity of the defendants, then the matter against the sub-contractors will never have been in the portal and will be in the Multi-Track. The court will then decide that Fixed Recoverable Costs do not apply.

In either of these scenarios that would leave, in costs terms, the claimant who had made a mistake by failing to issue against the sub-contractors initially, in a better position than the solicitor who had got it right and issued the whole claim in the portal and thus bound her or himself forever to Fixed Recoverable Costs.

Causation

If causation is denied the matter exits the portal.

Paragraph 6.15 provides that the claim will no longer continue under the portal process if the defendant does not admit liablity (6.15(3)).

Paragraph 1.1(1) reads:-

"(1) 'admission of liability' means the defendant admits that—

> (a) the breach of duty occurred;
>
> (b) the defendant thereby caused some loss to the claimant, the nature and extent of which is not admitted; and
>
> (c) the defendant has no accrued defence to the claim under the Limitation Act 1980;"

Thus admission of liability has a broader, and more common sense, meaning than in the law generally.

Having said that, there have been a number of recent cases where the courts have said that a denial of causation is denial of liability.

Costs consequences

CPR 45.24(2) provides that in certain circumstances only portal costs and disbursements shall be recoverable even if the matter has been issued and judgment entered for the claimant.

Those circumstances are that the claimant:-

- failed to utilise the portal at all despite the claim being within its scope; or
- unreasonably exited the portal;
- valued the claim at over £25,000.00 in order to avoid the portal;

- failed to provide sufficient information on the Claim Notification Form thus causing the defendant not proceed within the portal;
- in any other way reasonably causes the portal process to end.

Postscript

As set out above the one type of ex-portal claim that does not go into Fixed Recoverable Costs is industrial disease claims.

Speaking on 23 May 2016 at the Westminster Legal Policy Forum Lord Justice Jackson delivered a paper and explained that the reason why such claims do not go into Fixed Recoverable Costs is not because they are unsuitable for such a scheme but rather "was due to historical accident".

"3.
THE ANOMALY – EMPLOYER'S LIABILITY DISEASE FAST TRACK CASES

3.1 Why were ELD cases omitted from fast track fixed costs? One striking omission from the fast track fixed costs regime for personal injury cases is ELD cases where liability is disputed. People sometimes ask how this omission came about and whether it arose because ELD cases are unsuitable for fixed costs. The answer is that ELD cases are not unsuitable for fixed costs. The explanation for their omission is set out in paragraphs 3.2 and 3.3 below.

3.2 Preparation of fixed costs grid for other fast track PI cases. During the Review, with the help of Professor Paul Fenn, the CJC and others I prepared grids of fixed costs for fast track RTA, ELA and PL cases: see FR appendix 5. In relation to ELD I wrote at FR chapter 5:

"5.29 ELD data. The participants in the CJC's facilitative meetings reached the following agreement about Professor Fenn's data on ELD cases:

'It is agreed that the Fenn figures i.e. the analysis by Fenn of the data by Professor Fenn himself.'

At the time of the facilitative meetings the only data available to Professor Fenn had come from the claimant side. These data did not separate out multi-defendant cases or take account of apportionment. Professor Fenn stated that he would obtain supplementary data from insurers on ELD cases.

5.30 I propose that Professor Fenn continues his collection and analysis of ELD data and provides that material both to myself and to the claimant and defendant representatives from the CJC facilitative meetings by 31st March 2010. Those representatives can then have a period of six weeks to submit their written observations on that material. I will consider those written observations and then recommend a matrix of fixed costs for fast track ELD cases, drawing on the advice of the Senior Costs Judge and the CJC."

3.3 Subsequent events. Unfortunately, the planned work programme had to be suspended during the run up to the 2010 General Election, because the work was deemed to be 'political'. After the election the new Coalition Government had to decide (amongst much else) what to do with the FR recommendations. The Government initially accepted most of the FR recommendations, but not the proposals concerning fixed costs. So there was no point in doing further work on ELD cases. There matters rested for the next two years. Meanwhile, as the result of an operation in April 2012 and subsequent medical treatment, I ceased to be involved in the implementation of the FR reforms during 2012/2013. In late 2012 the Government had a change of mind and decided to proceed with fixed costs for fast track PI cases. Rules were made giving effect to the grids of fixed costs set out in FR appendix 5, subject to modest adjustments. Those rules came into force on 31st July 2013 (four months after the other reforms recommended in my report). But no grid for ELD cases was available for consideration, because the work which had been deferred in 2010 was never done.

3.4 The CJC working group. A working group of the CJC is currently seeking to develop a grid of fixed recoverable costs for noise induced hearing loss claims on the fast track. These represent the majority of fast track ELD cases. (Mesothelioma and other more serious ELD claims proceed on the multi-track.)

3.5 I am setting out the background facts, in order to explain why ELD cases were omitted from the fixed costs grids introduced into CPR Part 45 in July 2013. The omission was due to historical accident. It was not because the task was insuperable."

Chapter 42

Admissions and Evidence

ADMISSIONS AND EVIDENCE

The definition of an admission of liability in paragraph 1.1(1) of the Road Traffic Accident portal means that the defendant admits:

- an accident occurred;
- the accident was caused by the defendant's breach of duty;
- the defendant caused some loss to the claimant, the nature and extent of which is not admitted;
- there is no Limitation Act 1980 defence.

The definition in paragraph 1.1 of the EL/PL Portal is the same, save that the defendant admits that a breach of duty, rather than an accident, has occurred.

Is an admission made by an insurer within the Portal binding on the parties in future court action?

It now looks as though no admission is binding.

In *Simmons v City Hospitals Sunderland NHS [2016] EWHC 2953 (QB) (13 October 2016)*

the Queen's Bench Division of the High Court allowed the defendant's application under CPR 3.1(7) to withdraw certain admissions made in its defence and to vary an order for judgment by consent which had been based on those admissions.

The claim had been brought in 2014 and the defendant made certain admissions of breach of duty and causation and judgment was entered by consent.

The defendant's solicitors then instructed an expert on the remaining issues and that expert considered that the defendant, an NHS Trust, had wrongly admitted breach of duty and causation.

Here the court held that it was right to exercise its discretion to allow the defendant to withdraw the admissions and to allow the judgment to be set aside.

The general principle was that final orders are intended to be final and could only be set aside by way of appeal and that the power given to the court by CPR 3.1(7) ought not to be exercised in a way which undermines that principle.

However here the court took into account:-

- it was highly relevant that the admissions which the defendant was seeking to withdraw related to issues which were inextricably intertwined with issues which remained in dispute (paragraph 22, judgment).

- the considerations which made it just to allow withdrawal of the defendant's admissions under CPR 14.1(5) were also relevant; in particular, that the litigation was still at an early stage and that the claimant could not be prejudiced by their withdrawal because the action had not been progressed on the basis of them (paragraph 23, judgment).

- there was also a material difference between a provisional opinion of the kind the expert made before the order and the opinion now shared by the defendant's other experts (paragraph 21, judgment).

The case of Malak v Nasim (Watford County Court, 15 January 2015) also suggests that admissions under the protocol and portal are not binding in subsequent proceedings.

The Defendant in this case had submitted a Claim Notification Form (CNF) via the RTA portal. The Claimant then responded, admitting liability for the claim. The Claimant's insurers subsequently dealt with the Defendant's claim for damages and made payments in respect of damages for personal injury and vehicle-related expenses.

The Claimant then submitted their own CNF via the portal for the same accident and the Defendant denied liability, causing the claim to exit the portal.

Proceedings were issued and the Defendant filed a defence which stated that the Claimant was bound by its own prior admission of liability. The action was struck out on a without notice application. The Claimant applied to set aside that order and for an order allowing it to resile from the admission.

District Judge Wood held that an admission by an insurer under the Protocol *is* a binding admission on the parties (not just the insurer), provided it is not withdrawn. This admission remains binding even after a case has left the Protocol.

However DJ Wood also held that an admission made under the RTA Protocol is binding only in relation to the claim within which it was made and is *not* an admission of liability in relation to a potential counterclaim. Therefore in this case the admission made by the insurers within the Portal was not binding on the Claimant.

DJ Wood's reasoning for her decision is set out at paragraphs 10.6 and 10.7 as follows:

> "10.6 I do not accept the Defendant's submission that the possibility of there being inconsistent decisions on liability in the claim in the portal and the claim brought by the Claimant is a good policy reason against reaching the conclusion I have reached. There is no judicial decision made within the portal scheme and therefore there will not be two inconsistent judicial decisions: the most that can be said is that the Claimant's insurers decided to settle a claim brought by the Defendant in circumstances where, had liability been contested, they might have been successful in resisting that claim. The aim of the portal scheme is to provide a quick and cheap resolution, on the basis of a swift appraisal of the strengths of the case, without (in many instances) a full consideration of the merits. The possibility that a full examination of the facts might yield a different result does not detract from the desirability and utility of the scheme.
>
> 10.7 It follows that I accept the Claimant's submission that the reason there is no such provision is that the admission made by his insurer in response to the Defendant's claim within the

portal is not binding on him within the present proceedings, and that it was therefore not necessary for him to apply to withdraw it."

However earlier cases suggest that admissions within the portal *can* be binding, even in a counterclaim, and that an admission "subject to causation" is still an admission.

In *Cavell v Transport for London [2015] EWHC 2283 (QB)*

the Queen's Bench Division of the High Court held that an admission of liability "subject to causation" is still an admission and thus the defendant needed permission to withdraw the admission.

Here, there was no explanation for the "mistake" which it was said had led to the admission and it was not in the interests of justice to permit the admission to be withdrawn.

The claimant was injured whilst riding his bicycle. The defendant admitted liability for the defective highway. The admission was stated to be "subject to causation". The claimant pleaded the admission in the Particulars of Claim and the defendant applied to withdraw the admission.

The judge said:-

"The final consideration within the list set out in the Practice Direction is the interests of the administration of justice.

It cannot be in those interests to permit the withdrawal of an admission made after mature reflection of a claim by highly competent professional advisors when there is not a scintilla of evidence to suggest that the admission was not properly made. Were it to be otherwise civil litigation on any sensible basis would be impossible."

Provision is made for withdrawal of a pre-action admission in CPR 14.1A (4)(b). The relevant Practice Direction reads:-

"7.1 An admission made under Part 14 may be withdrawn with the court's permission.

7.2 In deciding whether to give permission for an admission to be withdrawn, the court will have regard to all the circumstances of the case, including –

(a) the grounds upon which the applicant seeks to withdraw the admission including whether or not new evidence has come to light which was not available at the time the admission was made;

(b) the conduct of the parties, including any conduct which led the party making the admission to do so;

(c) the prejudice that may be caused to any person if the admission is withdrawn;

(d) the prejudice that may be caused to any person if the application is refused;

(e) the stage in the proceedings at which the application to withdraw is made, in particular in relation to the date or period fixed for trial;

(f) the prospects of success (if the admission is withdrawn) of the claim or part of the claim in relation to which the offer was made; and

(g) the interests of the administration of justice."

The case of *Ullah v Jon* (Croydon County Court, 20th March 2013) was another case arising out of an RTA that was submitted via the portal. The Claimant's insurers admitted liability and settled within the portal, despite the Claimant's solicitors having written to the insurer asking that they do nothing to prejudice the Claimant's position.

The Claimant subsequently issued proceedings claiming that the Defendant in this case was responsible for the same accident. A defence was filed by the Defendant before they were aware of the earlier admission by the Claimant's insurers. On finding out about the admission the Defendant's solicitors made an application to amend the defence to rely on the previous admission.

The District Judge was very clear that the Claimant in this case could *not* withdraw his admission of liability within the portal.

The Judge undertook a comprehensive review of the principles underlying the RTA Protocol and rejected an argument that the admissions were only binding in relation to the RTA Protocol and the compromise of a specific dispute. The Judge held that CPR 14 1B applied and therefore the admission could only be withdrawn with permission from the court.

However the Judge was clear in the decision that the Claimant should not be given permission to withdraw the admission on the basis that the Claimant "chose to give his insurers the contractual right to make these admissions on his behalf" (Paragraph 11) and that "in any road traffic accident one would say that this was a 50:50 chance of success" (Paragraph 13).

Further, there would be uncertainty and potential prejudice to the Defendant if the Claimant was allowed to resile from his admissions.

District Judge Parker made important observations about the public interest at paragraph 13:

"Then looking at the public interest, there has to be a public interest in bringing finality to proceedings, particularly where a rigorous and tightly drawn set of rules and regulations have been set up to enable quick and relatively cheap way of resolving these issues and I find that this is an important element in this case…"

The District Judge therefore allowed the Defendant's application for summary judgment.

Ullah v Jon highlights the need for clear communication between a litigant and their insurer and demonstrates that an admission by the insurer binds their insured.

Although in this case District Judge Parker had held that the admission of liability was binding, he stated in paragraph 10 that:

"It is probably fair to say that in some situations there may be grounds for applying to withdraw these admissions…"

However insurance companies often rely on the case of *Ullah v Jon* to argue that an admission of liability made by a Claimant's insurer binds a Claimant personally.

Interestingly the definition of defendant as set out in 1.1(10) of the RTA Protocol is as follows:

"(10) 'defendant' means the insurer of the person who is subject to the claim under this Protocol, unless the context indicates that it means—

(a) the person who is subject to the claim;

(b) the defendant's legal representative;

(c) the Motor Insurers' Bureau ('MIB'); or

(d) a person falling within the exceptions in section 144 of the Road Traffic Act 1988 (a "self-insurer");"

Therefore it appears that the Protocol is directed at the insurance company and not the insured. The Protocol does not, in this sense, have anything to do with the insured party, that is the Defendant, and any admission within the Protocol is limited to the Defendant's insurer's liability. Arguably an admission in respect of the portal extends to the potential liability of the insurance company only and therefore the insurance company alone is bound by it.

The CPR

Part 14 of the CPR deals with admissions and in particular Rule 14.1B deals with admissions under the RTA Protocol or the EL/PL Protocol and reads:

"(1) This rule applies to a pre-action admission made in a case to which the Pre-Action Protocol for Low Value Personal Injury Claims in Road Traffic Accidents ('the RTA Protocol') or the Pre-action Protocol for Low Value Personal Injury (Employers' Liability and Public Liability) Claims ('the EL/PL Protocol') applies.

(2) The defendant may, by giving notice in writing withdraw an admission of causation –

(a) before commencement of proceedings –

(i) during the initial consideration period (or any extension to that period) as defined in the relevant Protocol; or

(ii) at any time if the person to whom the admission was made agrees; or

(b) after commencement of proceedings –

(i) if all the parties to the proceedings consent; or

(ii) with the permission of the court.

(3) The defendant may, by giving notice in writing withdraw any other pre-action admission after commencement of proceedings –

(a) if all the parties to the proceedings consent; or

(b) with the permission of the court.

(4) An application under rule 14.1B(2)(b)(ii) or (3)(b) to withdraw a pre-action admission must be made in accordance with Part 23."

Rule 14.1B(2) deals with the withdrawal of an admission of liability under one of the relevant Protocols and states:

"(2) The defendant may, by giving notice in writing withdraw an admission of causation –

(a) before commencement of proceedings –

(i) during the initial consideration period (or any extension to that period) as defined in the relevant Protocol; or

(ii) at any time if the person to whom the admission was made agrees; or

(b) after commencement of proceedings –

(i) if all the parties to the proceedings consent; or

(ii) with the permission of the court."

Therefore if proceedings have not been commenced, then an admission within the RTA Protocol or the EL/PL Protocol may be withdrawn either during the initial consideration period or at any time provided that the person to whom the admission was made agrees (presumably an unlikely prospect).

Given that it seems unlikely that all parties to the proceedings will consent to the withdrawal of an admission of liability, most parties in this position would need to make an application to the court for permission to withdraw the admission.

If proceedings have been commenced and a party wishes to withdraw an admission other than one amounting to liability, then rule 14.1B(3) onwards states:

> "(3) The defendant may, by giving notice in writing withdraw any other pre-action admission after commencement of proceedings –
>
> > (a) if all the parties to the proceedings consent; or
> >
> > (b) with the permission of the court.
>
> (4) An application under rule 14.1B(2)(b)(ii) or (3)(b) to withdraw a pre-action admission must be made in accordance with Part 23."

Rule 14.1B is largely the same, in principle, as Rule 14.1A, which deals with admissions made before commencement of proceedings in other claims. Again, an admission of liability can be withdrawn before the commencement of proceedings, if the person to whom the admission was made agrees, or after commencement of proceedings, if all parties to the proceedings consent or with the permission of the court.

However DJ Wood made it clear at paragraph 10.3 in *Malak v Nasim* that "CPR14.1B governs any withdrawal of the admission made by the Claimant's insurers in their Response to the CNF, and CPR14.1A is not applicable."

This reasoning is based on the fact that the Rules Committee felt it necessary to make provisions specifically relating to the RTA and EL/PL Protocols. DJ Wood went on to state at paragraph 10.4(2) that:

"Although, once the claim comes out of the portal, it proceeds under the pre-action protocol for personal injury claims, nevertheless I do not consider that this brings the claim within the types of claim to which CPR14.1A applies by virtue of PD14. 1B makes provision for withdrawal of admissions after proceedings have begun. This necessarily means that the claim would have left the portal."

District Judge Wood gave permission to the parties in *Malak v Nasim* to "leapfrog" the appeal to the Court of Appeal. However the Defendant has elected not to.

Therefore, for now at least, this issue appears to remain open to debate.

Withdrawal of Pre-Action Admission

In *Woods v Days Health UK Ltd & Others [2016] EWHC 1079 (QB) 9 May 2016*

the Queen's Bench Division of the High Court refused a defendant permission to withdraw a pre-action admission of liability in a personal injury claim concerning an alleged faulty wheelchair.

Proceedings had been issued against several defendants and when the wheelchair supplier discovered that another defendant had fitted components in the wheelchair that supplier sought to withdraw its pre-action admission.

The judge considered that the real ground for the application was an increase in the value of the claim and that was a risk inherent in any personal injury claim and that was why it was sensible for a defendant to settle at an early stage.

An increase in the value of the claim did not justify resiling from the admission. The admission had been made after the defendant had inspected the wheelchair and had it taken reasonable steps to investigate the matter it would have discovered the modifications made by the other defendant. No new evidence had come to light.

The defendant had brought matters upon itself but would not be prejudiced as it could claim a contribution from the second defendant and the fact that summary judgment had been obtained against another defendant was not a reason to allow withdrawal of the admission. The liability of one defendant did not distinguish that of another when there were different causes of action.

Note that generally the court's permission is not required to withdraw a pre-action admission either before or after proceedings have been commenced, but in personal injury claims a pre-action admission may be withdrawn only if the other party consents or the court gives permission.

Evidence

This section does not deal with the law and Civil Procedure Rules relating to evidence, except in relation to special issues in the portal/fixed costs process.

In chapter 29 I deal extensively with the portal process, including the requirement that all evidence is served during the stage 2 process and the fact that fresh evidence cannot be introduced at the stage 3 process – see *Mulholland v Hughes and Conjoined Appeals, No. AP20/15, Newcastle-upon-Tyne County Court, 18 September 2015.*

Once substantive Part 7 proceedings are issued the court appears to have unlimited discretion in relation to what evidence it should allow in and there is no rule that states that because a claimant failed to adduce evidence in stage 2 it cannot then adduce that evidence in Part 7 proceedings, even though it would have been prevented from adducing that evidence in stage 3.

It would seem sensible to introduce such a rule.

The unanswered question is whether the court has a discretion in Part 7 proceedings to refuse to admit evidence on the basis that it was not adduced in stage 2.

It is clear that the court has a discretion to limit costs in those circumstances, for example by restricting the claimant to stage 1 and stage 2 costs on the basis that if the evidence had been served then, the matter could have been resolved in within the portal process.

Clearly all evidence should be served during stage 2 and a claimant risks the court subsequently exercising a discretion and not allowing the evidence in, although that seems unlikely.

In practice a claimant faced with a problem of not having adduced evidence in stage 2 is better to exit the portal and hope that the court will allow the evidence in but the claimant can still be punished in costs.

Obviously being punished in costs is preferable to losing the claim because the evidence is not allowed to be presented.

As to the court's attitude to costs some help may be gathered from the decision in *Nicole Chapman v Tameside Hospital NHS Foundation Trust, Bolton County Court, 15 June 2016, Case number B74YN281,* where the defendant was ordered to pay the claimant's costs where the claimant discontinued shortly before trial, following disclosure by the defendant of documents which it should have disclosed during the portal process.

Thus the suggestion there is that such evidence is admissible, even though it was not disclosed during the portal process, but it had severe consequences for the successful defendant who was ordered to pay the unsuccessful claimant's costs.

Specifically the defendant was ordered to pay all of the post stage 2 costs on the basis that the matter would have reached stage 2 in any event and that the extra, effectively wasted costs, were all of those incurred thereafter.

Failure to engage the portal process, or failure to provide sufficient information on the Claim Notification Form, or exiting the portal unreasonably or unreasonably in any other way causing the process in the relevant protocol to be discontinued, are all specifically provided for in CPR 45. 24 as giving the court a discretion to allow only fixed portal costs and disbursements.

Failure to adduce evidence in stage 2 which is subsequently sought to be relied upon, appears to come within the definition of a claimant acting unreasonably in a way that causes the process in the relevant protocol to be discontinued.

Thus the court has a discretion to disallow, or restrict the costs of the claimant.

The rationale of the Chapman decision must surely apply to a claimant who fails to disclose evidence when it should and on the face of it gives the court power to order the claimant to pay all of the defendant's additional costs caused by the matter exiting the portal.

However the Civil Procedure Rules specifically provide for the successful claimant's costs to be restricted in such circumstances, but do not specifically make provision for the claimant to be ordered to pay the defendant's costs.

However the court appears to have that power under its general, very wide, discretionary powers in relation to costs.

That throws up the question of whether, in those circumstances, the claimant can rely on the protection afforded by Qualified One-Way Costs Shifting.

The answer appears to be yes and such a situation is not one of the exceptions to QOCS, unless the court strikes the matter out as an abuse of process.

That is not the scenario that I am looking at but rather that the claimant wins, but has been guilty of unreasonable behaviour.

That is not an exception to QOCS.

However in such circumstances the defendant is likely to succeed in obtaining a wasted costs order against the claimant solicitor personally and such a costs order does not attract the protection of QOCS.

All of this is dealt with in great detail in my book – Qualified One-Way Costs Shifting, Section 57 and Set-Off, but it should be noted here that in any QOCS protected case the court makes a costs order in the usual way and what QOCS does is to prevent enforcement of that order unless certain specific exceptions apply.

Thus if an order is made against the claimant, but is not enforceable against the claimant, that does not prevent a defendant seeking to enforce that order by way of a wasted costs order against the claimant solicitor.

All of this becomes of much greater importance as the portal fixed costs scheme spreads to non-personal injury work, where issues of evidence may be more difficult and where it is far more likely that one or both parties will be Litigants in Person, and where QOCS does not apply.

In personal injury cases the defendant is virtually always an insurance company.

Chapter 43

CPR 45: the text

PART 45 - FIXED COSTS

This chapter contains Public Sector information licensed under the Open Government Licence V3.0.

Contents of this Part

Scope and interpretation	Rule 45.16
Application of fixed costs, and disbursements	Rule 45.17
Amount of fixed costs	Rule 45.18
Disbursements	Rule 45.19
Where the claimant obtains judgment for an amount more than the defendant's relevant Protocol offer	Rule 45.20
Settlement at Stage 2 where the claimant is a child	Rule 45.21
Settlement at Stage 3 where the claimant is a child	Rule 45.22
Where the court orders that the claim is not suitable to be determined under the Stage 3 Procedure and the claimant is a child	Rule 45.23
Settlement before proceedings are issued under Stage 3	Rule 45.23A
Additional advice on value of claim	Rule 45.23B
Failure to comply or electing not to continue with the relevant Protocol – costs consequences	Rule 45.24
Where the parties have settled after proceedings have started	Rule 45.25
Where the claimant obtains judgment for an amount equal to or less than the defendant's RTA Protocol offer	Rule 45.26
Adjournment	Rule 45.27
Account of payment of Stage 1 fixed costs	Rule 45.28
Costs-only application after a claim is started under Part 8 in accordance with Practice Direction 8B	Rule 45.29
IIIA CLAIMS WHICH NO LONGER CONTINUE UNDER THE RTA AND EL/PL PRE-ACTION PROTOCOLS – FIXED RECOVERABLE COSTS	
Scope and interpretation	Rule 45.29A
Application of fixed costs and disbursements – RTA Protocol	Rule 45.29B
Amount of fixed costs – RTA Protocol	Rule 45.29C
Application of fixed costs and disbursements – EL/PL Protocol	Rule 45.29D
Amount of fixed costs – EL/PL Protocol	Rule 45.29E
Defendants' costs	Rule 45.29F
Counterclaims under the RTA Protocol	Rule 45.29G
Interim applications	Rule 45.29H

I FIXED COSTS

Scope of this Section

45.1

(1) This Section sets out the amounts which, unless the court orders otherwise, are to be allowed in respect of legal representatives' charges.

(2) This Section applies where –

(a) the only claim is a claim for a specified sum of money where the value of the claim exceeds £25 and –

(i) judgment in default is obtained under rule 12.4(1);

(ii) judgment on admission is obtained under rule 14.4(3);

(iii) judgment on admission on part of the claim is obtained under rule 14.5(6);

(iv) summary judgment is given under Part 24;

(v) the court has made an order to strike out a defence under rule 3.4(2)(a) as disclosing no reasonable grounds for defending the claim; or

(vi) rule 45.4 applies;

(b) the only claim is a claim where the court gave a fixed date for the hearing when it issued the claim and judgment is given for the delivery of goods, and the value of the claim exceeds £25;

(c) the claim is for the recovery of land, including a possession claim under Part 55, whether or not the claim includes a claim for a sum of money and the defendant gives up possession, pays the amount claimed, if any, and the fixed commencement costs stated in the claim form;

(d) the claim is for the recovery of land, including a possession claim under Part 55, where one of the grounds for possession is arrears of rent, for which the court gave a fixed date for the hearing when it issued the claim and judgment is given for the possession of land (whether or not the order for possession is suspended on terms) and the defendant –

(i) has neither delivered a defence, or counterclaim, nor otherwise denied liability; or

(ii) has delivered a defence which is limited to specifying his proposals for the payment of arrears of rent;

(e) the claim is a possession claim under Section II of Part 55 (accelerated possession claims of land let on an assured shorthold tenancy) and a possession order is made where the defendant has neither delivered a defence, or counterclaim, nor otherwise denied liability;

(f) the claim is a demotion claim under Section III of Part 65 or a demotion claim is made in the same claim form in which a claim for possession is made under Part 55 and that demotion claim is successful; or

(g) a judgment creditor has taken steps under Parts 70 to 73 to enforce a judgment or order.

(Practice Direction 7B sets out the types of case where a court will give a fixed date for a hearing when it issues a claim.)

(3) No sum in respect of legal representatives' charges will be allowed where the only claim is for a sum of money or goods not exceeding £25.

(4) Any appropriate court fee will be allowed in addition to the costs set out in this Section.

(5) The claim form may include a claim for fixed commencement costs.

Amount of fixed commencement costs in a claim for the recovery of money or goods

45.2

(1) The amount of fixed commencement costs in a claim to which rule 45.1(2)(a) or (b) applies –

(a) will be calculated by reference to Table 1; and

(b) the amount claimed, or the value of the goods claimed if specified, in the claim form is to be used for determining the band in Table 1 that applies to the claim.

(2) The amounts shown in Table 4 are to be allowed in addition, if applicable.

TABLE 1

Fixed costs on commencement of a claim for the recovery of money or goods

Relevant band	Where the claim form is served by the court or by any method other than personal service by the claimant	Where – • the claim form is served personally by the claimant; and • there is only one defendant	Where there is more than one defendant, for each additional defendant personally served at separate addresses by the claimant
Where – • the value of the claim exceeds £25 but does not exceed £500	£50	£60	£15
Where – • the value of the claim exceeds £500 but does not exceed £1,000	£70	£80	£15

Fixed costs on commencement of a claim for the recovery of money or goods

Where – • the value of the claim exceeds £1,000 but does not exceed £5,000; or • the only claim is for delivery of goods and no value is specified or stated on the claim form	£80	£90	£15
Where – • the value of the claim exceeds £5,000	£100	£110	£15

When defendant only liable for fixed commencement costs

45.3 Where –

(a) the only claim is for a specified sum of money; and

(b) the defendant pays the money claimed within 14 days after being served with the particulars of claim, together with the fixed commencement costs stated in the claim form,

the defendant is not liable for any further costs unless the court orders otherwise.

Costs on entry of judgment in a claim for the recovery of money or goods

45.4 Where –

(a) the claimant has claimed fixed commencement costs under rule 45.2; and

(b) judgment is entered in a claim to which rule 45.1(2)(a) or (b) applies in the circumstances specified in Table 2, the amount to be included in the judgment for the claimant's legal representative's charges is the total of –

(i) the fixed commencement costs; and

(ii) ii) the relevant amount shown in Table 2.

TABLE 2

Fixed Costs on Entry of Judgment in a claim for the recovery of money or goods

	Where the amount of the judgment exceeds £25 but does not exceed £5,000	Where the amount of the judgment exceeds £5,000
Where judgment in default of an acknowledgment of service is entered under rule 12.4(1) (entry of judgment by request on claim for money only)	£22.00	£30.00
Where judgment in default of a defence is entered under rule 12.4(1) (entry of judgment by request on claim for money only)	£25.00	£35.00
Where judgment is entered under rule 14.4 (judgment on admission), or rule	£40.00	£55.00

Fixed Costs on Entry of Judgment in a claim for the recovery of money or goods

14.5 (judgment on admission of part of claim) and claimant accepts the defendant's proposal as to the manner of payment		
Where judgment is entered under rule 14.4 (judgment on admission), or rule 14.5 (judgment on admission of part of claim) and court decides the date or time of payment	£55.00	£70.00
Where summary judgment is given under Part 24 or the court strikes out a defence under rule 3.4(2)(a), in either case, on application by a party	£175.00	£210.00
Where judgment is given on a claim for delivery of goods under a regulated agreement within the meaning of the Consumer Credit Act 1974[1] and no other entry in this table applies	£60.00	£85.00

Amount of fixed commencement costs in a claim for the recovery of land or a demotion claim

45.5

(1) The amount of fixed commencement costs in a claim to which rule 45.1(2)(c), (d) or (f) applies will be calculated by reference to Table 3.

(2) The amounts shown in Table 4 are to be allowed in addition, if applicable.

TABLE 3

Fixed costs on commencement of a claim for the recovery of land or a demotion claim

	Where –	
Where the claim form is served by the court or by any method other than personal service by the claimant	• the claim form is served personally by the claimant; and • there is only one defendant	Where there is more than one defendant, for each additional defendant personally served at separate addresses by the claimant
£69.50	£77.00	£15.00

Costs on entry of judgment in a claim for the recovery of land or a demotion claim

45.6

(1) Where –

(a) the claimant has claimed fixed commencement costs under rule 45.5; and

(b) judgment is entered in a claim to which rule 45.1(2)(d) or (f) applies, the amount to be included in the judgment for the claimant's legal representative's charges is the total of –

(i) the fixed commencement costs; and

(ii) the sum of £57.25.

(2) Where an order for possession is made in a claim to which rule 45.1(2)(e) applies, the amount allowed for the claimant's legal representative's charges for preparing and filing –

(a) the claim form;

(b) the documents that accompany the claim form; and

(c) the request for possession,

is £79.50.

Miscellaneous fixed costs

45.7 Table 4 shows the amount to be allowed in respect of legal representative's charges in the circumstances mentioned.

TABLE 4

Miscellaneous Fixed Costs

For service by a party of any document other than the claim form required to be served personally including preparing and copying a certificate of service for each individual served	£15.00
Where service by an alternative method or at an alternative place is permitted by an order under rule 6.15 for each individual served	£53.25
Where a document is served out of the jurisdiction –	
(a) in Scotland, Northern Ireland, the Isle of Man or the Channel Islands;	£68.25
(b) in any other place	£77.00

Fixed enforcement costs

45.8 Table 5 shows the amount to be allowed in respect of legal representatives' costs in the circumstances mentioned. The amounts shown in Table 4 are to be allowed in addition, if applicable.

TABLE 5

Fixed Enforcement Costs	
For an application under rule 70.5(4) that an award may be enforced as if payable under a court order, where the amount outstanding under the award:	
exceeds £25 but does not exceed £250	£30.75
exceeds £250 but does not exceed £600	£41.00
exceeds £600 but does not exceed £2,000	£69.50
exceeds £2,000	£75.50
On attendance to question a judgment debtor (or officer of a company or other corporation) who has been ordered to attend court under rule 71.2 where the questioning takes place before a court officer, including attendance by a responsible representative of the legal representative	for each half hour or part, £15.00
On the making of a final third party debt order under rule 72.8(6)(a) or an order for the payment to the judgment creditor of money in court under rule 72.10(1)(b):	
if the amount recovered is less than £150	one-half of the amount recovered

otherwise	£98.50
On the making of a final charging order under rule 73.10(7)(a) or 73.10A(3)(a):	£110.00
	The court may also allow reasonable disbursements in respect of search fees and the registration of the order.
Where a certificate is issued and registered under Schedule 6 to the Civil Jurisdiction and Judgments Act 1982[2], the costs of registration	£39.00
Where permission is given under rule 83.13 to enforce a judgment or order giving possession of land and costs are allowed on the judgment or order, the amount to be added to the judgment or order for costs –	
(a) basic costs	£42.50
(b) where notice of the proceedings is to be to more than one person, for each additional person	£2.75
Where a writ of control as defined in rule 83.1(2)(k) is issued against any party	£51.75
Where a writ of execution as defined in rule 83.1(2)(l) is issued against any party	£51.75
Where a request is filed for the issue of a warrant of control under rule 83.15 for a sum exceeding £25	£2.25

Fixed Enforcement Costs

Where a request is filed for the issue of a warrant of delivery under rule 83.15 for a sum exceeding £25	£2.25
Where an application for an attachment of earnings order is made and costs are allowed under rule 89.10 or CCR Order 28, rule 10, for each attendance on the hearing of the application	£8.50

II ROAD TRAFFIC ACCIDENTS – FIXED RECOVERABLE COSTS

Scope and interpretation

45.9

(1) Subject to paragraph (3), this Section sets out the costs which are to be allowed in –

(a) proceedings to which rule 46.14(1) applies (costs-only proceedings); or

(b) proceedings for approval of a settlement or compromise under rule 21.10(2),

in cases to which this Section applies.

(2) This Section applies where –

(a) the dispute arises from a road traffic accident occurring on or after 6 October 2003;

(b) the agreed damages include damages in respect of personal injury, damage to property, or both;

(c) the total value of the agreed damages does not exceed £10,000; and

(d) if a claim had been issued for the amount of the agreed damages, the small claims track would not have been the normal track for that claim.

(3) This Section does not apply where –

(a) the claimant is a litigant in person; or

(b) Section III or Section IIIA of this Part applies.

(4) In this Section –

'road traffic accident' means an accident resulting in bodily injury to any person or damage to property caused by, or arising out of, the use of a motor vehicle on a road or other public place in England and Wales;

'motor vehicle' means a mechanically propelled vehicle intended for use on roads; and

'road' means any highway and any other road to which the public has access and includes bridges over which a road passes.

Application of fixed recoverable costs

45.10 Subject to rule 45.13, the only costs which are to be allowed are –

(a) fixed recoverable costs calculated in accordance with rule 45.11; and

(b) disbursements allowed in accordance with rule 45.12.

(Rule 45.13 provides for where a party issues a claim for more than the fixed recoverable costs.)

Amount of fixed recoverable costs

45.11

(1) Subject to paragraphs (2) and (3), the amount of fixed recoverable costs is the total of –

(a) £800;

(b) 20% of the damages agreed up to £5,000; and

(c) 15% of the damages agreed between £5,000 and £10,000.

(2) Where the claimant –

(a) lives or works in an area set out in Practice Direction 45; and

(b) instructs a legal representative who practises in that area,

the fixed recoverable costs will include, in addition to the costs specified in paragraph (1), an amount equal to 12.5% of the costs allowable under that paragraph.

(3) Where appropriate, VAT may be recovered in addition to the amount of fixed recoverable costs and any reference in this Section to fixed recoverable costs is a reference to those costs net of any such VAT.

Disbursements

45.12

(1) The court –

(a) may allow a claim for a disbursement of a type mentioned in paragraph (2); but

(b) will not allow a claim for any other type of disbursement.

(2) The disbursements referred to in paragraph (1) are –

(a) the cost of obtaining –

(i) medical records;

(ii) a medical report;

(iii) a police report;

(iv) an engineer's report; or

(v) a search of the records of the Driver Vehicle Licensing Authority;

(b) where they are necessarily incurred by reason of one or more of the claimants being a child or protected party as defined in Part 21 –

(i) fees payable for instructing counsel; or

(ii) court fees payable on an application to the court; or

(c) any other disbursement that has arisen due to a particular feature of the dispute.

Claims for an amount of costs exceeding fixed recoverable costs

45.13

(1) The court will entertain a claim for an amount of costs (excluding any success fee or disbursements) greater than the fixed recoverable costs but only if it considers that there are exceptional circumstances making it appropriate to do so.

(2) If the court considers such a claim appropriate, it may –

(a) summarily assess the costs; or

(b) make an order for the costs to be subject to detailed assessment.

(3) If the court does not consider the claim appropriate, it will make an order for fixed recoverable costs (and any permitted disbursements) only.

Failure to achieve costs greater than fixed recoverable costs

45.14

(1) This rule applies where –

(a) costs are assessed in accordance with rule 45.13(2); and

(b) the court assesses the costs (excluding any VAT) as being an amount which is less than 20% greater than the amount of the fixed recoverable costs.

(2) The court must order the defendant to pay to the claimant the lesser of –

(a) the fixed recoverable costs; and

(b) the assessed costs.

Costs of the costs-only proceedings or the detailed assessment

45.15 Where –

(a) the court makes an order for fixed recoverable costs in accordance with rule 45.13(3); or

(b) rule 45.14 applies, the court may –

(i) decide not to make an award of the payment of the claimant's costs in bringing the proceedings under rule 46.14; and

(ii) make orders in relation to costs that may include an order that the claimant pay the defendant's costs of defending those proceedings.

III THE PRE-ACTION PROTOCOLS FOR LOW VALUE PERSONAL INJURY CLAIMS IN ROAD TRAFFIC ACCIDENTS AND LOW VALUE PERSONAL INJURY (EMPLOYERS' LIABILITY AND PUBLIC LIABILITY) CLAIMS

Scope and interpretation

45.16

(1) This Section applies to claims that have been or should have been started under Part 8 in accordance with Practice Direction 8B ('the Stage 3 Procedure').

(2) Where a party has not complied with the relevant Protocol rule 45.24 will apply.

'The relevant Protocol' means

(a) the Pre-Action Protocol for Personal Injury Claims in Road Traffic Accidents ("the RTA Protocol"); or

(b) the Pre-action Protocol for Low Value Personal Injury Claims (Employers' Liability and Public Liability) Claims ('the EL/PL Protocol').

(3) A reference to 'Claim Notification Form' or Court Proceedings Pack is a reference to the form used in the relevant Protocol.

Application of fixed costs, and disbursements

45.17 The only costs allowed are –

(a) fixed costs in rule 45.18; and

(b) disbursements in accordance with rule 45.19; and

(c) where applicable, fixed costs in accordance with rule 45.23A or 45.23B.

Amount of fixed costs

45.18

(1) Subject to paragraph (4), the amount of fixed costs is set out in Tables 6 and 6A.

(2) In Tables 6 and 6A –

'Type A fixed costs' means the legal representative's costs;

'Type B fixed costs' means the advocate's costs; and

'Type C fixed costs' means the costs for the advice on the amount of damages where the claimant is a child.

(3) 'Advocate' has the same meaning as in rule 45.37(2)(a).

(4) Subject to rule 45.24(2) the court will not award more or less than the amounts shown in Tables 6 or 6A.

(5) Where the claimant –

(a) lives or works in an area set out in Practice Direction 45; and

(b) instructs a legal representative who practises in that area,

the fixed costs will include, in addition to the costs set out in Tables 6 or 6A, an amount equal to 12.5% of the Stage 1 and 2 and Stage 3 Type A fixed costs.

(6) Where appropriate, VAT may be recovered in addition to the amount of fixed costs and any reference in this Section to fixed costs is a reference to those costs net of any such VAT.

TABLE 6

Fixed costs in relation to the RTA Protocol			
Where the value of the claim for damages is not more than £10,000		**Where the value of the claim for damages is more than £10,000, but not more than £25,000**	
Stage 1 fixed costs	£200	Stage 1 fixed costs	£200
Stage 2 fixed costs	£300	Stage 2 fixed costs	£600
Stage 3 - Type A fixed costs	£250	Stage 3 - Type A fixed costs	£250
Stage 3 - Type B fixed costs	£250	Stage 3 - Type B fixed costs	£250
Stage 3 - Type C fixed costs	£150	Stage 3 - Type C fixed costs	£150

TABLE 6A

Fixed costs in relation to the EL/PL Protocol			
Where the value of the claim for damages is not more than £10,000		**Where the value of the claim for damages is more than £10,000, but not more than £25,000**	
Stage 1 fixed costs	£300	Stage 1 fixed costs	£300
Stage 2 fixed costs	£600	Stage 2 fixed costs	£1300
Stage 3 - Type A fixed costs	£250	Stage 3 - Type A fixed costs	£250

Stage 3 - Type B fixed costs	£250	Stage 3 - Type B fixed costs	£250
Stage 3 - Type C fixed costs	£150	Stage 3 - Type C fixed costs	£150

Disbursements

45.19

(1) Subject to paragraphs (2A) to (2E), the court –

(a) may allow a claim for a disbursement of a type mentioned in paragraphs (2) or (3); but

(b) will not allow a claim for any other type of disbursement.

(2) In a claim to which either the RTA Protocol or EL/PL Protocol applies, the disbursements referred to in paragraph (1) are –

(a) the cost of obtaining –

(i) medical records;

(ii) a medical report or reports or non-medical expert reports as provided for in the relevant Protocol;

(aa) Driver Vehicle Licensing Authority;

(bb) Motor Insurance Database;

(b) court fees as a result of Part 21 being applicable;

(c) court fees payable where proceedings are started as a result of a limitation period that is about to expire;

(d) court fees in respect of the Stage 3 Procedure; and

(e) any other disbursement that has arisen due to a particular feature of the dispute.

(2A) In a soft tissue injury claim to which the RTA Protocol applies, the only sums (exclusive of VAT) that are recoverable in respect of the cost of obtaining a fixed cost medical report or medical records are as follows—

(a) obtaining the first report from an accredited medical expert selected via the MedCo Portal: £180;

(b) obtaining a further report where justified from an expert from one of the following disciplines—

(i) Consultant Orthopaedic Surgeon (inclusive of a review of medical records where applicable): £420;

(ii) Consultant in Accident and Emergency Medicine: £360;

(iii) General Practitioner registered with the General Medical Council: £180; or

(iv) Physiotherapist registered with the Health and Care Professions Council: £180;

(c) obtaining medical records: no more than £30 plus the direct cost from the holder of the records, and limited to £80 in total for each set of records required. Where relevant records are required from more than one holder of records, the fixed fee applies to each set of records required;

(d) addendum report on medical records (except by Consultant Orthopaedic Surgeon): £50; and

(e) answer to questions under Part 35: £80.

(2B) Save in exceptional circumstances, no fee may be allowed for the cost of obtaining a report to which paragraph (2A) applies where the medical expert—

(a) has provided treatment to the claimant;

(b) is associated with any person who has provided treatment; or

(c) proposes or recommends treatment that they or an associate then provide.

(2C) The cost of obtaining a further report from an expert not listed in paragraph (2A)(b) is not fixed, but the use of that expert and the cost must be justified.

(2D) Where appropriate, VAT may be recovered in addition to the cost of obtaining a fixed cost medical report or medical records.

(2E) In this rule, 'accredited medical expert', 'associate', 'associated with', 'fixed cost medical report' 'MedCo' and 'soft tissue injury claim' have the same meaning as in paragraph 1.1(A1), (1A), (10A), (12A), and (16A), respectively, of the RTA Protocol.

(3) In a claim to which the RTA Protocol applies, the disbursements referred to in paragraph (1) are also the cost of—

(a) an engineer's report; and

(b) a search of the records of the—

(i) Driver Vehicle Licensing Authority; and

(ii) Motor Insurance Database.

Where the claimant obtains judgment for an amount more than the defendant's relevant Protocol offer

45.20

Where rule 36.29(1)(b) or (c) applies, the court will order the defendant to pay –

(a) where not already paid by the defendant, the Stage 1 and 2 fixed costs;

(b) where the claim is determined –

(i) on the papers, Stage 3 Type A fixed costs;

(ii) at a Stage 3 hearing, Stage 3 Type A and B fixed costs; or

(iii) at a Stage 3 hearing and the claimant is a child, Type A, B and C fixed costs; and

(c) disbursements allowed in accordance with rule 45.19.

Settlement at Stage 2 where the claimant is a child

45.21

(1) This rule applies where –

(a) the claimant is a child;

(b) there is a settlement at Stage 2 of the relevant Protocol; and

(c) an application is made to the court to approve the settlement.

(2) Where the court approves the settlement at a settlement hearing it will order the defendant to pay –

(a) the Stage 1 and 2 fixed costs;

(b) the Stage 3 Type A, B and C fixed costs; and

(c) disbursements allowed in accordance with rule 45.19.

(3) Where the court does not approve the settlement at a settlement hearing it will order the defendant to pay the Stage 1 and 2 fixed costs.

(4) Paragraphs (5) and (6) apply where the court does not approve the settlement at the first settlement hearing but does approve the settlement at a second settlement hearing.

(5) At the second settlement hearing the court will order the defendant to pay –

(a) the Stage 3 Type A and C fixed costs for the first settlement hearing;

(b) disbursements allowed in accordance with rule 45.19; and

(c) the Stage 3 Type B fixed costs for one of the hearings.

(6) The court in its discretion may also order –

(a) the defendant to pay an additional amount of either or both the Stage 3 –

(i) Type A fixed costs;

(ii) Type B fixed costs; or

(b) the claimant to pay an amount equivalent to either or both the Stage 3 –

(i) Type A fixed costs;

(ii) Type B fixed costs.

Settlement at Stage 3 where the claimant is a child

45.22

(1) This rule applies where –

(a) the claimant is a child;

(b) there is a settlement after proceedings are started under the Stage 3 Procedure;

(c) the settlement is more than the defendant's relevant Protocol offer; and

(d) an application is made to the court to approve the settlement.

(2) Where the court approves the settlement at the settlement hearing it will order the defendant to pay –

(a) the Stage 1 and 2 fixed costs;

(b) the Stage 3 Type A, B and C fixed costs; and

(c) disbursements allowed in accordance with rule 45.19.

(3) Where the court does not approve the settlement at the settlement hearing it will order the defendant to pay the Stage 1 and 2 fixed costs.

(4) Paragraphs (5) and (6) apply where the court does not approve the settlement at the first settlement hearing but does approve the settlement at the Stage 3 hearing.

(5) At the Stage 3 hearing the court will order the defendant to pay –

(a) the Stage 3 Type A and C fixed costs for the settlement hearing;

(b) disbursements allowed in accordance with rule 45.19; and

(c) the Stage 3 Type B fixed costs for one of the hearings.

(6) The court in its discretion may also order –

(a) he defendant to pay an additional amount of either or both the Stage 3 –

(i) Type A fixed costs;

(ii) Type B fixed costs; or

(b) the claimant to pay an amount equivalent to either or both of the Stage 3 –

(i) Type A fixed costs;

(ii) Type B fixed costs.

(7) Where the settlement is not approved at the Stage 3 hearing the court will order the defendant to pay the Stage 3 Type A fixed costs.

Where the court orders that the claim is not suitable to be determined under the Stage 3 Procedure and the claimant is a child

45.23 Where –

(a) the claimant is a child; and

(b) at a settlement hearing or the Stage 3 hearing the court orders that the claim is not suitable to be determined under the Stage 3 Procedure,

the court will order the defendant to pay –

(i) the Stage 1 and 2 fixed costs; and

(ii) the Stage 3 Type A, B and C fixed costs.

Settlement before proceedings are issued under Stage 3

45.23A Where—

(a) there is a settlement after the Court Proceedings Pack has been sent to the defendant but before proceedings are issued under Stage 3; and

(b) the settlement is more than the defendant's relevant Protocol offer,

the fixed costs will include an additional amount equivalent to the Stage 3 Type A fixed costs.

Additional advice on the value of the claim

45.23B Where—

(a) the value of the claim for damages is more than £10,000;

(b) an additional advice has been obtained from a specialist solicitor or from counsel;

(c) that advice is reasonably required to value the claim,

the fixed costs may include an additional amount equivalent to the Stage 3 Type C fixed costs.

Failure to comply or electing not to continue with the relevant Protocol – costs consequences

45.24

(1) This rule applies where the claimant –

(a) does not comply with the process set out in the relevant Protocol; or

(b) elects not to continue with that process,

and starts proceedings under Part 7.

(2) Subject to paragraph (2A), where a judgment is given in favour of the claimant but –

(a) the court determines that the defendant did not proceed with the process set out in the relevant Protocol because the claimant provided insufficient information on the Claim Notification Form;

(b) the court considers that the claimant acted unreasonably –

(i) by discontinuing the process set out in the relevant Protocol and starting proceedings under Part 7;

(ii) by valuing the claim at more than £25,000, so that the claimant did not need to comply with the relevant Protocol; or

(iii) except for paragraph (2)(a), in any other way that caused the process in the relevant Protocol to be discontinued; or

(c) the claimant did not comply with the relevant Protocol at all despite the claim falling within the scope of the relevant Protocol,

the court may order the defendant to pay no more than the fixed costs in rule 45.18 together with the disbursements allowed in accordance with rule 45.19.

(2A) Where a judgment is given in favour of the claimant but the claimant did not comply with the process in paragraph 6.3A(2) of the RTA Protocol, the court may not order the defendant to pay the claimant's costs and disbursements save in exceptional circumstances.

(3) Where the claimant starts proceedings under paragraph 7.28 of the RTA Protocol or paragraph 7.26 of the EL/PL Protocol and the court orders the defendant to make an interim payment of no more than the interim payment made under paragraph 7.14(2) or (3) of the RTA Protocol or paragraph 7.17(2) or (3) of the EL/PL Protocol the court will, on the final determination of the proceedings, order the defendant to pay no more than –

(a) the Stage 1 and 2 fixed costs; and

(b) the disbursements allowed in accordance with rule 45.19.

Where the parties have settled after proceedings have started

45.25

(1) This rule applies where an application is made under rule 45.29 (costs-only application after a claim is started under Part 8 in accordance with Practice Direction 8B).

(2) Where the settlement is more than the defendant's relevant Protocol offer the court will order the defendant to pay –

(a) the Stage 1 and 2 fixed costs where not already paid by the defendant;

(b) the Stage 3 Type A fixed costs; and

(c) disbursements allowed in accordance with rule 45.19.

(3) Where the settlement is less than or equal to the defendant's relevant Protocol offer the court will order the defendant to pay –

(a) the Stage 1 and 2 fixed costs where not already paid by the defendant; and

(b) disbursements allowed in accordance with rule 45.19.

(4) The court may, in its discretion, order either party to pay the costs of the application.

Where the claimant obtains judgment for an amount equal to or less than the defendant's relevant Protocol offer

45.26 Where rule 36.29(1)(a) applies, the court will order the claimant to pay –

(a) where the claim is determined –

(i) on the papers, Stage 3 Type A fixed costs; or

(ii) at a hearing, Stage 3 Type A and B fixed costs;

(b) any Stage 3 disbursements allowed in accordance with rule 45.19.

Adjournment

45.27 Where the court adjourns a settlement hearing or a Stage 3 hearing it may, in its discretion, order a party to pay –

(a) an additional amount of the Stage 3 Type B fixed costs; and

(b) any court fee for that adjournment.

Account of payment of Stage 1 and Stage 2 fixed costs

45.28 Where a claim no longer continues under the relevant Protocol the court will, when making any order as to costs including an order for fixed recoverable costs under Section II or Section IIIA of this Part, take into account the Stage 1 and Stage 2 fixed costs that have been paid by the defendant.

Costs-only application after a claim is started under Part 8 in accordance with Practice Direction 8B

45.29

(1) This rule sets out the procedure where –

(a) the parties to a dispute have reached an agreement on all issues (including which party is to pay the costs) which is made or confirmed in writing; but

(b) they have failed to agree the amount of those costs; and

(c) proceedings have been started under Part 8 in accordance with Practice Direction 8B.

(2) Either party may make an application for the court to determine the costs.

(3) Where an application is made under this rule the court will assess the costs in accordance with rule 45.22 or rule 45.25.

(4) Rule 44.5 (amount of costs where costs are payable pursuant to a contract) does not apply to an application under this rule.

SECTION IIIA CLAIMS WHICH NO LONGER CONTINUE UNDER THE RTA OR EL/PL PRE-ACTION PROTOCOLS – FIXED RECOVERABLE COSTS

Scope and interpretation

45.29A

(1) Subject to paragraph (3), this section applies where a claim is started under—

(a) the Pre-Action Protocol for Low Value Personal Injury Claims in Road Traffic Accidents ('the RTA Protocol'); or

(b)the Pre-Action Protocol for Low Value Personal Injury (Employers' Liability and Public Liability) Claims ('the EL/PL Protocol'),

but no longer continues under the relevant Protocol or the Stage 3 Procedure in Practice Direction 8B.

(2) This section does not apply to a disease claim which is started under the EL/PL Protocol.

(3) Nothing in this section shall prevent the court making an order under rule 45.24.

Application of fixed costs and disbursements – RTA Protocol

45.29B

Subject to rules 45.29F, 45.29G, 45.29H and 45.29J, if, in a claim started under the RTA Protocol, the Claim Notification Form is submitted on or after 31st July 2013, the only costs allowed are—

(a) the fixed costs in rule 45.29C;

(b) disbursements in accordance with rule 45.29I.

Amount of fixed costs – RTA Protocol

45.29C

(1) Subject to paragraph (2), the amount of fixed costs is set out in Table 6B.

(2) Where the claimant—

(a) lives or works in an area set out in Practice Direction 45; and

(b) instructs a legal representative who practises in that area,
the fixed costs will include, in addition to the costs set out in Table 6B, an amount equal to 12.5% of the costs allowable under paragraph (1) and set out in Table 6B.

(3) Where appropriate, VAT may be recovered in addition to the amount of fixed recoverable costs and any reference in this Section to fixed costs is a reference to those costs net of VAT.

(4) In Table 6B—

(a) in Part B, 'on or after' means the period beginning on the date on which the court respectively—

(i) issues the claim;

(ii) allocates the claim under Part 26; or

(iii) lists the claim for trial; and

(b) unless stated otherwise, a reference to 'damages' means agreed damages; and

(c) a reference to 'trial' is a reference to the final contested hearing.

TABLE 6B

Fixed costs where a claim no longer continues under the RTA Protocol				
A. If Parties reach a settlement prior to the claimant issuing proceedings under Part 7				
Agreed damages	At least £1,000, but not more than £5,000	More than £5,000, but not more than £10,000	More than £10,000, but not more than £25,000	
Fixed costs	The greater of— (a) £550; or (b) the total of— (i) £100; and (ii) 20% of the damages	The total of— (a) £1,100; and (b) 15% of damages over £5,000	The total of— (a) £1,930; and (b) 10% of damages over £10,000	
B. If proceedings are issued under Part 7, but the case settles before trial				
Stage at which case is settled	On or after the date of issue, but prior to the date of allocation under Part 26	On or after the date of allocation under Part 26, but prior to the date of listing	On or after the date of listing but prior the date of trial	
Fixed costs	The total of— (a) £1,160; and (b) 20% of the damages	The total of— (a) £1,880; and (b) 20% of the damages	The total of— (a) £2,655; and (b) 20% of the damages	
C. If the claim is disposed of at trial				

Fixed costs	The total of— (a) £2,655; and (b) 20% of the damages agreed or awarded; and (c) the relevant trial advocacy fee			
D. Trial advocacy fees				
Damages agreed or awarded	Not more than £3,000	More than £3,000, but not more than £10,000	More than £10,000, but not more than £15,000	More than £15,000
Trial advocacy fee	£500	£710	£1,070	£1,705

Application of fixed costs and disbursements – EL/PL Protocol

45.29D Subject to rules 45.29F, 45.29H and 45.29J, in a claim started under the EL/PL Protocol the only costs allowed are—

(a) fixed costs in rule 45.29E; and

(b) disbursements in accordance with rule 45.29I.

Amount of fixed costs – EL/PL Protocol

45.29E

(1) Subject to paragraph (2), the amount of fixed costs is set out—

(a) in respect of employers' liability claims, in Table 6C; and

(b) in respect of public liability claims, in Table 6D.

(2) Where the claimant—

(a) lives or works in an area set out in Practice Direction 45; and

(b) instructs a legal representative who practises in that area,

the fixed costs will include, in addition to the costs set out in Tables 6C and 6D, an amount equal to 12.5% of the costs allowable under paragraph (1) and set out in table 6C and 6D.

(3) Where appropriate, VAT may be recovered in addition to the amount of fixed recoverable costs and any reference in this Section to fixed costs is a reference to those costs net of VAT.

(4) In Tables 6C and 6D—

(a) in Part B, 'on or after' means the period beginning on the date on which the court respectively—

(i) issues the claim;

(ii) allocates the claim under Part 26; or

(iii) lists the claim for trial; and

(b) unless stated otherwise, a reference to 'damages' means agreed damages; and

(c) a reference to 'trial' is a reference to the final contested hearing.

TABLE 6C

Fixed costs where a claim no longer continues under the EL/PL Protocol – employers' liability claims				
A. If Parties reach a settlement prior to the claimant issuing proceedings under Part 7				
Agreed damages	At least £1,000, but not more than £5,000	More than £5,000, but not more than £10,000	More than £10,000, but not more than £25,000	
Fixed costs	The total of— (a) £950; and (b) 17.5% of the damages	The total of— (a) £1,855; and (b) 12.5% of damages over £5,000	The total of— (a) £2,500; and (b) 10% of damages over £10,000	
B. If proceedings are issued under Part 7, but the case settles before trial				
Stage at which case is settled	On or after the date of issue, but prior to the date of allocation under Part 26	On or after the date of allocation under Part 26, but prior to the date of listing	On or after the date of listing but prior the date of trial	
Fixed costs	The total of— (a) £2,630; and (b) 20% of the damages	The total of— (a) £3,350; and (b) 25% of the damages	The total of— (a) £4,280; and (b) 30% of the damages	
C. If the claim is disposed of at trial				

Fixed costs	The total of— (a) £4,280; (b) 30% of the damages agreed or awarded; and (c) the relevant trial advocacy fee			
D. Trial advocacy fees				
Damages agreed or awarded	Not more than £3,000	More than £3,000, but not more than £10,000	More than £10,000, but not more than £15,000	More than £15,000
Trial advocacy fee	£500	£710	£1,070	£1,705

TABLE 6D

<table>
<tr><th colspan="5">Fixed costs where a claim no longer continues under the EL/PL Protocol – public liability claims</th></tr>
<tr><td colspan="5">A. If Parties reach a settlement prior to the claimant issuing proceedings under Part 7</td></tr>
<tr><td>Agreed damages</td><td>At least £1,000, but not more than £5,000</td><td>More than £5,000, but not more than £10,000</td><td>More than £10,000, but not more than £25,000</td><td></td></tr>
<tr><td>Fixed costs</td><td>The total of—
(a) £950; and
(b) 17.5% of the damages</td><td>The total of—
(a) £1,855; and
(b) 10% of damages over £5,000</td><td>The total of—
(a) £2,370; and
(b) 10% of damages over £10,000</td><td></td></tr>
<tr><td colspan="5">B. If proceedings are issued under Part 7, but the case settles before trial</td></tr>
<tr><td>Stage at which case is settled</td><td>On or after the date of issue, but prior to the date of allocation under Part 26</td><td>On or after the date of allocation under Part 26, but prior to the date of listing</td><td>On or after the date of listing but prior the date of trial</td><td></td></tr>
<tr><td>Fixed costs damages</td><td>The total of—
(a) £2,450; and
(b) 17.5% of the damages</td><td>The total of—
(a) £3,065; and
(b) 22.5% of the damages</td><td>The total of—
(a) £3,790; and
(b) 27.5% of the damages</td><td></td></tr>
</table>

C. If the claim is disposed of at trial				
Fixed costs	The total of— (a) £3,790; (b) 27.5% of the damages agreed or awarded; and (c) the relevant trial advocacy fee			
D. Trial advocacy fees				
Damages agreed or awarded	Not more than £3,000	More than £3,000, but not more than £10,000	More than £10,000, but not more than £15,000	More than £15,000
Trial advocacy fee	£500	£710	£1,070	£1,705

Defendants' costs

45.29F

(1) In this rule—

(a) paragraphs (8) and (9) apply to assessments of defendants' costs under Part 36;

(b) paragraph (10) applies to assessments to which the exclusions from qualified one way costs shifting in rules 44.15 and 44.16 apply; and

(c) paragraphs (2) to (7) apply to all other cases under this Section in which a defendant's costs are assessed.

(2) If, in any case to which this Section applies, the court makes an order for costs in favour of the defendant—

(a) the court will have regard to; and

(b) the amount of costs order to be paid shall not exceed,

the amount which would have been payable by the defendant if an order for costs had been made in favour of the claimant at the same stage of the proceedings.

(3) For the purpose of assessing the costs payable to the defendant by reference to the fixed costs in Table 6, Table 6A, Table 6B, Table 6C and Table 6D, "value of the claim for damages" and "damages" shall be treated as references to the value of the claim.

(4) For the purposes of paragraph (3), "the value of the claim" is—

(a) the amount specified in the claim form, excluding—

(i) any amount not in dispute;

(ii) in a claim started under the RTA Protocol, any claim for vehicle related damages;

(iii) interest;

(iv) costs; and

(v) any contributory negligence;

(b) if no amount is specified in the claim form, the maximum amount which the claimant reasonably expected to recover according to the statement of value included in the claim form under rule 16.3; or

(c) £25,000, if the claim form states that the claimant cannot reasonably say how much is likely to be recovered.

(5) Where the defendant—

(a) lives, works or carries on business in an area set out in Practice Direction 45; and

(b) instructs a legal representative who practises in that area,
the costs will include, in addition to the costs allowable under paragraph (2), an amount equal to 12.5% of those costs.

(6) Where an order for costs is made pursuant to this rule, the defendant is entitled to disbursements in accordance with rule 45.29I

(7) Where appropriate, VAT may be recovered in addition to the amount of any costs allowable under this rule.

(8) Where, in a case to which this Section applies, a Part 36 offer is accepted, rule 36.20 will apply instead of this rule.

(9) Where, in a case to which this Section applies, upon judgment being entered, the claimant fails to obtain a judgment more advantageous than the defendant's Part 36 offer, rule 36.21 will apply instead of this rule.

(10) Where, in a case to which this Section applies, any of the exceptions to qualified one way costs shifting in rules 44.15 and 44.16 is established, the court will assess the defendant's costs without reference to this rule.

Counterclaims under the RTA Protocol

45.29G

(1) If in any case to which this Section applies—

(a) the defendant brings a counterclaim which includes a claim for personal injuries to which the RTA Protocol applies;

(b) the counterclaim succeeds; and

(c) the court makes an order for the costs of the counterclaim,

rules 45.29B, 45.29C, 45.29I, 45.29J, 45.29K and 45.29L shall apply.

(2) Where a successful counterclaim does not include a claim for personal injuries—

(a) the order for costs of the counterclaim shall be for a sum equivalent to one half of the applicable Type A and Type B costs in Table 6;

(b) where the defendant—

(i) lives, works, or carries on business in an area set out in Practice Direction 45; and

(ii) instructs a legal representative who practises in that area,

the costs will include, in addition to the costs allowable under paragraph (a), an amount equal to 12.5% of those costs;

(c) if an order for costs is made pursuant to this rule, the defendant is entitled to disbursements in accordance with rule 45.29I; and

(d)where appropriate, VAT may be recovered in addition to the amount of any costs allowable under this rule.

Interim applications

45.29H

(1) Where the court makes an order for costs of an interim application to be paid by one party in a case to which this Section applies, the order shall be for a sum equivalent to one half of the applicable Type A and Type B costs in Table 6 or 6A.

(2) Where the party in whose favour the order for costs is made—

(a) lives, works or carries on business in an area set out in Practice Direction 45; and

(b) instructs a legal representative who practises in that area,
the costs will include, in addition to the costs allowable under paragraph (1), an amount equal to 12.5% of those costs.

(3) If an order for costs is made pursuant to this rule, the party in whose favour the order is made is entitled to disbursements in accordance with rule 45.29I.

(4) Where appropriate, VAT may be recovered in addition to the amount of any costs allowable under this rule.

Disbursements

45.29I

(1) Subject to paragraphs (2A) to (2E), the court—

(a) may allow a claim for a disbursement of a type mentioned in paragraphs (2) or (3); but

(b) will not allow a claim for any other type of disbursement.

(2) In a claim started under either the RTA Protocol or the EL/PL Protocol, the disbursements referred to in paragraph (1) are—

(a) the cost of obtaining medical records and expert medical reports as provided for in the relevant Protocol;

(b) the cost of any non-medical expert reports as provided for in the relevant Protocol;

(c) the cost of any advice from a specialist solicitor or counsel as provided for in the relevant Protocol;

(d) court fees;

(e) any expert's fee for attending the trial where the court has given permission for the expert to attend;

(f) expenses which a party or witness has reasonably incurred in travelling to and from a hearing or in staying away from home for the purposes of attending a hearing;

(g) a sum not exceeding the amount specified in Practice Direction 45 for any loss of earnings or loss of leave by a party or witness due to attending a hearing or to staying away from home for the purpose of attending a hearing; and

(h) any other disbursement reasonably incurred due to a particular feature of the dispute.

(2A) In a soft tissue injury claim started under the RTA Protocol, the only sums (exclusive of VAT) that are recoverable in respect of the cost of obtaining a fixed cost medical report or medical records are as follows—

(a) obtaining the first report from an accredited medical expert selected via the MedCo Portal: £180;

(b) obtaining a further report where justified from an expert from one of the following disciplines—

(i) Consultant Orthopaedic Surgeon (inclusive of a review of medical records where applicable): £420;

(ii) Consultant in Accident and Emergency Medicine: £360;

(iii) General Practitioner registered with the General Medical Council: £180; or

(iv) Physiotherapist registered with the Health and Care Professions Council: £180;

(c) obtaining medical records: no more than £30 plus the direct cost from the holder of the records, and limited to £80 in total for each set of records required. Where relevant records are required from more than one holder of records, the fixed fee applies to each set of records required;

(d) addendum report on medical records (except by Consultant Orthopaedic Surgeon): £50; and

(e) answer to questions under Part 35: £80.

(2B) Save in exceptional circumstances, no fee may be allowed for the cost of obtaining a report to which paragraph (2A) applies where the medical expert—

(a) has provided treatment to the claimant;

(b) is associated with any person who has provided treatment; or

(c) proposes or recommends treatment that they or an associate then provide.

(2C) The cost of obtaining a further report from an expert not listed in paragraph (2A)(b) is not fixed, but the use of that expert and the cost must be justified.

(2D) Where appropriate, VAT may be recovered in addition to the cost of obtaining a fixed cost medical report or medical records.

(2E) In this rule, 'accredited medical expert', 'associate', 'associated with', 'fixed cost medical report' 'MedCo' and 'soft tissue injury claim' have the same meaning as in paragraph 1.1(A1), (1A), (10A), (12A), and (16A), respectively, of the RTA Protocol.

(3) In a claim started under the RTA Protocol only, the disbursements referred to in paragraph (1) are also the cost of—

(a) an engineer's report; and

(b) a search of the records of the—

(i) Driver Vehicle Licensing Authority; and

(ii) Motor Insurance Database.

Claims for an amount of costs exceeding fixed recoverable costs

45.29J

(1) If it considers that there are exceptional circumstances making it appropriate to do so, the court will consider a claim for an amount of costs (excluding disbursements) which is greater than the fixed recoverable costs referred to in rules 45.29B to 45.29H.

(2) If the court considers such a claim to be appropriate, it may—

(a) summarily assess the costs; or

(b) make an order for the costs to be subject to detailed assessment.

(3) If the court does not consider the claim to be appropriate, it will make an order—

(a) if the claim is made by the claimant, for the fixed recoverable costs; or

(b) if the claim is made by the defendant, for a sum which has regard to, but which does not exceed the fixed recoverable costs,

and any permitted disbursements only.

Failure to achieve costs greater than fixed recoverable costs

45.29K

(1) This rule applies where—

(a) costs are assessed in accordance with rule 45.29J(2); and

(b) the court assesses the costs (excluding any VAT) as being an amount which is in a sum less than 20% greater than the amount of the fixed recoverable costs.

(2) The court will make an order for the party who made the claim to be paid the lesser of—

(a) the fixed recoverable costs; and

(b) the assessed costs.

Costs of the costs-only proceedings or the detailed assessment

45.29L

(1) Where—

(a) the court makes an order for costs in accordance with rule 45.29J(3); or

(b) rule 45.29K applies,

the court may—

(i) decide not to award the party making the claim the costs of the costs only proceedings or detailed assessment; and

(ii) make orders in relation to costs that may include an order that the party making the claim pay the costs of the party defending those proceedings or that assessment.

IV SCALE COSTS FOR CLAIMS IN THE INTELLECTUAL PROPERTY ENTERPRISE COURT

Scope and interpretation

45.30

(1) Subject to paragraph (2), this Section applies to proceedings in the Intellectual Property Enterprise Court.

(2) This Section does not apply where –

(a) the court considers that a party has behaved in a manner which amounts to an abuse of the court's process; or

(b) the claim concerns the infringement or revocation of a patent or registered design or registered trade mark the validity of which has been certified by a court or by the Comptroller-General of Patents, Designs and Trade Marks in earlier proceedings.

(3) The court will make a summary assessment of the costs of the party in whose favour any order for costs is made. Rules 44.2(8), 44.7(b) and Part 47 do not apply to this Section.

(4) 'Scale costs' means the costs set out in Table A and Table B of the Practice Direction supplementing this Part.

Amount of scale costs

45.31

(1) Subject to rule 45.32, the court will not order a party to pay total costs of more than –

(a) £50,000 on the final determination of a claim in relation to liability; and

(b) £25,000 on an inquiry as to damages or account of profits.

(2) The amounts in paragraph (1) apply after the court has applied the provision on set off in accordance with rule 44.12(a).

(3) The maximum amount of scale costs that the court will award for each stage of the claim is set out in Practice Direction 45.

(4) The amount of the scale costs awarded by the court in accordance with paragraph (3) will depend on the nature and complexity of the claim.

(4A) Subject to assessment where appropriate, the following may be recovered in addition to the amount of the scale costs set out in Practice Direction 45 – Fixed Costs—

(a) court fees;

(b) costs relating to the enforcement of any court
order; and

(c) wasted costs.

(5) Where appropriate, VAT may be recovered in addition to the amount of the scale costs and any reference in this Section to scale costs is a reference to those costs net of any such VAT.

Summary assessment of the costs of an application where a party has behaved unreasonably

45.32 Costs awarded to a party under rule 63.26(2) are in addition to the total costs that may be awarded to that party under rule 45.31.

V FIXED COSTS: HM REVENUE AND CUSTOMS

Scope, interpretation and application

45.33

(1) This Section sets out the amounts which, unless the court orders otherwise, are to be allowed in respect of HM Revenue and Customs charges in the cases to which this Section applies.

(2) For the purpose of this Section –

(a) 'HMRC Officer' means a person appointed by the Commissioners under section 2 of the Commissioners for Revenue and Customs Act 2005[3] and authorised to conduct County Court proceedings for recovery of debt under section 25(1A)[4] of that Act;

(b) 'Commissioners' means commissioners for HMRC appointed under section 1 of the Commissioners for Revenue and Customs Act 2005;

(c) 'debt' means any sum payable to the Commissioners under or by virtue of an enactment or under a contract settlement; and

(d) 'HMRC charges' means the fixed costs set out in Tables 7 and 8 in this Section.

(3) HMRC charges must, for the purpose of this Section, be claimed as 'legal representative's costs' on relevant court forms.

(4) This Section applies where the only claim is a claim conducted by an HMRC Officer in the County Court for recovery of a debt and the Commissioners obtain judgment on the claim.

(5) Any appropriate court fee will be allowed in addition to the costs set out in this Section.

(6) The claim form may include a claim for fixed commencement costs.

Amount of fixed commencement costs in a County Court claim for the recovery of money

45.34 The amount of fixed commencement costs in a claim to which rule 45.33 applies –

(a) will be calculated by reference to Table 7; and

(b) the amount claimed in the claim form is to be used for determining which claim band in Table 7 applies.

TABLE 7

Fixed costs on commencement of a County Court claim conducted by an HMRC Officer

Where the value of the claim does not exceed £25	Nil
Where the value of the claim exceeds £25 but does not exceed £500	£33.00
Where the value of the claim exceeds £500 but does not exceed £1,000	£47.00
Where the value of the claim exceeds £1,000 but does not exceed £5,000	£53.00
Where the value of the claim exceeds £5,000 but does not exceed £15,000	£67.00
Where the value of the claim exceeds £15,000 but does not exceed £50,000	£90.00
Where the value of the claim exceeds £50,000 but does not exceed £100,000	£113.00

Fixed costs on commencement of a County Court claim conducted by an HMRC Officer

Where the value of the claim exceeds £100,000 but does not exceed £150,000	£127.00
Where the value of the claim exceeds £150,000 but does not exceed £200,000	£140.00
Where the value of the claim exceeds £200,000 but does not exceed £250,000	£153.00
Where the value of the claim exceeds £250,000 but does not exceed £300,000	£167.00
Where the value of the claim exceeds £300,000	£180.00

Costs on entry of judgment in a County Court claim for recovery of money

45.35 Where –

(a) an HMRC Officer has claimed fixed commencement costs under Rule 45.34; and

(b) judgment is entered in a claim to which rule 45.33 applies,

(i) the fixed commencement costs; and

(ii) the amount in Table 8 relevant to the value of the claim.

TABLE 8

Fixed costs on entry of judgment in a County Court claim conducted by an HMRC Officer

Where the value of the claim does not exceed £5,000	£15.00
Where the value of the claim exceeds £5,000	£20.00

When the defendant is only liable for fixed commencement costs

45.36 Where –

(a) the only claim is for a specified sum of money; and

(b) the defendant pays the money claimed within 14 days after service of the particulars of claim, together with the fixed commencement costs stated in the claim form,

the defendant is not liable for any further costs unless the court orders otherwise.>

VI FAST TRACK TRIAL COSTS

Scope of this Section

45.37

(1) This Section deals with the amount of costs which the court may award as the costs of an advocate for preparing for and appearing at the trial of a claim in the fast track (referred to in this rule as 'fast track trial costs').

(2) For the purposes of this Section –

'advocate' means a person exercising a right of audience as a representative of, or on behalf of, a party;

'fast track trial costs' means the costs of a party's advocate for preparing for and appearing at the trial, but does not include –

(i) any other disbursements; or

(ii) any value added tax payable on the fees of a party's advocate; and

'trial' includes a hearing where the court decides an amount of money or the value of goods following a judgment under Part 12 (default judgment) or Part 14 (admissions) but does not include –

(i) the hearing of an application for summary judgment under Part 24; or

(ii) the court's approval of a settlement or other compromise under rule 21.10.

Amount of fast track trial costs

45.38

(1) Table 9 shows the amount of fast track trial costs which the court may award (whether by summary or detailed assessment).

TABLE 9

Value of the claim	Amount of fast track trial costs which the court may award
No more than £3,000	£485.00
More than £3,000 but not more than £10,000	£690.00
More than £10,000 but not more than £15,000	£1,035.00
For proceedings issued on or after 6th April 2009, more than £15,000	£1,650.00

(2) The court may not award more or less than the amount shown in the table except where –

(a) it decides not to award any fast track trial costs; or

(b) rule 45.39 applies,

but the court may apportion the amount awarded between the parties to reflect their respective degrees of success on the issues at trial.

(3) Where the only claim is for the payment of money –

(a) for the purpose of quantifying fast track trial costs awarded to a claimant, the value of the claim is the total amount of the judgment excluding –

(i) interest and costs; and

(ii) any reduction made for contributory negligence; and

(b) for the purpose of quantifying fast track trial costs awarded to a defendant, the value of the claim is –

(i) the amount specified in the claim form (excluding interest and costs);

(ii) if no amount is specified, the maximum amount which the claimant reasonably expected to recover according to the statement of value included in the claim form under rule 16.3; or

(iii) more than £15,000, if the claim form states that the claimant cannot reasonably say how much is likely to be recovered.

(4) Where the claim is only for a remedy other than the payment of money, the value of the claim is deemed to be more than £3,000 but not more than £10,000, unless the court orders otherwise.

(5) Where the claim includes both a claim for the payment of money and for a remedy other than the payment of money, the value of the claim is deemed to be the higher of –

(a) the value of the money claim decided in accordance with paragraph (3); or

(b) the deemed value of the other remedy decided in accordance with paragraph (4),

unless the court orders otherwise.

(6) Where –

(a) a defendant has made a counterclaim against the claimant;

(b) the counterclaim has a higher value than the claim; and

(c) the claimant succeeds at trial both on the claim and the counterclaim, for the purpose of quantifying fast track trial costs awarded to the claimant, the value of the claim is the value of the defendant's counterclaim calculated in accordance with this rule.

Power to award more or less than the amount of fast track trial costs

45.39

(1) This rule sets out when a court may award –

(a) an additional amount to the amount of fast track trial costs shown in Table 9 in rule 45.38(1); or

(b) less than those amounts.

(2) If –

(a) in addition to the advocate, a party's legal representative attends the trial;

(b) the court considers that it was necessary for a legal representative to attend to assist the advocate; and

(c) the court awards fast track trial costs to that party,

the court may award an additional £345 in respect of the legal representative's attendance at the trial.

(3) If the court considers that it is necessary to direct a separate trial of an issue then the court may award an additional amount in respect of the separate trial but that amount is limited in accordance with paragraph (4) of this rule.

(4) The additional amount the court may award under paragraph (3) will not exceed two-thirds of the amount payable for that claim, subject to a minimum award of £485.

(5) Where the party to whom fast track trial costs are to be awarded is a litigant in person, the court will award –

(a) if the litigant in person can prove financial loss, two-thirds of the amount that would otherwise be awarded; or

(b) if the litigant in person fails to prove financial loss, an amount in respect of the time spent reasonably doing the work at the rate specified in Practice Direction 46.

(6) Where a defendant has made a counterclaim against the claimant, and –

(a) the claimant has succeeded on his claim; and

(b) the defendant has succeeded on his counterclaim,

the court will quantify the amount of the award of fast track trial costs to which –

(i) but for the counterclaim, the claimant would be entitled for succeeding on his claim; and

(ii) but for the claim, the defendant would be entitled for succeeding on his counterclaim,

and make one award of the difference, if any, to the party entitled to the higher award of costs.

(7) Where the court considers that the party to whom fast track trial costs are to be awarded has behaved unreasonably or improperly during the trial, it may award that party an amount less than would otherwise be payable for that claim, as it considers appropriate.

(8) Where the court considers that the party who is to pay the fast track trial costs has behaved improperly during the trial the court may award such additional amount to the other party as it considers appropriate.

Fast track trial costs where there is more than one claimant or defendant

45.40

(1) Where the same advocate is acting for more than one party –

(a) the court may make only one award in respect of fast track trial costs payable to that advocate; and

(b) the parties for whom the advocate is acting are jointly entitled to any fast track trial costs awarded by the court.

(2) Where –

(a) the same advocate is acting for more than one claimant; and

(b) each claimant has a separate claim against the defendant,
the value of the claim, for the purpose of quantifying the award in respect of fast track trial costs is to be ascertained in accordance with paragraph (3).

(3) The value of the claim in the circumstances mentioned in paragraph (2) or (5) is –

(a) where the only claim of each claimant is for the payment of money –

(i) if the award of fast track trial costs is in favour of the claimants, the total amount of the judgment made in favour of all the claimants jointly represented; or

(ii) if the award is in favour of the defendant, the total amount claimed by the claimants, and in either case, quantified in accordance with rule 45.38(3);

(b) where the only claim of each claimant is for a remedy other than the payment of money, deemed to be more than £3,000 but not more than £10,000; and

(c) where claims of the claimants include both a claim for the payment of money and for a remedy other than the payment of money, deemed to be –

(i) more than £3,000 but not more than £10,000; or

(ii) if greater, the value of the money claims calculated in accordance with subparagraph (a) above.

(4) Where –

(a) there is more than one defendant; and

(b) any or all of the defendants are separately represented,
the court may award fast track trial costs to each party who is separately represented.

(5) Where –

(a) there is more than one claimant; and

(b) a single defendant,
the court may make only one award to the defendant of fast track trial costs, for which the claimants are jointly and severally liable.

(6) For the purpose of quantifying the fast track trial costs awarded to the single defendant under paragraph (5), the value of the claim is to be calculated in accordance with paragraph (3) of this rule.

VII COSTS LIMITS IN AARHUS CONVENTION CLAIMS

Scope and interpretation

45.41

(1) This Section provides for the costs which are to be recoverable between the parties in Aarhus Convention claims.

(2) In this Section, 'Aarhus Convention claim' means a claim for judicial review of a decision, act or omission all or part of which is subject to the provisions of the UNECE Convention on Access to Information, Public Participation in Decision-Making and Access to Justice in Environmental Matters done at Aarhus, Denmark on 25 June 1998, including a claim which proceeds on the basis that the decision, act or omission, or part of it, is so subject.

(Rule 52.19 makes provision in relation to costs of an appeal.)

Opting out

45.42

Rules 45.43 to 45.44 do not apply where the claimant –

(a) has not stated in the claim form that the claim is an Aarhus Convention claim; or

(b) has stated in the claim form that –

(i) the claim is not an Aarhus Convention claim, or

(ii) although the claim is an Aarhus Convention claim, the claimant does not wish those rules to apply.

Limit on costs recoverable from a party in an Aarhus Convention claim

45.43

(1) Subject to rule 45.44, a party to an Aarhus Convention claim may not be ordered to pay costs exceeding the amount prescribed in Practice Direction 45.

(2) Practice Direction 45 may prescribe a different amount for the purpose of paragraph (1) according to the nature of the claimant.

Challenging whether the claim is an Aarhus Convention claim 45.44

(1) If the claimant has stated in the claim form that the claim is an Aarhus Convention claim, rule 45.43 will apply unless –

(a) the defendant has in the acknowledgment of service filed in accordance with rule 54.8 –

(i) denied that the claim is an Aarhus Convention claim; and

(ii) set out the defendant's grounds for such denial; and

(b) the court has determined that the claim is not an Aarhus Convention claim.

(2) Where the defendant argues that the claim is not an Aarhus Convention claim, the court will determine that issue at the earliest opportunity.

(3) In any proceedings to determine whether the claim is an Aarhus Convention claim –

(a) if the court holds that the claim is not an Aarhus Convention claim, it will normally make no order for costs in relation to those proceedings;

(b) if the court holds that the claim is an Aarhus Convention claim, it will normally order the defendant to pay the claimant's costs of those proceedings on the indemnity basis, and that order may be enforced notwithstanding that this would increase the costs payable by the defendant beyond the amount prescribed in Practice Direction 45.

Index

PERSONAL INJURY SMALL CLAIMS, PORTALS AND FIXED COSTS

VOLUMES I-III INDEX